THE CAMBRIDGE CO
POSTMODERN AMERI

Few previous periods in the history of American literature could rival the richness of the postmodern era – the diversity of its authors, the complexity of its ideas and visions, and the multiplicity of its subjects and forms. This volume offers an authoritative, comprehensive, and accessible guide to the American fiction of this remarkable period. It traces the development of postmodern American fiction over the past half century and explores its key aesthetic, cultural, and political contexts. It examines its principal styles and genres, from the early experiments with metafiction to the most recent developments, such as the graphic novel and digital fiction, and offers concise, compelling readings of many of its major works. An indispensable resource for students, scholars, and the general reader, the *Companion* both highlights the extraordinary achievements of postmodern American fiction and provides illuminating critical frameworks for understanding it.

PAULA GEYH is Associate Professor of English at Yeshiva University. She is the author of *Cities, Citizens, and Technologies: Urban Life and Postmodernity*, and a coeditor, with Fred G. Leebron and Andrew Levy, of *Postmodern American Fiction: A Norton Anthology*. Her articles on postmodern literature and culture have appeared in such journals as *Contemporary Literature*, *Twentieth-Century Literature*, *PARADOXA*, and *Criticism*.

THE CAMBRIDGE
COMPANION TO
POSTMODERN
AMERICAN FICTION

EDITED BY
PAULA GEYH
Yeshiva University

CAMBRIDGE
UNIVERSITY PRESS

CAMBRIDGE
UNIVERSITY PRESS

University Printing House, Cambridge CB2 8BS, United Kingdom

One Liberty Plaza, 20th Floor, New York, NY 10006, USA

477 Williamstown Road, Port Melbourne, VIC 3207, Australia

4843/24, 2nd Floor, Ansari Road, Daryaganj, Delhi - 110002, India

79 Anson Road, #06-04/06, Singapore 079906

Cambridge University Press is part of the University of Cambridge.

It furthers the University's mission by disseminating knowledge in the pursuit of education, learning and research at the highest international levels of excellence.

www.cambridge.org
Information on this title: www.cambridge.org/9781107103443
DOI: 10.1017/9781316216514

© Cambridge University Press 2017

First published 2017

Printed in the United States of America by Sheridan Books, Inc.

A catalog record for this publication is available from the British Library

Library of Congress Cataloging-in-Publication data
Names: Geyh, Paula, editor.
Title: The Cambridge companion to postmodern American fiction / edited by Paula Geyh.
Description: New York, NY : Cambridge University Press, 2017. | Series: Cambridge companions to literature | Includes bibliographical references and index.
Identifiers: LCCN 2016047831 | ISBN 9781107103443 (hardback) |
ISBN 9781107502772 (paperback)
Subjects: LCSH: American fiction – 20th century – History and criticism. | American fiction – 21st century – History and criticism. | Postmodernism (Literature) – United States.
Classification: LCC PS374.P64 C36 2017 | DDC 813/.5409 – dc23
LC record available at https://lccn.loc.gov/2016047831

ISBN 978-1-107-10344-3 Hardback
ISBN 978-1-107-50277-2 Paperback

CONTENTS

CONTENTS

CONTRIBUTORS

DAVID COWART, Louise Fry Scudder Professor at the University of South Carolina, is the author of several books on contemporary fiction, including *Don DeLillo: The Physics of Language* (2002), *Trailing Clouds: Immigrant Fiction in Contemporary America* (2006), *Thomas Pynchon and the Dark Passages of History* (2011), and *The Tribe of Pyn: Literary Generations in the Postmodern Period* (2015).

JONATHAN P. EBURNE is Associate Professor of Comparative Literature and English at the Pennsylvania State University. He is the founding coeditor of *ASAP/Journal*, the scholarly journal of ASAP: The Association for the Study of the Arts of the Present. He is the author of *Surrealism and the Art of Crime* (2008) and the coeditor, most recently, of *The Year's Work in the Oddball Archive* (with Judith Roof; 2016). He also edits a book series, "Refiguring Modernism," at the Penn State University Press.

ASTRID ENSSLIN is Professor of Media and Digital Communication at the University of Alberta. Her key publications are *Literary Gaming* (2014), *Analyzing Digital Fiction* (2014), *The Language of Gaming* (2011), *Creating Second Lives: Community, Identity and Spatiality as Constructions of the Virtual* (2011), *Canonizing Hypertext* (2007), and *Language in the Media: Representations, Identities, Ideologies* (2007).

DEAN FRANCO is Professor of English and Director of Jewish Studies at Wake Forest University. He is the author of *Ethnic American Literature: Comparing Chicano, Jewish, and African American Writing* (2006) and *Race, Rights, and Recognition: Jewish American Literature Since 1969* (2012). His essays on American literature appear in such journals as *NOVEL*, *Prooftexts*, *MFS*, and *PMLA*.

PAULA GEYH is Associate Professor of English at Yeshiva University. She is the author of *Cities, Citizens, and Technologies: Urban Life and Postmodernity* (2009) and a coeditor, with Fred G. Leebron and Andrew Levy, of *Postmodern American Fiction: A Norton Anthology* (1998).

ELANA GOMEL is Associate Professor at the Department of English and American Studies at Tel Aviv University. She has taught and done research at Princeton, Stanford, the University of Hong Kong, and Venice International University. She is the author of six books and numerous articles on subjects such as postmodernism, narrative theory, science fiction, Dickens, and Victorian culture. Her latest books are *Narrative Space and Time: Representing Impossible Topologies in Literature* (2014) and *Science Fiction, Alien Encounters, and the Ethics of Posthumanism: Beyond the Golden Rule* (2014). She is currently working on a project about history and zombies.

CAREN IRR is Professor of English at Brandeis University. She is the author, most recently, of *Toward the Geopolitical Novel: U.S. Fiction in the 21st Century* (2013).

PATRICK O'DONNELL is Professor of Twentieth and Twenty-First Century American and British Literature at Michigan State University. He is the author or editor of over a dozen books on modern and contemporary fiction, most recently *A Temporary Future: The Fiction of David Mitchell* (2015), *The Encyclopedia of Twentieth Century American Fiction*, coedited with Justus Nieland and David W. Madden (2011), and *The American Novel Now: Reading American Fiction Since 1980* (2010). Currently, he is completing a book on Henry James and contemporary cinema.

TIMOTHY PARRISH is Professor of English at Virginia Tech. He is the author of three books, including *Ralph Ellison and the Genius of America* (2012). He has published widely on American literature and culture, and is the editor of both *The Cambridge Companion to American Novelists* (2013) and *The Cambridge Companion to Philip Roth* (2007). His story "Philip Roth's Final Hours" (2016) is part of a larger cycle of creative essays and stories.

ARKADY PLOTNITSKY is Distinguished Professor of English at Purdue University, where he is also Director of the Theory and Cultural Studies Program. He has published extensively on critical theory, continental philosophy, Romanticism, modernism and postmodernism, the philosophy of mathematics and physics, and the relationships among literature, philosophy, and science. His latest book is *The Principles of Quantum Theory, From Planck's Quanta to the Higgs Boson: The Nature of Quantum Reality and the Spirit of Copenhagen* (2016).

SALLY ROBINSON is Associate Professor of English at Texas A&M University, where she is also affiliate faculty in Women's and Gender Studies. She is the author of *Engendering the Subject: Gender and Self-Representation in Contemporary Women's Fiction* (1991) and *Marked Men: White Masculinity in Crisis* (2000). She has recently published essays in *Genders* and *Postmodern Culture*, and is completing a book on gender and anti-consumerism in postwar American culture.

CHRONOLOGY

1960   John F. Kennedy elected president
        Black students hold sit-in at Woolworth lunch counter in
        Greensboro, North Carolina
        Birth control pill becomes available for use as a contraceptive
        Laser invented
        John Barth, *The Sot-Weed Factor*

1961   Construction of the Berlin Wall
        Freedom Rides organized by CORE
        Soviet cosmonaut Yuri Gagarin first man in space
        William S. Burroughs, *The Soft Machine*
        Joseph Heller, *Catch-22*

1962   Cuban Missile Crisis
        Telstar, the first telecommunications satellite
        John Glenn first American astronaut to orbit the Earth
        James Baldwin, *Another Country*
        Jorge Luis Borges, *Ficciones* (English translation)
        William S. Burroughs, *The Ticket That Exploded*
        Philip K. Dick, *The Man in the High Castle*
        Ken Kesey, *One Flew Over the Cuckoo's Nest*
        Vladimir Nabokov, *Pale Fire*

1963   Dr. Martin Luther King Jr.'s "I Have a Dream" speech
        President John F. Kennedy assassinated
        Lyndon B. Johnson becomes president
        James Baldwin, *The Fire Next Time*
        Thomas Pynchon, *V.*
        Betty Friedan, *The Feminine Mystique*

1964   Lyndon B. Johnson elected president
       Civil Rights Act
       President Johnson declares War on Poverty
       Donald Barthelme, *Come Back, Dr. Caligari*
       William S. Burroughs, *Nova Express*
       Hubert Selby Jr., *Last Exit to Brooklyn*
       Susan Sontag, "Against Interpretation"

1965   Malcolm X assassinated
       Civil Rights March from Selma to Montgomery led by
       Dr. Martin Luther King Jr.
       Truman Capote, *In Cold Blood*

1966   China's Cultural Revolution begins
       Black Panthers founded by Bobby Seale and Huey P. Newton
       National Organization of Women (NOW) founded
       Julio Cortázar, *Hopscotch* (English translation)
       William H. Gass, *Omensetters Luck*
       Thomas Pynchon, *The Crying of Lot 49*
       Jean Rhys, *Wide Sargasso Sea*
       Tom Stoppard, *Rosencrantz and Guildenstern Are Dead*
       Jacques Derrida, "Structure, Sign, and Play in the Discourse of
       the Human Sciences"

1967   Six-Day War
       Summer of Love
       Donald Barthelme, *Snow White*
       Richard Brautigan, *Trout Fishing in America*
       Gabriel García Márquez, *One Hundred Years of Solitude*
       Susan Sontag, *Death Kit*
       John Barth, "The Literature of Exhaustion"
       Roland Barthes, "The Death of the Author"

1968   Richard Nixon elected president
       Dr. Martin Luther King Jr. and Senator Robert Kennedy assas-
       sinated
       Prague Spring
       May 1968 protests in France
       John Barth, *Lost in the Funhouse*
       Donald Barthelme, *Unspeakable Practices, Unnatural Acts*
       Richard Brautigan, *In Watermelon Sugar*
       Robert Coover, *The Universal Baseball Association*

William H. Gass, *In the Heart of the Heart of the Country*
William H. Gass, *Willie Masters' Lonesome Wife*
Michael Herr, *Dispatches*
Norman Mailer, *The Armies of the Night*
Tayeb Salih, *Season of Migration to the North*

1969   United States lands men on the moon
Creation of the ARPANET, forerunner of the Internet
Robert Coover, *Pricksongs and Descants: Fictions*
Ursula K. Le Guin, *The Left Hand of Darkness*
Ishmael Reed, *Yellow Back Radio Broke-Down*
Kurt Vonnegut, *Slaughterhouse-Five*

1970   United States invades Cambodia
Kent State Massacre of antiwar protesters
Environmental Protection Agency (EPA) founded
Donald Barthelme, *City Life*
Joan Didion, *Play It As It Lays*
Toni Morrison, *The Bluest Eye*

1971   Pentagon Papers scandal
Invention of the microchip
E. L. Doctorow, *The Book of Daniel*
John Gardner, *Grendel*
Hunter S. Thompson, *Fear and Loathing in Las Vegas*

1972   Richard Nixon re-elected president
Nixon goes to China
Equal Rights Amendment approved by Congress
John Barth, *Chimera*
John Gardner, *The Sunlight Dialogues*
Ishmael Reed, *Mumbo Jumbo*
Gene Wolfe, *The Fifth Head of Cerberus*

1973   Skylab launched
Roe v. Wade Supreme Court decision
Kathy Acker, *The Childlike Life of the Black Tarantula by the
Black Tarantula*
Toni Morrison, *Sula*
Thomas Pynchon, *Gravity's Rainbow*
Kurt Vonnegut, *Breakfast of Champions*

1974   Richard Nixon resigns; Gerald Ford becomes president

1975   Vietnam War ends
        Bill Gates and Paul Allen found Microsoft
        Samuel R. Delany, *Dhalgren*
        E. L. Doctorow, *Ragtime*
        William Gaddis, *JR*
        Gayl Jones, *Corregidora*
        Joanna Russ, *The Female Man*

1976   Jimmy Carter elected president
        Mao Zedong dies; China's Cultural Revolution ends
        Steve Jobs and Steve Wozniak found Apple
        Maxine Hong Kingston, *Woman Warrior*
        Marge Piercy, *Woman on the Edge of Time*
        Manuel Puig, *Kiss of the Spider Woman*
        Ishmael Reed, *Flight to Canada*
        Tom Robbins, *Even Cowgirls Get the Blues*

1977   Voyager spacecraft launched
        Robert Coover, *The Public Burning*
        Toni Morrison, *Song of Solomon*
        Leslie Marmon Silko, *Ceremony*

1978   First test-tube baby born
        Israel and Egypt sign Camp David Peace Accords
        Gerald Vizenor, *Darkness in Saint Louis Bearheart*

1979   Margaret Thatcher becomes prime minister of the United
        Kingdom
        Three Mile Island nuclear plant accident
        John Barth, *LETTERS*
        Norman Mailer, *The Executioner's Song*
        V. S. Naipaul, *A Bend in the River*
        Philip Roth, *The Ghost Writer*
        Gilbert Sorrentino, *Mulligan Stew*
        Jean-François Lyotard, *The Postmodern Condition: A Report
        on Knowledge*

1980   Ronald Reagan elected president
        Toni Cade Bambara, *The Salt Eaters*
        Maxine Hong Kingston, *China Men*
        Marilynne Robinson, *Housekeeping*
        Adrienne Rich, "Compulsory Heterosexuality and Lesbian
        Existence"

1981   First Space Shuttle flight
IBM introduces personal computer
President of Egypt Anwar Sadat assassinated
Sandra Day O'Connor becomes first woman Supreme Court
justice
Donald Barthelme, *Sixty Stories*
Philip K. Dick, *VALIS*
Salman Rushdie, *Midnight's Children*
Alexander Theroux, *D'Arconville's Cat*
Jean Baudrillard, *Simulacra and Simulation*

1982   Kathy Acker, *Great Expectations*
Theresa Hak Kyung Cha, *Dictee*
Audre Lorde, *Zami: A New Spelling of My Name*
Ntozake Shange, *Sassafrass, Cypress & Indigo*
Alice Walker, *The Color Purple*

1983   Thomas Bernhard, *The Loser*
Samuel R. Delany, *Return to Neveryón*
Katherine Dunn, *Geek Love*
Wendy Law-Yone, *The Coffin Tree*
Paule Marshall, *Praisesong for the Widow*
Steve Meretzky, *Planetfall*
Jean Baudrillard, *Simulations*

1984   HIV identified as the cause of AIDS
Ronald Reagan re-elected president
Octavia Butler, *Dawn* (Part 1 of the *Xenogenesis* trilogy)
Joan Didion, *Democracy*
Louise Erdrich, *Love Medicine*
William Gibson, *Neuromancer*

1985   Mikhail Gorbachev becomes premier of the Soviet Union
DNA fingerprinting
Paul Auster, *City of Glass*
Don DeLillo, *White Noise*
Gloria Naylor, *Linden Hills*
Donna Haraway, "A Cyborg Manifesto"

1986   US Space Shuttle *Challenger* explodes
Nuclear reactor accident at Chernobyl
Iran–Contra scandal
Kathy Acker, *Don Quixote, which was a dream*
Art Spiegelman, *Maus*

1987	Ronald Reagan and Mikhail Gorbachev sign Strategic Arms Reduction Treaty

1987   Ronald Reagan and Mikhail Gorbachev sign Strategic Arms
Reduction Treaty
US stock market crash
Gloria Anzaldúa, *Borderlands/La Frontera: The New Mestiza*
Jay Cantor, *Krazy Kat*
Robert Coover, *A Night at the Movies, or, You Must Remember This*
Michael Joyce, *afternoon, a story* (hypertext)
Maxine Hong Kingston, *Tripmaster Monkey: His Fake Book*
Toni Morrison, *Beloved*
Cynthia Ozick, *The Messiah of Stockholm*
William T. Vollmann, *You Bright and Risen Angels*
David Foster Wallace, *The Broom of the System*
Brian McHale, *Postmodernist Fiction*

1988   George H. W. Bush elected president
Perestroika begins
Harvard patents genetically altered mouse
Kathy Acker, *In the Realm of the Senseless*
Octavia Butler, *Adulthood Rites* (Part 2 of the *Xenogenesis* trilogy)
Don DeLillo, *Libra*
Gloria Naylor, *Mama Day*
Cynthia Ozick, *The Shawl*
Linda Hutcheon, *A Poetics of Postmodernism: History, Theory, Fiction*

1989   Berlin Wall falls; collapse of Soviet bloc in Europe
Tiananmen Square Massacre
US government bails out savings-and-loan banks
Octavia Butler, *Imago* (Part 3 of the *Xenogenesis* trilogy)
Rikki Ducornet, *Fountains of Neptune*
Oscar Hijuelos, *The Mambo Kings Play Songs of Love*
Bharati Mukherjee, *Jasmine*
William T. Vollmann, *The Rainbow Stories*

1990   Reunification of West and East Germany
Creation of the World Wide Web
Hubble Space Telescope launched
Iraq invades Kuwait; Gulf War begins
Lynda Barry, *Come Over, Come Over*
Jessica Hagedorn, *Dogeaters*

Charles Johnson, *Middle Passage*
Valerie Martin, *Mary Reilly*
Tim O'Brien, *The Things They Carried*
Thomas Pynchon, *Vineland*
Kim Stanley Robinson, *A Short, Sharp Shock*
Karen Tei Yamashita, *Through the Arc of the Rainforest*
Judith Butler, *Gender Trouble*

1991   Dissolution of the Soviet Union
Gulf War ends
Julia Alvarez, *How the García Girls Lost Their Accents*
Sandra Cisneros, *Woman Hollering Creek*
Douglas Coupland, *Generation X*
Bret Easton Ellis, *American Psycho*
Stuart Moulthrop, *Victory Garden*
Leslie Marmon Silko, *Almanac of the Dead*
Jane Smiley, *A Thousand Acres*
Art Spiegelman, *Maus II*
Gerald Vizenor, *Feral Lasers*
Gerald Vizenor, *Landfill Meditations: Crossblood Stories*
Homi Bhabha, *The Location of Culture*
Fredric Jameson, *Postmodernism, or, The Cultural Logic of Late Capitalism*

1992   Maastricht Treaty creates the European Union
Bill Clinton elected president
Bosnian Wars begin
Cristina García, *Dreaming in Cuban*
Neal Stephenson, *Snow Crash*
Toni Morrison, *Playing in the Dark: Whiteness and the Literary Imagination*

1993   Oslo Accords signed by Israel and the Palestine Liberation Organization (PLO)
Ana Castillo, *So Far from God*
Philip Roth, *Operation Shylock*
Tei Yamashita, *Brazil-Maru*

1994   South Africa ends apartheid; Nelson Mandela elected president
North American Free Trade Agreement (NAFTA) goes into effect
Netscape introduced

Edwidge Danticat, *Breath, Eyes, Memory*
Gerald Vizenor, *Manifest Manners*
George Landow, *Hyper/Text/Theory*

1995   World Trade Organization (WTO) established
Oklahoma City bombing
Dayton Accords end Bosnian War
Marie Cardinal, *The Words to Say It*
Rikki Ducornet, *Phosphor in Dreamland*
William H. Gass, *The Tunnel*
Shelley Jackson, *Patchwork Girl*
Chang-Rae Lee, *Native Speaker*
Richard Powers, *Galatea 2.2*

1996   Bill Clinton re-elected president
Dolly the sheep cloned
Margaret Atwood, *Alias Grace*
Percival Everett, *Watershed*
David Foster Wallace, *Infinite Jest*

1997   Don DeLillo, *Underworld*
Nora Okja Keller, *Comfort Woman*
Toni Morrison, *Paradise*
Thomas Pynchon, *Mason & Dixon*
Philip Roth, *American Pastoral*
Gerald Vizenor, *Hotline Healers*

1998   International Space Station launched
Google founded
Adam Cadre, *Photopia*
Michael Cunningham, *The Hours*

1999   Rikki Ducornet, *The Fan-Maker's Inquisition*
Viktor Pelevin, *Generation P*
Colson Whitehead, *The Intuitionist*

2000   George W. Bush elected president
Vladimir Putin elected president of Russia
Michael Chabon, *The Amazing Adventures of Kavalier &
Clay*
Mark Z. Danielewski, *House of Leaves*
Mario Vargas Llosa, *The Feast of the Goat*
Nick Montfort, *Ad Verbum*
Judd Morrissey, *The Jew's Daughter*

Philip Roth, *The Human Stain*
Emily Short, *Galatea*
Franco Moretti, "Conjectures on World Literature"

2001   Al-Qaeda attacks United States on September 11
Afghan War begins
Wikipedia launched
Apple introduces iPod
Percival Everett, *Erasure*
Jonathan Franzen, *The Corrections*

2002   Euro enters circulation
Lydia Davis, *Samuel Johnson Is Indignant*
Kelley Eskridge, *Solitaire*
Jeffrey Eugenides, *Middlesex*
Aleksandar Hemon, *Nowhere Man*

2003   Human Genome Project completed
United States and allies invade Iraq
Don DeLillo, *Cosmopolis*

2004   NATO and EU expand to include most of the former Eastern
Bloc
Web 2.0
Facebook introduced
Mars Rover explores planet surface
George W. Bush re-elected president
Sarah Shun-Lien Bynum, *Madeleine Is Sleeping*
Rikki Ducornet, *Gazelle*
Kate Pullinger, Stefan Schemat, and babel, *The Breathing Wall*
Philip Roth, *The Plot Against America*
Art Spiegelman, *In the Shadow of No Towers*

2005   Angela Merkel becomes first woman chancellor of Germany
YouTube launched
Kyoto Protocol to reduce greenhouse gas emissions commences
Hurricane Katrina floods New Orleans

2006   Twitter launched
Alison Bechdel, *Fun Home: A Family Tragicomic*
Max Brooks, *World War Z: An Oral History of the Zombie War*
Dave Eggers, *What is the what*

Jonathan Safran Foer, *Extremely Loud and Incredibly Close*
Shelley Jackson, *Half Life*
Kate Pullinger, Chris Joseph, and Andy Campbell, *Inanimate Alice* begins
Thomas Pynchon, *Against the Day*
Gary Shteyngart, *Absurdistan*

2007   Global economic crisis
Apple introduces the iPhone
Michael Chabon, *The Yiddish Policemen's Union*
Junot Díaz, *The Brief Wondrous Life of Oscar Wao*
Helena María Viramontes, *Their Dogs Came with Them*

2008   Barack Obama elected president
Nicholson Baker, *Human Smoke: The Beginnings of World War II, the End of Civilization*
Matt Richtel, *Twiller*

2009   Dave Eggers, *Zeitoun*
Tao Lin, *Shoplifting from American Apparel*
Thomas Pynchon, *Inherent Vice*
Tale of Tales, *The Path*

2010   European sovereign debt crisis
Arab Spring
Jennifer Egan, *A Visit from the Goon Squad*
Jonathan Franzen, *Freedom*
Ben Marcus, *The Flame Alphabet*

2011   Iraq War ends
David Foster Wallace, *The Pale King*

2012   Higgs boson discovered
Barack Obama re-elected president
Chris Ware, *Building Stories*

2013   Edward Snowden releases documents proving mass surveillance by National Security Agency (NSA)
Chimamanda Ngozi Adichie, *Americanah*
Jonathan Franzen, *The Kraus Project: Essays by Karl Kraus*
Thomas Pynchon, *Bleeding Edge*

2014   Chang-Rae Lee, *On Such a Full Sea*
Jeff Vandermeer, *Southern Reach* trilogy

PAULA GEYH

Introduction

In the late 1960s, the young American artist Bruce Nauman created "A Cast of the Space Under My Chair," a concrete materialization of a "void," negative space made positive. On the concrete block, one can see the imprint of what was rarely, if ever, seen – the underside of the chair, the inside of its legs, and, above all, that seemingly empty space below, now filled, the absent made present. And, although the sculpture might not look entirely comfortable, one could sit on it, too.

The story of postmodern American fiction could also be seen as the making present of that which was absent throughout the previous history of American literature. The first of the two most significant new presences was that of the author within the narrative itself, which was a formal, metafictional development (admittedly one with precursors). These authors, initially mostly white men, stepped onto the pages of their metafictional narratives, joining their characters and reflecting on what was happening. This development went hand in hand with other early postmodernist formal experiments. The second new presence, crucial for postmodern literature and culture alike, was that of the multiple "others," authors who moved from the margins of literature to its, now in turn multiple, centers. These "other" authors – women in historically unprecedented numbers, and then Native Americans, African Americans, Latina/o Americans, Asian Americans, and more – emerged as major creative forces and joined the ongoing conversation that is American literature, a process that has continued ever since. These new voices *changed* this conversation by telling the stories of those who had always been on the margins of or absent from American literature, and thus gave presence to these absences in turn.

This proliferation of narratives from below and from outside can be seen as one of the manifestations of the "incredulity toward [grand] narratives" that, as the philosopher Jean-François Lyotard argued, defined the "postmodern" in general, the cultural formation that arose because of the transformation of knowledge in postindustrial, computerized societies.[1] The extraordinary range and power of postmodernism's challenges to traditional structures of knowledge, and to the social and cultural hierarchies that define these structures, dominant in the post-World War II world and still in place now, explain many of the controversies still surrounding postmodernism, beginning with those over the term itself. The debates among literary scholars and critics about what the term meant, or whether it meaningfully designated anything at all or was merely another word for "late modernism," began early on and persist to this day. In the meantime, "postmodernism" became widely used, especially in the mainstream media, as a general term of disapproval for contentious aspects of both academic and popular culture. In one form or another, then, the term "postmodernism" and the phenomena associated (for good or bad reasons) with it have been around for nearly half a century now. Indeed, recent academic debates concerning postmodernism are often about whether it has ended, and if so, when, and, inevitably, "what it was."

This book is not likely to settle these debates about postmodernism. I hope, however, it will lend support to the view, assumed here, that "postmodernism" remains our best overarching designation for the most characteristic and significant aspects of the American and (although this exceeds this volume's purview) European literature and culture of the past five decades. With this half-century mark, we have also now arrived at a point where it is possible, with a reasonable degree of confidence, to demarcate and survey the field of postmodern American fiction. Although its canon is still fluid and new works are likely to be added to it, there is a substantial critical consensus on the essential authors and works of postmodern American fiction, and on its key ideas, thematic preoccupations, and stylistic hallmarks. This *Companion* aims to offer an engaging guide to this fiction, to highlight its achievements, supply illuminating frameworks for understanding it, and provide concise, compelling readings of many of its most important works.

Before I outline the content of this volume, I shall define some key terms, beginning with "postmodernity" and "postmodernism," and lay some conceptual groundwork for this outline. Postmodernity is a historical category designating the period that is generally agreed to have begun in the late 1960s; its endpoint is a matter of no small dispute, but, for reasons to be explained below, this editor's view is that we are still somewhere in its midst (a view shared by many, even if not all, of the volume's contributors). Postmodernism, by contrast, is a cultural and conceptual category that refers to the literature, art, and culture of postmodernity, and its defining ideas and modes of thought. Postmodernist is the adjective that applies to these works, although "postmodern" is often used, as in this volume's title and in several of its chapters, interchangeably with it.

Admittedly, these definitions may be too broad and somewhat simplified. "Postmodernity," in particular, may ultimately be more useful as a periodizing term referring to cultural (including literary) and intellectual history than as a general, historical term encompassing the last half-century's events that began, in the advanced industrial and now postindustrial countries, with the political upheavals of the late 1960s. (It is noteworthy that professional historians generally do not use the term, except occasionally when negatively referring to some trends associated with it.) At the same time, as many scholars – perhaps most prominently Lyotard and Fredric Jameson – have argued, there are profound relationships between literature and the political, social, economic, technological, or other, as they are sometimes termed, "dominants" of its historical era. These relationships may be more oblique and reciprocal than Jameson's Marxist schema of the (economic) base–(cultural) superstructure suggests, but the historical context within which postmodern American fiction has developed is important. Thus, the equal rights and social liberation movements of the past half-century undoubtedly helped to bring about the opening of the canon of American literature, making it fully inclusive and representative for the first time. Reciprocally, the works of women, African Americans, and all the other "others" mentioned above gave voice to their experiences and helped to define these movements and their guiding ideas. These ideas became, in turn, integral parts of postmodern thought.

At the same time, an examination of some of the key works of postmodern American fiction could easily lead one to conclude that, rather than being simply the mirror of its time, it is often remarkably ahead of it, as if conforming to Oscar Wilde's famous statement, made long ago, that "Life imitates art far more than Art imitates life."[2] Thus, in a remarkable scene in Thomas Pynchon's 1966 novel *The Crying of Lot 49*, its heroine Oedipa Maas stands on a hillside in Southern California, looking down at the vast sprawl of San Narciso, with its "ordered swirl of houses and streets," which makes her think "of the time she'd opened a transistor radio to replace a battery and seen her first printed circuit."[3] Pynchon's startling and subtle metaphor introduces the emerging landscape of postmodernity, already suggested by his immediately preceding description of San Narciso as "less an identifiable city than a grouping of concepts."[4] The printed circuit will evolve into the microchip, making possible the personal computer and the Internet, two of the defining technologies of postmodernity. Later, but still years before the Internet went public (1991) and Netscape (1994) enabled us to navigate the emerging World Wide Web, William Gibson coined the term "cyberspace" and imagined it in his 1984 cyberpunk novel *Neuromancer* as "a graphic representation of data abstracted from the banks of every computer in the human system."[5]

Computerized information and communication technologies have profound effects on how we experience and understand the postmodern world. Indeed, as Lyotard argues, the postmodern shift or even revolution in the nature of knowledge has largely been brought about by these technologies (which were still in their early stages when he wrote *The Postmodern Condition* in 1979). This revolution in thought is, I believe, still underway, which is why I think that we are still in the midst of the postmodern era. Bioengineering and cyborg technologies are also part of this postmodern transformation, and they are changing our senses of subjectivity and even of what it means to be human. Perhaps, as N. Katherine Hayles, Cary Wolfe, and others have argued, we are already "posthuman," insofar as our subjectivity is not defined merely phenomenologically but instead, as it were, techno-phenomenologically. Postmodern literature depicts these new ways of thinking and experiencing the world, enacts them through its formal and conceptual structures, and helps us to make sense of them. As the world changes, new experiences demand new modes of thought and forms of expression. What Frank Lentricchia wrote of Don DeLillo's novels is largely true of all postmodern novels: they "could not have been written before the mid-1960s," and they are remarkable for "the unprecedented degree to which they prevent their readers from gliding off into the comfortable sentiment that the real problems of the human race have always been about what they are today."[6]

As indicated earlier, some theorists of postmodernism deem it to be reaching its end or even to have already ended. Brian McHale, who has done much to help to establish postmodernism as a literary and cultural category (he is among the most-quoted theorists in this book, along with Lyotard, Jameson, and Linda Hutcheon), begins *The Cambridge Introduction to Postmodernism* (2015) with a chapter entitled "What Was Postmodernism?" He argues that "perhaps the only consensus that has ever been reached about postmodernism has to do with its end: postmodernism, it is generally agreed, is now 'over.'"[7] McHale aims to locate the end of postmodernism in historical events and suggests 9/11 as "a convenient shorthand for postmodernism's endgame."[8] If, however, postmodernism is defined (as I assume it to be) less by historical events than by revolutions in thought and modes of existence, by epistemologies and ontologies that emerged in the late 1960s and do not yet seem to have played themselves out, then we still live in the postmodern world, or, rather, in many postmodern worlds. Postmodern literature continues to reflect on, shape, and illuminate these worlds.

Introduction

I now turn to an outline of the book's chapters, which explore in greater depth and detail the subjects just considered, beginning with different definitions of and perspectives on postmodernity and postmodernism. The book's organization is defined by several key interrelated problems and themes.

The first three chapters situate postmodern American fiction in its relation to, and as, literary history, on the one hand, and in relation to global literature, on the other. In Chapter 1, Jonathan P. Eburne considers the history of the definitions of postmodernism and their relations to different trajectories of modernism. He argues that postmodern writers create their own literary pantheons of precursors across periods and use literary-historical categories like postmodernism "as part of their very medium of experimentation." In Chapter 2, David Cowart traces the development of postmodern American fiction over three generations, from the late 1960s through the present. He surveys its characteristic forms and key ideas as they have been worked out by the successive, yet interrelated, generations of postmodernists, including the "aesthetic dissent" of several very recent authors. In Chapter 3, Caren Irr explores the networks of connections between postmodern American fiction and global literature, and how "a quest for affiliations and affinities scattered across a global landscape unifies late postmodern writing as its practitioners work to make sense on a human scale of transformations wrought by global capital."

The next two chapters on theory and history address key issues in postmodern thought and how they shape – and are shaped by – postmodern fiction. In Chapter 4, Arkady Plotnitsky examines paradigms of postmodern thinking, found in theory and literature alike, that define and are defined by "the postmodern condition" and explains their relations with preceding modes of modern or (a separate category) modernist thinking. Using Thomas Pynchon's and Don DeLillo's novels as examples, he demonstrates how literature engages with scientific conceptions of chance, contingency, and probability. Postmodern thinking and skepticism extend far beyond science, however, to virtually every other discipline of knowledge, including history, and they have, as Lyotard put it, "altered the game rules" for all of them in some way.[9] The postmodern skepticism, or incredulity, toward the received (and grand) narratives of the past and traditional notions of history is explored by Timothy Parrish in Chapter 5. Noting the preoccupation of postmodern American fiction with "how history is made, received, and understood," he looks at how the critical awareness of the constructed nature of both literature and history has informed the ways this fiction reimagines the past and rewrites history from previously marginalized or absent perspectives.

The advent of postmodern forms of subjectivity constitutes a decisive break or paradigm shift from earlier forms, particularly from the Cartesian or Enlightenment subject, which was assumed to be unified, fully self-conscious (at least in principle), and, not incidentally, male. This "Cartesian subject" could, however, hardly be claimed to be universal, given that it was constructed in opposition to female, racial, or ethnic "others," who were considered as lesser beings, neither sovereign subjects nor selves in any philosophical or political sense. Postmodern subjectivity or, rather, subjectivities are, in contrast, inherently fragmented, contingent, and "positional." They emerge at the intersection of diverse and fluctuating subject positions as nodes of interacting forces of language and social constructions, such as those of gender, race, ethnicity, and class. Beyond, but relating to all of these transformations, are the technological changes that challenge the very definition of "human" and the lines we have drawn between human and machine, and human and animal. The next three chapters explore how postmodern fiction depicts – and participates in – the construction of these new forms of subjectivity, and, moreover, imagines others beyond them.

In Chapter 6, Sally Robinson examines how postmodern American fiction contests and disrupts traditional ideas of gender and sexuality by questioning the master "narratives that script us as masculine and feminine" and as heterosexual or homosexual, and equally importantly, how these works provide alternative conceptual frameworks that go beyond such binary constructions. She also considers works, particularly science fiction novels, that envision new forms of gendered and sexual subjectivity that are not constrained by these inherited and limiting binaries. In Chapter 7, Dean Franco explores the ethnic and racial diversity of postmodern fiction as "an insurgent body of work that radically challenges social norms and stories of national formation." He looks at how these works both add new racial and "ethnic geographical itineraries and historical trajectories to traditional [narratives]" of American history, while at the same time positing "simultaneous yet incommensurate histories and geographies ... bringing forth the uncanny and the irresolvable plurality of nations within the nation that constitutes the United States." In Chapter 8, Elana Gomel argues that our scientific and technological advances profoundly affect not just how we live, but also "the way we are," and that postmodern fiction, especially science fiction, develops new narrative techniques to depict these "new ways of being" in the posthuman world. She considers such sci-fi figures as the cyborg, alien, AI, and zombie as icons of new postmodern subjectivities, and shows how they emerge in concert with postmodernism's philosophical, political, and ethical critiques of humanism and the human subject.

The last three chapters focus on postmodern fiction's ongoing experimentation with form and style. In Chapter 9, Patrick O'Donnell surveys postmodern American fiction's experiments with language and narrative form, and the ways in which they challenged traditional assumptions concerning the relationship between readers and texts. He focuses in particular on reflexivity, encyclopedism, and pastiche – hallmarks of early postmodernism – and explains how these features waned over time or evolved into new types of experimentation.

The history of postmodern culture has also been marked by constant renegotiations of the connections and boundaries between literature, the visual arts, and electronic media. These renegotiations are the subject of the final two chapters of the volume. Chapter 10, which is my own contribution, explores the relationships between word and image in postmodern fiction. The chapter specifically considers three types of works: those that experiment with typography and other visual and material aspects of the book itself; those that incorporate visual images into the text; and finally graphic novels, an important new genre of postmodern fiction. Rather than merely illustrating the written text, the chapter argues, the images in these works "are integral to the narrative," and they produce effects that demand new approaches to reading and literary interpretation. Postmodernity's omnipresent information and communication technologies are having profound effects on postmodern literature, spurring the creation of new, "digital-born" genres. In Chapter 11, Astrid Ensslin traces the development of these new genres, including interactive fiction, hypertext and hypermedia fiction, app fiction written for smart phones and tablets, and literary (video) gaming, and also examines the new forms of reading and reader interaction they produce. Finally, she offers a speculative vision of the future of digital fiction and of literary "reading" itself.

Whatever is the future of the debates concerning postmodernism or of postmodernism itself, this volume makes a compelling case for the extraordinary value of what postmodern American writers have accomplished over the past half century. Few previous periods in the history of American literature have given us works that could rival the richness of postmodern fiction – the diversity of its authors and cultures, the complexity of its ideas and visions, the multiplicity of its subjects and forms. While one might be uncertain about the fate of postmodernity, which one day must be replaced by a different cultural formation, one may be reasonably confident that postmodern American fiction will live on, whatever name the future will give it.

NOTES

1 "Grand narratives" are narratives – philosophical, scientific, religious, political, economic, or other – that seek to provide a totalizing worldview through particular legitimating historical or political teleologies and that rely upon some form of purportedly universal and transcendent truth. See Jean-François Lyotard, *The Postmodern Condition: A Report on Knowledge*, trans. Geoff Bennington and Brian Massumi (Minneapolis: University of Minnesota Press, 1984). In this text, Lyotard's term is translated as "metanarratives," but to avoid confusion with the genre known as metafiction, "grand narratives" is the generally preferred term, which will be used throughout this volume as well.
2 Oscar Wilde, "The Decay of Lying," in *The Critical Tradition: Classic Texts and Contemporary Trends*, ed. David H. Richter (Boston and New York: Bedford/St. Martin's, 1998), 448–468, 461.
3 Thomas Pynchon, *The Crying of Lot 49* (New York: Bantam, 1966), 24.
4 Ibid.
5 William Gibson, *Neuromancer* (New York: Ace Books, 1984), 52.
6 "Introduction," in *New Essays on White Noise*, ed. Frank Lentricchia (Cambridge: Cambridge University Press, 1991), 6.
7 Brian McHale, *The Cambridge Introduction to Postmodernism* (New York: Cambridge University Press, 2015), 171.
8 Ibid., 175.
9 Lyotard, *The Postmodern Condition*, xxiii.

I

JONATHAN P. EBURNE

Postmodern Precursors

Among its other technological marvels, the Internet can teach us to read. The website *wikiHow*, a compilation of how-to and DIY instructions presented for a general audience, features an illustrated step-by-step recipe for "How to Read a Thomas Pynchon Novel." After basic steps (#1) advising us about which novel to choose and instructing us (#2) to relax, (#3) to sit down while reading, and (#4) to "read at a brisk, but not manic, pace," the article then offers a capsule statement on the very nature of our undertaking. In choosing to read Pynchon, we are entering into a kind of aesthetic contract with a work of postmodern fiction. To do so, the *wikiHow* essay suggests, is to undertake a demanding task that necessitates a novel or at least unfamiliar way of reading, at once active enough to warrant instructions and yet curiously receptive and accommodating. The essay exhorts us, therefore, (#5) to

> **Be patient.** Keep reading, even if you feel you don't get it. Thomas Pynchon is a post-modern author, which means his stories can tend to stray towards self-reflexive, fragmented, and shifting forms and identity. If you're not understanding what's going on now, something completely different will happen later that will get you back on track. If he's going on what seems to be a long tangent, the tangent may have taken over the narrative. No matter what, however, whether it's a sex scene, a musical number, a play on scientific ideas, or something else, it will not be that long of a wait before something else happens that will re-awaken your interest (if your interest is lost in the first place).[1]

Step #5 of "How to Read a Thomas Pynchon Novel" offers both a literary-historical judgment and a categorical definition of that judgment. As the work of a "post-modern author," a novel by Pynchon is designed, we are told, to draw away from our capacity to "get it" and instead "stray toward self-reflexive, fragmented, and shifting forms and identity."

The *wikiHow* assessment of literary postmodernism is hardly an outlandish one. The definition is not that far off from the many critical assessments of postmodern American fiction published by critics and scholars over the past four decades, especially with regard to the history of US fiction. Scholars such as Amy Elias, Linda Hutcheon, and Joseph Tabbi have approached literary postmodernism in terms of its paradoxical relationship to history; characterized by a "sublime desire" for historical understanding, but also by irony and skepticism toward the possibility of any such understanding, postmodernism extends the difficulty of "getting it" to a general problem of historical experience.[2] It wasn't just stories that changed; the very ideas about history that undergirded them no longer seemed quite so straightforward in the wake of World War II, the Holocaust, and a seemingly endless series of international wars, conflicts, and assassinations. At the same time, critics remind us that literary postmodernism also resides *within* history, as a cultural phenomenon related to but distinct from the artistic and epistemological tendencies that preceded it. Thus, as one scholar has recently summarized it, postmodern American fiction bears "only a faint resemblance" to the fiction published in the first half of the century, breaking free from the "traditional aesthetic innovation" of earlier literature. After the 1950s, the "heavy seriousness" of modernist writing gives way "to a strangely comic irony" in works such as Pynchon's.[3] Difficult, indeed, but guaranteed to reawaken our flagging interest.

But it all depends on where we look. The tangents and ellipses of postmodernist fiction may seem to have strayed from an American literary family tree whose branches bear the names of Ernest Hemingway, F. Scott Fitzgerald, William Faulkner, John Steinbeck, Theodore Dreiser, Edith Wharton, and Henry James. If we look instead to the French writers Alfred Jarry (1873–1907) and Raymond Roussel (1877–1933), for instance, we find no shortage of narrative-devouring tangents and plays on scientific ideas that form the shifting terrain attributed to postmodernism. More Père Ubu or Dr. Faustroll than Gatsby or Jake Barnes, the resemblances between postmodern American fiction and literary history – or world history – depend very much on *which* history we designate. Like the novels themselves (according to *wikiHow*), the histories within which postmodern fiction situates itself have a tendency to stray toward reflexive, fragmented, and shifting forms.

Literary critics have tended to agree upon the digressiveness and recursion of postmodern narrative, but less so upon the prior histories from which it emerges or "breaks free." For many scholars, literary history seems to have been fairly predictable before postmodernism reared its head. By this logic, Pynchon's novels and other works of postmodern literature and art derive their characteristic idiosyncrasy from their collective abandonment of the "heavy seriousness" ascribed to pre–World War II literary modernism – or, perhaps more accurately, from our own critical suspicion or fatigue toward this seriousness. The literary modernism of the United States – often characterized as a catchall term for writing produced between the World Wars – might be described as both experimental in form and eschatological in political tenor. Though certainly continuous with the types of ambiguity at work within poetic language in general, the modernist project of experimenting with such properties was vested with deep cultural and political significance, whether in shoring up the fragments of the contemporary against our own ruins, or in seeking a "Revolution of the Word," to cite the editors of the Paris-based American journal *transition*. Postmodernism, the logic goes, gazed back at the struggles and engagements of the Faulkners and Hemingways from a historical remove. The formal and political difficulties of experimental US literature were no longer something to take at face value; in losing all that heavy seriousness, postmodern fiction does us the service of liberating us from modernism's lugubrious (and increasingly specious-sounding) claims to political agency or life-altering transcendence. This divide, too, has often been celebrated as the literary-historical or even epochal shift that constitutes the postmodern liberation from the "master narratives" of industrial modernity, suggesting a break not only from its literary modes – the romance, the epic, the poetic cycle, the encyclopedia – but from its historiographical incarnations as well: the revolutionary horizon of socialism, the fascist "final solution," or the forward thrust of industrial capitalism. In place of fiction that strives to give form to the unrepresentable scale of such phenomena, postmodernist fiction "denies itself the solace of good forms," as the philosopher Jean-François Lyotard puts it in his paradigmatic 1979 study of *The Postmodern Condition*.[4] "Postmodernism" refers here, Lyotard explains, to "the state of our culture following the transformations which, since the end of the nineteenth century, have altered the game rules for science, literature, and the arts," a condition that demands a corresponding "incredulity toward the kinds of large-scale metanarratives that form and legitimate our knowledge of the changing world."[5] Instead of placing knowledge in the service of legitimation and authority, postmodern knowledge "refines our sensitivity to differences and reinforces our ability to tolerate the incommensurable."[6] Relieved of the false comforts of formal totality, postmodernism instead impels us to "wage war on totality" itself.[7] Stories, to rehearse our *wikiHow* instructions, tend to stray toward self-reflexive, fragmented, and shifting forms and identities because it's the right thing to do.

Such critical appraisals of postmodernism co-opt the liberatory rhetoric of modernist art movements in the service of literary history itself: breaking with totality will set you free – at least from the authority-serving comforts of totality. "Postmodernism" as a literary-historical category thus marks a rupture in the logic of historical continuity ascribed to its modernist precursor, and the logic of this rupture is that of revolutionary time: a paradigm shift, an epistemic break, an event. Something definitive, in other words, has happened to divorce post-1950s writing from its precursors. Such claims are unreliable, however. Fredric Jameson's signal insight in *A Singular Modernity* (2002) is that such notions of rupture and break are merely the dialectical inversion of the narratives of continuity they purport to overthrow.[8] The radical break and the master narrative are, by this logic, cut from the same historical cloth. The interval between a "modernist" text and a "postmodernist" text is measured according to the same criteria, the same periodizing historical logic, as their sequential relationship. And indeed, these literary-historical categories have become somewhat fatiguing in themselves, subject to a critical exhaustion that has become virtually paradigmatic in the field of contemporary literary study. Do postmodernist novels and modernist novels differ in degree or kind? Do the very terms "modern" and "postmodern" designate historical periods, or do they specify discrete modes of storytelling and forms of knowledge? The fiction may be full of events that reawaken our interest, but the scholarly framework seems disconcertingly subject to its own self-reflexive, fragmented, and shifting forms. Not only has it become commonplace to interrogate the very parameters of so-called postmodernist literature, from its start date to its essential tendencies, but it has also become just as commonplace to cite its eclipse, both as a literary phenomenon and as a viable descriptive contemporary category.[9] After all, the *wikiHow* instructions no longer presume that "postmodern" is an emergent category: like any other atomic age classic, it merely takes some getting used to.

Such notions of literary periodicity – and the larger world-historical grand narratives with which they remain bound up dialectically – have become one of the zombie categories of literary and intellectual history. Evoking the hordes of walking dead familiar from Cold War horror films, the notion of a "zombie category" refers in this sense to sociological concepts that continue to organize our thinking in spite of their exhaustion as viable terms for understanding contemporary reality.[10] The terms "modernist" and "postmodernist" are two such categories. So, too, is the very imperative to organize literary creation according to sequential historical periods. My point here is not to be polemical, however; rather than rejecting such terms, I propose that we recognize this very exhaustion as an active historical phenomenon contemporary with the literary work it describes. As early as 1964, the critic and novelist Susan Sontag diagnosed this exhaustion, lamenting the "thick incrustations of interpretation" that had taken hold of canonical modern authors such as Marcel Proust, James Joyce, William Faulkner, Rainer

Maria Rilke, D. H. Lawrence, and André Gide, and which conditioned any modern approach to their works.[11] Sontag, true to postmodernism's "sublime desire," sought to reawaken our senses in the face of literary history's stultifying accumulations. Yet even to make this claim was to recognize interpretive exhaustion as a form in itself, a concrete medium for experience. Not only do such "incrustations" influence the way critics, readers, and authors approach the field of contemporary literature, but they also constitute a medium for aesthetic experience in their own right.

This is an argument made by the novelist John Barth in a 1967 essay on contemporary experimental literature, entitled "The Literature of Exhaustion." In his essay, a signal contribution to literary discussions of what became known as postmodernism, Barth extends Sontag's critique of interpretation toward the "exhaustion" of contemporary experimental writing and art in general. Whereas plenty of contemporary writers continued to write imitations of Dickens or Dostoyevsky, others dedicated themselves so formulaically to innovation that they ended up throwing the baby (of artistic creativity and continuity) out with the bathwater (of stultifying tradition). Some even went so far, Barth argues, as to dispense with "the very idea of the controlling artist" altogether, condemning authorship as "politically reactionary, authoritarian, even fascist."[12] In the name of sloughing off one set of "incrustations," contemporary writers ended up building up another. Yet rather than seeking a reactionary return to heroic ideas of artistic prowess, Barth redefines literary history and literary experimentation according to an author's ability to recast creative exhaustion as a medium for continual artistic pursuit. To this end, he singles out the Argentine writer Jorge Luis Borges as an ideal contemporary. Borges's "artistic victory" in stories such as "Pierre Menard, Author of the *Quixote*" (1939; trans. 1962) is that "he confronts an intellectual dead end and employs it against itself to accomplish new human work," Barth writes.[13] Instead of struggling to create or re-create a great literary masterpiece, Borges dramatizes "the difficulty, perhaps the unnecessity, of writing original works of literature" by inventing a minor *fin-de-siècle* writer who strives to re-compose *Don Quixote* himself, as if for the first time. Borges's metafiction is significant to the extent that "it turns the artist's mode or form into a metaphor for his concerns," Barth writes, "as does the diary-ending of [James Joyce's] *Portrait of the Artist as a Young Man* or the cyclical construction of *Finnegans Wake.*... In short, it's a paradigm of or metaphor for itself; not just the *form* of the story but the *fact* of the story is symbolic; the medium is (part of) the message."[14] Literary history – even a literary history confronted with its own exhaustion, its own tired persistence as a zombie category – becomes the medium upon and within which writers can sustain the possibility of invention. The result is both a recourse to anachronism and, in the words of *wikiHow*, a reawakening of interest: Borges, James Joyce, and Miguel de Cervantes all become contemporaries. So too do Pynchon, Raymond Roussel, and say, Herman Melville, another notable disgressionist whose fictions "tend to stray toward reflexive, fragmentary, and shifting forms and identity." This owes less to their proximity in time and space or to the bonds of lineage or influence, than to their mutual entanglement within the literature of exhaustion: that is, the extent to which the historical conditions and historiographical conventions for writing become both the medium and (part of) the message of a literary work. Such imbrication also owes much to the machinations of the book market and the conventions of public and scholarly criticism: Borges's *Ficciones* was published in English translation in 1962, rendering Borges's prewar work contemporary not only with Barth, but also with the Latin American Boom, the name for a surge in experimental fiction throughout the Americas, whose worldwide circulation contributed substantively to the artistic and political preoccupations of literary postmodernism.[15]

As a literary-historical category, "postmodernism" is a second-order category, and a provisional, heuristic one at that. This means that whatever explanatory prestige it might hold is predicated on the no-less-provisional status of the term "modernism," within and against whose terms its own project can be articulated. Modernism is hardly a stable categorical reference point from which to deduce the essential features of postmodernism. Both terms, at one point, had designated something resembling "newness," gaining literary-historical traction on account of a presumed stylistic, epistemological, or political shift from an older order. Such shifts may correspond to real, world-historical conditions characterized by global industrial development or warfare. Indeed, terms such as "modern" and "postmodern" still describe the general set of historical and political-economic conditions that influence our institutions of knowledge, our media of expression, the book market, the production of literary taste, and even our experience of reading. Even so, such conditions do not simply dictate concomitant shifts in literary creativity. As explanatory categories, the exhaustion of terms such as "modernism" and "postmodernism" is virtually self-evident; yet they persist all the same as ways for readers and literary critics to classify and explain our knowledge of history.

Authors themselves rarely adhere to the models of literary succession to which scholarly and critical genealogies assign them, drawing on ancient works, historical epics, and vanguard traditions alike as "contemporaries" in the same blithe manner as they refuse to read only the writers of their own period and nation. Such myths of direct succession and the "anxiety of influence" nonetheless remain available as zombie categories, however. Kathy

Acker, writing in 1990, identifies her admiration for William S. Burroughs, as well as for the avant-garde French writers Jean Genet, Antonin Artaud, and Georges Bataille, as substitutes for "those in the pantheon of great living American writers. The big men. Norman Mailer, macho of machos; Philip Roth; John Cheever; etc. Perhaps at the head of the class, Saul Bellow. There weren't many, any, women."[16] Acker's alternative canon of experimental writers is roughly a generation older than the "big men" of US letters, but they are far more contemporary to her work. So, too, is Cervantes's *Don Quixote* likewise contemporary insofar as Acker, like Borges's Pierre Menard, recasts it as the title of her own 1986 novel. Analogously, literary texts betray their own tendency to disclose entanglements with texts and traditions that may have only marginally to do with the intentions and reading habits even of their authors. The paradoxical desire for and skepticism toward historical understanding cited by critics such as Elias, Hutcheon, and others is no less characteristic of the literary-historical status of modernism and postmodernism themselves as descriptive categories.

The poet David Antin's 1972 remark that "from the modernism you choose you get the postmodernism you deserve" is an apt expression for describing such entanglements.[17] It is also reversible. For indeed, as a number of critics have noted, the very notion of what we consider "modernism" has changed dramatically over the past century, and especially during the past several decades, both within the academy and without. The rise of the "new modernism studies" in literary scholarship has canonized figures once marginalized from traditional white, male ideas about the experimental triumphs of the early part of the twentieth century; in place of a restricted pantheon of great poets – T. S. Eliot, Ezra Pound, W. H. Auden, Rainer Maria Rilke – or two-fisted male American novelists – Hemingway, Faulkner, John Steinbeck, John Dos Passos, Dashiell Hammett, Henry Miller, Jack Kerouac, Richard Wright – "modernism" has come to designate a broad international system of literary and artistic creativity whose aesthetic and historical criteria for demarcation are increasingly provisional. The pantheon comprised of "the big men" now offers a variety of entrances and corridors – or, rather, it is but one of many such imaginary structures. Such are the critical commonplaces that have arisen in tandem with the period of mid- to late-twentieth-century cultural life we associate with postmodernity: the death of the author, the pleasure of the text, the anxiety of influence. The result, as Steven Connor has written, is that "modernism" has shifted to reflect what it is we mean by "postmodernism."[18] Acker's French genealogy of Bataille, Artaud, and Genet is but one of innumerable "modernist" pantheons; others have looked to Roussel, Jarry, and Raymond Queneau; or to Mina Loy, Marcel Duchamp, Gertrude Stein, and Djuna Barnes; or to Franz Kafka, Karel

Čapek, Joseph Roth, Alfred Döblin, and Bruno Schulz. There are left-wing pantheons – John Reed, Dora Marsden, Claude McKay, Langston Hughes, Muriel Rukeyser – and more right-wing pantheons – T. S. Eliot, John Crowe Ransom, Allen Tate, Wendell Berry, and even Ayn Rand. The condition of postmodernism in literature might perhaps be said to enact, on the order of literary-historical categories, Borges's insight that "every writer creates his [sic] own precursors. His work modifies our conception of the past, as it will modify the future."[19] This is hardly to suggest that authors writing before 1950 did not invent their own idiosyncratic pantheons as well; rather, the point is that literary postmodernism is unimaginable without the spectrum of possibility such pantheons offer in their very multiplication. In his essay on the literature of exhaustion, John Barth invokes Borges's formulation – as a self-fulfilling gesture – to diagnose as well as confront the anachronistic demands of literary periodization. I wish to invoke it again here as a way to think about the continuities between postmodernist American fiction and its so-called literary precursors. Such continuities are often doubly anachronistic: authors, or their books, can invent their own contemporaries and precursors alike – sometimes literally, in the case of Borges's Pierre Menard. By the same logic, the forms and narratives of historical rupture and continuity that constitute "zombie categories" of literary history and criticism also function as a medium for changes or intensifications in that history. Postmodern American fiction did not invent the literary recourse to such historical forms; all the same, the creative reuse and re-appropriation of such zombie categories represent a signal artistic technology of US writing in the later decades of the twentieth century.

Ironic Seriousness: The Bourdon Gauge

The cultural forms within and upon which postmodern American fiction experimented are legion. Much as T. S. Eliot drew upon the folklore study of Jessie Weston in composing *The Waste Land* – not to mention his anxious recourse to centuries of Western culture – so too are the fictional works associated with literary postmodernism written on the backs of earlier stories and studies. These connections reach back throughout the history of the novel from the seventeenth century onward, but incorporate, too, an ever-expanding range of historical media, from occult traditions and archeological discoveries to radio, cinema, television, and popular science. Likewise, as I have claimed, the very forms used to describe both historical change and literary history also offer a medium for literary creation – even when, or precisely because, we consider those forms to have encountered a dead end. In the postmodernism of an author such as Thomas Pynchon, such dead ends multiply and proliferate in a fictional universe characterized by the force of entropy, itself the title of one of Pynchon's earliest short stories. In *V.* (1963), Pynchon's first novel, we find formal structures from literary, scholarly, military, and scientific history integrated within the novel's architecture at every turn, from Boccaccio and Wittgenstein in the "Foppl's Siege Party" chapter, to Edwardian Egyptology in the philosophical and geometric overtones of its bifurcated plot.[20] As if reflecting on this architecture, protagonist Benny Profane experiences the world as a tangle of media and often feels conspired against by the malice of the "inanimate objects" that surround him. In the storyline parallel to Profane's, the chimerical title character is herself composed of such objects, a living medium for (inanimate) media. Like Profane, we may never fully "get it," we may not fully comprehend the logic or cause for such structures; nevertheless, we witness the deployment of inanimate cultural forms – whether objects, patterns, or metaphysical constructs – as vehicles for tireless recombination and experiment.

Most prosaically, postmodern recombination and experiment tend toward the metafictional. This means that postmodern American fiction not only draws attention to its own status as fiction, but also literally adopts extant works of fiction, concepts, and historical categories as its medium. Some of the key literary-historical reference points of postmodern American fiction are texts and formal concepts disinterred from literary history and rendered contemporary. Sigmund Freud may have resuscitated a Sophoclean family tragedy as a structure of unconscious desire and aggression; and James Joyce may have named his 1922 novel after Homer's wandering hero; but throughout the late twentieth century, the rewriting of canonical texts becomes quite literally a commonplace. This owes less to the alleged timelessness of great literary masterpieces than, as Barth and Borges each suggest, to their very historicity, their evolving status and meaning on account of the changing opinions of readers, critics, and forms of media circulation.

No less readily do historical myths and ideological state apparatuses find themselves interpolated into US fiction of the Cold War years as a medium for fictional recombination. Tellingly, the nineteenth-century concept of Manifest Destiny – a journalistic term justifying the annexation of Texas and the Pacific Northwest into the United States – became one of the very "master narratives" used to describe and legitimate US colonial expansion from the moment of its coinage in 1845. With the formal incorporation of Alaska and Hawai'i as the 49th and 50th American states in 1959, the now-exhausted category of Manifest Destiny found new Cold War life in the Space Race, and even in the culture of surveillance and conspiracy that rendered the domestic and interior ideological landscapes as frontiers to be "overspread" in the name of national security. The repurposing of Manifest

Destiny (itself a journalistic construct) during the Cold War is attributable as much to the literary imagination as to explicit public policy – as suggested in the work of writers such as Don DeLillo (particularly in *White Noise* [1985]), William Gaddis (particularly in *JR* [1975]), Philip K. Dick (particularly in *VALIS* [1981]), Madeleine L'Engle (particularly in *A Wrinkle in Time* [1963]), and Gerald Vizenor (in *Darkness in Saint Louis Bearheart* [1978] and *Hotline Healers* [1997], as well as in his scholarly *Manifest Manners* [1994]), among many others. The notion of Manifest Destiny as a self-evident incarnation of historical "progress" is not simply challenged by such writers, who manifest their incredulity and opposition toward such ideological projects. Rather, it forms the very framework for their fictional experiments. Colonial expansion, surveillance, and conspiracy are not simply the "real" historical phenomena represented in fiction; their availability as self-evident ideological concepts is part of the very machinery of the postmodernist literary imagination – forming both its medium and (part of) its message.

The emergence of postmodernist American fiction in the decades after World War II owes much, moreover, to the critical environments that enfolded its distribution and reception, as well as its creation: this included the consolidation of a Cold War–era critical consensus in an increasingly regulated public sphere, as well as the emergence of universities as a key institution in postwar cultural discourse, especially after the G.I. Bill brought new generations of students to college.[21] On the one hand, the post–World War II years see changes in the cultural and political landscape of the United States – and even, as Daniel Grausam has argued, in the very understanding of historical time altogether after the Holocaust and the advent of the nuclear age.[22] On the other hand, the postwar years also saw a consolidation of literary critical interest in US fiction as a major scholarly concern, as parodied in Vladimir Nabokov's 1962 novel *Pale Fire*. The professionalization of literary studies, as well as the consolidation of its methods and preconceptions, applied as strongly to canon formation as to the interpretation of recent fiction; as formulated by critics such as F. O. Matthiesson, Leslie Fiedler, Lionel Trilling, and Edmund Wilson, the nineteenth century forwarded Henry David Thoreau, Nathaniel Hawthorne, Ralph Waldo Emerson, Walt Whitman, and Herman Melville as the key figures of its American Renaissance, and a critical enshrinement of white male authors of the twentieth century, such as Hemingway, Faulkner, and Steinbeck. Alongside the more open genealogies and traditions of modernism, and in contrast to the polyglot and historically self-conscious global affiliations that emerged with the rise of "magical realism" in Latin America, Europe, and Africa, the postwar decades saw the formation of a distinctively national, and nationalist,

"American" canon among major critics. One of the reasons that novelists such as Coover, DeLillo, and others could so readily forge recognizable pastiches of the Cold War US cultural landscape was that it was so explicitly carved out in both literary and political terms. Even so, this exceptionalism was far from perfect; as Brian McHale and others have argued, the same decades that saw a professionalization and restriction of the American canon also witnessed a profusion of "contemporary" literatures, both internationally and throughout the Americas.[23]

The effort to consolidate and legitimate a canon of distinctly *American* fiction – a master narrative on the literary-historical front – took on particular urgency during and after World War II. In addition to the work of Matthiesson and other major scholars, for instance, the influential critic and editor Malcolm Cowley championed modernist US writers of the 1920s and early 1930s in the pages of *The New Republic*. Cowley, a champion of Hemingway, Faulkner, Dos Passos, and Steinbeck – white US male authors who had animated popular debates about contemporary American literature since the mid-1930s – strived to forge an argument for recognizing the critical value and social responsibility of the literature of the 1920s, as he called it. Cowley defended this writing precisely for its refusal to depict "the smiling parts, the broad farmlands, the big Sunday dinners after coming home from church." In fact, he continues, "these authors were rebelling against another picture of American life that was dominant and accepted, that was preached in the churches, proclaimed at Rotary luncheons and romanticized by the *Saturday Evening Post*."[24] Cowley celebrates the "rebellious" distance from the ideology of social realism that opened up in the fiction of Lost Generation authors, whose irony, even cynicism, toward American modernity became the very logic for canonizing it. Cowley argues that modern US literature becomes most serious in pulling away from seriousness, the dutiful or even propagandistic depiction of social reality. Such critical appraisals of so-called modernist US fiction would soon become commonplace, and indeed would condition the critical consensus from which postwar fiction emerged, and according to whose terms it would be judged.

The possibility that literature, and literary history, could function at an ironic remove from literary and political realism and yet still carry out an important social function came to be part of the critical consensus among a number of US critics during the Cold War. Not only did the CIA famously promote American experimental art abroad – especially the disinterested and seemingly apolitical formalism of Abstract Expressionism – as a form of Cold War propaganda, but critics also shifted their notions of irony and seriousness in a manner constitutive of the commonly understood literary devices of postmodernism.[25] The critic Edmund Wilson was, like Cowley, an admirer of Hemingway; as Wilson wrote in 1940, Hemingway "has expressed with genius the terrors of the modern man at the danger of losing control of his world."[26] Wilson places a high demand on artistic genius in his concern for distinguishing a politically relevant mode of writing from what he called the "Russian" "disparagement of works of art in comparison with political action."[27] Wilson thus privileged literary genius as the ability, through talent, to give art a social function. What Wilson describes as the "moral victories" of Hemingway's art epitomize this social function; as Wilson explains in a telling analogy, his fiction works according to "the principle of a Bourdon gauge," a device for measuring pressure.[28] Hemingway's fiction – like his characters and career alike – succumbs to the social pressures of the moment, and in doing so, registers the laws these pressures obey. Their ironic distance emerges as a second-order product of their very susceptibility to social pressures; this irony, in turn, becomes the key to their social relevance, the very principle of its function as a Bourdon gauge. Herein lay Hemingway's genius.

Wilson's Bourdon gauge pointedly recalls T. S. Eliot's famous analogy for describing the significance of artistic depersonalization – another form of distance, if hardly an ironic one – in his 1919 essay on "Tradition and the Individual Talent." Eliot describes the impersonal poet as "a bit of finely filiated platinum" that, when introduced into a certain environment – here, a jar of oxygen and sulfur dioxide – catalyzes the creation of a new chemical compound, an acid. Eliot describes this chemical reaction in terms of the poet's function in creating new kinds of feelings, but the analogy might more accurately be said to introduce the notion that artistic creation has less to do with expression, of having "more to say," than with the process through which a writer becomes "a more finely perfected medium" for literary precursors ("tradition") and new emotions to mutually recombine.[29] Wilson's Bourdon gauge extrapolates this notion across Hemingway's body of fictional work and, by extension, to other Lost Generation writing: precisely in falling prey to social pressure, such writers and works become a medium for registering its effects, but also for enabling new combinations of "feeling" to emerge.

Such devices – gauges, catalysts, bits of metal – proliferate throughout the fiction of the American Cold War. Nominated as precursors for the fictions that emerged after the war, the very acceptance of Cowley's modernists as canonical, and the devices through which their importance becomes demonstrable, render them ironically available to Cold War writers as contemporary media for their continued experimental work. Ralph Ellison's nameless protagonist in *Invisible Man* (1952) traverses a veritable anthology of African American thought throughout the novel, from the Booker T. Washingtonesque discourses of his Southern black college to the pan-Africanism of the Marcus Garvey-esque Ras the Exhorter. Ellison's protagonist, while perhaps not fully "impersonal" in Eliot's sense, nonetheless functions as both catalyst and gauge. Not only does he register the effects of long-accumulating pressures of racism and racial non-relation in the United States, but he also manages, time and again, inadvertently to set them into violent action as well; he thereby serves as a fictional means for formalizing their effects.

The multiplication of impersonal gauges and catalysts throughout US fiction of the later twentieth century is too widespread to delineate fully here, yet it comprises one of the signal means through which critical and literary "precursors" become a medium for contemporary artistic creativity. Toni Morrison, herself a former editor at Random House and thus firmly embedded within the very technology of literary production and distribution, describes her own synthetic practice of accumulating catalysts in her 1992 essay *Playing in the Dark*. The book begins by describing a moment in *The Words to Say It*, a 1975 autobiographical novel by the Algerian-born French writer Marie Cardinal, in which a unique note in a Louis Armstrong solo sets off a series of strong emotional and physical responses that both enact and represent the real psychic pressures of Cardinal's life. Constructing her own version of Wilson's gauge or Eliot's bit of finely filiated platinum, Morrison remarks upon the power of Armstrong's solo as a catalyst in Cardinal's text; most notably, she draws attention to the extent to which this chain of precursors already registers the recombinatory effects of a borrowed tradition: Cardinal's visceral reaction to Armstrong's jazz solo also comprises a white Frenchwoman's "conceptual response to a black, that is, nonwhite, figuration."[30] Such moments form the basis of Morrison's observation about the history and criticism of US literature: "I was interested," she writes, "as I had been for a long time, in the way black people ignite critical moments of discovery or change or emphasis in literature not written by them. In fact I had started, casually like a game, keeping a file of such instances."[31] Morrison's work as an author, editor, and critic is dedicated to working though the power and significance of such intense concentrations of historical meaning. She thus nominates as important literary precursors an archive of non-white figuration within the very canon of traditional white writing erected at midcentury. Whereas her editorial work was instrumental in promoting the literary careers of African American authors such as Gayl Jones, Toni Cade Bambara, Henry Dumas, and Angela Davis, her attention in *Playing in the Dark* is directed toward the tendency of critics and scholars to disavow blackness within the established "white" canon of American literature. Morrison renders visible the mediating function of such critical commonplaces, taking issue with the ways in which "agendas in criticism have disguised themselves and, in so doing, impoverished the literature it studies."[32] In a manner that recalls Susan Sontag's critique of "interpretation," Morrison establishes her own project on the terrain of literary canonicity as a zombie category. Far from discarding the canon, or rejecting the categories of literary history altogether, her "game-like" accumulation of catalysts inaugurates a means of reassessing, of reinhabiting, the zombie categories themselves. In writing about Poe, Hemingway, Willa Cather, Mark Twain, and others, Morrison retains the same set of literary precursors as many Cold War critics (or, perhaps more accurately, returns to them at a 30-year remove); yet in nominating them once more as precursors, she draws attention to the way we read and invest in them as the critical environment that mediates our own continued artistic and political experience. The "impoverished" categories of literary study remain important frameworks within and against which Morrison gathers and deploys the catalysts of nonwhite figuration she collects, engendering new combinations from what would otherwise be a critical dead end.

What Goes Around Comes Around

Morrison, Pynchon, Acker, Barth, and numerous other postmodern authors throughout the United States and the Americas construct literary genealogies that extend across established literary periods. In doing so, they do not so much reject established critical and literary-historical categories, as I have suggested, as appropriate such categories as part of their very medium of experimentation. There is nothing especially new about this, nor specific to postmodernism. As recent scholars have attested, beyond the exhaustion of the categories themselves, their adoption as formal considerations within postmodern fiction represents an intensification of, rather than a break with, the historiographical and critical frameworks adopted in earlier literary forms. Indeed, we find metacritical tendencies throughout literary history, from the recourse to historical book burning in *Don Quixote* as a poetics of erasure, to the play on editorial timing and the mechanics of printing in *Tristram Shandy*; from commentaries on Shakespeare scholarship in Joyce's *Ulysses* to footnote references to Jessie Weston's folklore study in Eliot's *The Waste Land*. The "zombie categories" of literary periodization and canonicity that continue to organize our understanding of American literature have their precedents in the historiographical and critical categories of the nineteenth and twentieth centuries, in the theories of transhistorical continuity and residual ancientness that often undergird the production and reception of earlier modernist literature. Indeed, the master narratives once attributed to modernist literature themselves took shape in scholarly or historical works whose claims to science, or at least to methodological consistency, have become subject to the same claims of obsolescence (or worse) as "master narratives" themselves. The nineteenth and twentieth centuries are rife with archetypes and narratives of progress and degeneration, cycles of decay and regeneration, epochal shifts, family trees, and romances of Ancient Mysteries. Yet as scholars of postmodernism from the 1960s to the present remind us time and again, we have never fully departed from the era of master narratives; the discourses of world history, comparative folklore, Egyptology, psychoanalysis, and hermetic mysticism that inform so many works of modern literature continue to inform the way we think about literature and history alike. Rather than reflecting a quaint recourse to myth or a more troublesome longing for totalization, this body of work staggers on obstinately through the twentieth century and into the twenty-first. Modernist ideas about historical continuity and rupture are themselves zombie categories, as Jameson notes: two sides of the same dialectical coin. The meaning of such residual categories is not reducible to their historical origins, however, nor is their status as the basis of master narratives reducible to their outdated and often unsavory ideological content. They may, in fact, be bound up in very bad histories, and often are. But as zombie concepts, such models of recursion and continuity become something other than the stable bearers of these effects. Recast by postmodern authors as the very framework within which literary precursors become identifiable, it is no longer possible to say that the recourse to dialecticism makes one not only a Hegelian but a champion of Imperial Consciousness; or that the invocation of Osirian cycles of dismemberment and return (or of the waxing and waning Moon or King) exposes one's proclivities as a potential fascist. This may be a perfectly obvious point to make, but our tendency in literary studies to identify such metahistorical figurations as "source material" or "historical context" for modern literature often risks invoking such identifications as some sort of ideological guarantee.

Such forms not only persist but also threaten to get out of hand. Indeed, it is this very capacity that makes it possible for such critical and metahistorical forms to be taken up as an apparatus for continued experimentation. In *Mumbo Jumbo* (1972), Ishmael Reed's brilliant allegory of the Civil Rights era, the Jazz-Age United States becomes the immediate historical setting for an epic struggle to secure a hermetic power – at once a holy Grail, a secret book, and a spontaneous force that "Jes Grew" – whose origins date from antiquity. Set in a Prohibition-era New York scarred by segregation, lynching, and colonial expansion, this millennial crusade plays out intradiegetically as a racial struggle with mortal consequences. But for Reed, the stakes of this war are not limited to the immediate conditions of racism and oppression alone, but extend to the long historical legacy of their perpetuation as well. That is, the struggle between the regressive bureaucratic rationalism of the "Atonists" and the liberatory unreason of "Jes Grew" is nothing less than the epochal clash of universal histories: the white supremacist narratives of Western Civilization such as those of nineteenth-century universal histories of Marc Gaborieau, Max Nordau, and even G. W. F. Hegel, which contrast starkly with competing historiographies of ancient African empires, as forwarded by Edgar Wylmot Blyden, J. A. Rogers, and Frank Snowden. Such texts flesh out the back pages of Reed's novel, which features a bibliography: Reed's novel explicitly names its precursors, both in its literary recourse to epic historiography (Reed's characters cite Johann Wolfgang von Goethe, Sigmund Freud, and Marcus Garvey, for instance) and in its scholarly apparatus. The novel ascribes living agency to such metahistorical precursors, its fictional characters fighting to "teach ... the difference between a healer, a holy man, and a duppy who returns from the grave and causes mischief."[33] In its clash of universal historical forms and theories, *Mumbo Jumbo* seeks less to enforce the demarcation between good and bad historical forms themselves, than to dramatize the stakes of their intelligibility, as well as their persistence and recursion as a medium for contemporary postmodern art and experience.

In *Mumbo Jumbo*, the zombie categories of modern history become literal in their persistence and recursion: Reed's novel at once figures the repressive work of zombification itself – the instrumental reason of slavery, colonialism, monotheism, and capitalism – as well as its spiritual countermeasures in jazz, experimental black writing, and Haitian Voudon. Such living forms become the measure of how historical forms continue to structure experience in spite of their exhaustion. As Papa LaBas, the novel's protagonist, reflects on his career as a *houngan*, a male Voudon priest, at the novel's close: "What are you driving at? they would say in Detroit in the 1950s. In the 40s he haunted the stacks of a ghost library. In the 30s he sought to recover his losses like everybody else. In the 20s they know. And the 20s were back again. Better, Arna Bontemps was correct in his new introduction to *Black Thunder*. Time is a pendulum. Not a river. More akin to what goes around comes around."[34] Such pendulum swings figure at once the possibility of historical justice and the recursivity of time itself. Like the Bourdon gauge or the concept of "master narratives" itself, such figurations not only document the political and epistemological imperatives of a postmodernist novel such as *Mumbo Jumbo*, but they also constitute the novel's historical relationship to its medium, that is, the body of fictional and scholarly precursors it nominates both implicitly and explicitly as the bearers of its zombie categories.

Like other works of postmodern American fiction, *Mumbo Jumbo* demonstrates the extent to which the lessons of *wikiHow* apply to contemporary literary history in general. "If you're not understanding what's going on now, something completely different will happen later that will get you back on track." We find here good advice for reading a Thomas Pynchon novel, certainly; but we also find a model for historical recursion, and even for justice, that characterizes how postmodern fiction both nominates and works through its own precursors.

Further Reading

James, David. *Modernist Futures: Innovation and Inheritance in the Contemporary Novel*. Cambridge: Cambridge University Press, 2012.

Jameson, Fredric. *The Ancients and the Postmoderns: On the Historicity of Forms*. London: Verso, 2015.

Levine, Caroline. *Forms: Whole, Rhythm, Hierarchy, Network*. Princeton, NJ: Princeton University Press, 2015.

Morrison, Toni. *Playing in the Dark: Whiteness and the Literary Imagination*. New York: Vintage, 1992.

Moten, Fred. *In the Break: The Aesthetics of the Black Radical Tradition*. Minneapolis: University of Minnesota Press, 2003.

Nealon, Jeffrey. *Post-Postmodernism, or, the Cultural Logic of Just-in-Time Capitalism*. Palo Alto, CA: Stanford University Press, 2012.

Peterson, Nancy J. *Against Amnesia: Contemporary Women Writers and the Crises of Historical Memory*. Philadelphia: University of Pennsylvania Press, 2001.

NOTES

1 "How to Read a Thomas Pynchon Novel." *WikiHow*, accessed February 1, 2015, http://www.wikihow.com/Read-a-Thomas-Pynchon-Novel.

2 See Amy Elias, *Sublime Desire: History and Post-1960s Fiction* (Baltimore, MD: Johns Hopkins University Press, 2001); Linda Hutcheon, *A Poetics of Postmodernism: History, Theory, Fiction* (New York: Routledge, 1988); Joseph Tabbi, *Postmodern Sublime: Technology and American Writing from Mailer to Cyberpunk* (Ithaca, NY: Cornell University Press, 1996).

3 Linda Wagner-Martin, *A History of American Literature: 1950 to the Present* (London: Wiley-Blackwell, 2013), 1.

4 Jean-François Lyotard, *The Postmodern Condition: A Report on Knowledge* (1979), trans. Geoff Bennington and Brian Massumi (Minneapolis: University of Minnesota Press, 1984), 81.

5 Ibid., xxiii, xxiv.

6 Ibid., xxv.

7 Ibid., 82.

8 Fredric Jameson, *A Singular Modernity: Essay on the Ontology of the Present* (London: Verso, 2002), e.g., 25.

9 There have been a number of special journal issues looking retrospectively at postmodernist American fiction, such as "Postmodernism, Then" and "After

Postmodernism." See esp. Jason Gladstone and Daniel Worden, "Introduction: Postmodernism, Then," *Twentieth-Century Literature* 57, no. 3–4 (2011): 292–294; see also Andrew Hoberek, "Introduction: After Postmodernism," *Twentieth-Century Literature* 53, no. 3 (2007): 233–247. Brian McHale, "1966 Nervous Breakdown; or, When Did Postmodernism Begin?," *Modern Language Quarterly* 69, no. 3 (2008): 391–413. See also Jeffrey T. Nealon, *Post-Postmodernism, or, The Cultural Logic of Just-in-Time Capitalism* (Stanford, CA: Stanford University Press, 2012).

10 See, for instance, Ulrich Beck and Elisabeth Beck-Gernscheim, *Individualization: Institutionalized Individualism and Its Social and Political Consequences* (London: Sage, 2001), esp. Jonathan Rutherford, "Zombie Categories: An Interview with Ulrich Beck," 202–213.

11 Susan Sontag, "Against Interpretation" (1964), in *Against Interpretation and Other Essays* (New York: Farrar, Straus and Giroux, 1966), 9.

12 John Barth, "The Literature of Exhaustion" (1967), in *The Friday Book: Essays and Other Non-Fiction* (Baltimore, MD: John Hopkins University Press, 1984), 65.

13 Ibid., 69–70.

14 Ibid., 71.

15 On the relation of the Latin American Boom to US postmodernism, see Brian McHale's "Afterword: Reconstructing Postmodernism," *Narrative* 21, no. 3 (2013): 357–364.

16 Kathy Acker, "William Burroughs's Realism" (1990), in *Bodies of Work: Essays* (London: Serpent's Tail, 1997), 1.

17 David Antin, "Modernism and Postmodernism," *Boundary* 2 (1972), 1.

18 Steven Connor, "Postmodernism and Literature," in *The Cambridge Companion to Postmodernism*, ed. Steven Connor (Cambridge: Cambridge University Press, 2004), 63.

19 Jorge Luis Borges, "Kafka and His Precursors," trans. James Irby, in *Labyrinths: Selected Stories and Other Writings* (New York: New Directions, 1964), 201.

20 Thomas Pynchon, *V.* (1963) (New York: Harper, 2005).

21 See Mark McGurl, *The Program Era: Postwar Fiction and the Rise of Creative Writing* (Cambridge, MA: Harvard University Press, 2011), 209.

22 See Daniel Grausam, *On Endings: American Postmodern Fiction and the Cold War* (Charlottesville: University of Virginia Press, 2011), 71.

23 See McHale, "Afterword," 357–364; also *Postmodernist Fiction* (New York: Methuen, 1987), 3–26.

24 Cowley, "In Defense of the 1920s," *New Republic* CX (April 24, 1933): 564–565.

25 See Frances Stonor Saunders, *The Cultural Cold War: The CIA and the World of Arts and Letters* (New York: New Press, 1999); see also Giles Scott-Smith, *The Politics of Apolitical Culture: The Congress for Cultural Freedom, the CIA, and Post-War American Hegemony* (London: Routledge, 2002).

26 Edmund Wilson, "Hemingway: Gauge of Morale," *Atlantic Monthly* (July 19, 1939), reprinted in *Literary Essays and Reviews of the 1930s and 1940s* (New York: Library of America, 2007), 436.

27 Edmund Wilson, "The Historical Interpretation of Literature," in *Literary Essays and Reviews of the 1930s and 1940s*, ed. Lewis M. Dabney (New York: Library of America, 2007), 262.

28 Wilson, "Hemingway: Gauge of Morale," *Literary Essays and Reviews*, 436.

29 T. S. Eliot, "Tradition and the Individual Talent" (1919), in *Selected Prose*, ed. Frank Kermode (New York: Harcourt, 1975), 40 and 41.

30 Toni Morrison, *Playing in the Dark: Whiteness and the Literary Imagination* (New York: Vintage, 1992), viii.

31 Ibid.

32 Ibid., 9.

33 Ishmael Reed, *Mumbo Jumbo* (New York: Scribner, 1972), 104.

34 Ibid., 218.

2

DAVID COWART

Prolonged Periodization

American Fiction After 1960

This sentence may be pregnant, it missed its period.
– Tom Robbins

Serious, discriminating readers can, if challenged, say a number of cogent things about the character of, say, literary Romanticism – the gulf between a Keats and a Wordsworth (or a Wordsworth and a Byron) notwithstanding. Somehow, by the same token, James Joyce and D. H. Lawrence and Willa Cather and Virginia Woolf are all recognizably modernists. Their postmodern successors, however, remain diverse in ways that can frustrate the periodizing impulse. Surveying contemporary letters, the theoretical Theseus enters again the Daedalian labyrinth, its forking paths generated not only by the energy of varied practitioners, all striving to make "making it new" new, but also by the earnest (and perhaps premature) attempts of readers, reviewers, and academic critics to discern the occasional principle of order – the kind of order that will presumably reveal itself to critical retrospect. A postmodern Pope would be hard pressed to affirm the "plan" in this "mighty maze." Nevertheless, one can still, like the poet, explore "this ample field" and assess the energy of its denizens.

From writers born in the 1920s to those born (virtually) yesterday, one discerns three or so generations of postmodern literary endeavor. By tracing the sequent toil of these cohorts, I hope to sketch a literary period that remains robust, even as younger writers rightly resist fitting themselves too uncritically into parental or grandparental aesthetic molds. I will not attempt, in a single essay, to cover everything going on in American fiction for the last half century (and more); rather, I will identify a number of significant personalities, titles, events, and dates that define a recognizable aesthetic postmodernity – from auguries in the work of Gertrude Stein (1874–1946), Nathanael West (1903–1940), and the Beats to efflorescence in fictions clustering in the 1960s (by the likes of William Gaddis and William H. Gass, Grace Paley and Thomas Pynchon, John Barth and Donald Barthelme) and on to an aesthetic consolidation that continues, in the work of younger artists, to this day. Across this spectrum, I will note formal and ideational markers that characterize these decades of postmodern literary practice. By way of periodizing postmodern American fiction, that is, I propose briefly to characterize the aesthetic principles to which it answers and to discuss the logic of this kind of literary demarcation. After a glance at the work of that modern–postmodern amphibium, Vladimir Nabokov, and a brief inventory of already canonized texts from the 1960s and 1970s, I will consider the postmodernity of fictions by younger, more contemporary practitioners: Richard Powers, Jennifer Egan, and Mark Z. Danielewski. I will also consider the vexed question of postmodernism's putative attenuation, as signaled, perhaps, in the aesthetic dissent of writers – Jonathan Franzen, David Foster Wallace – who chafe at the epistemic tether. These artists, I suggest, have as little hope of prevailing against postmodernism's inexorable sea as the legendary hero Cuchulain who, in his madness, fought the invading waves with his sword.

From Modern to Postmodern

Early in the twentieth century, as faith dwindled and war left lives and landscape lorn, literary artists crafted an aesthetic characterized by the embrace of language stripped of rhetorical sophistry (sincere yet apotropaically ironic); by formal fragmentation; by a desire to shock and a willingness to alienate a complacent, unimaginative middle class; by an interest in time and consciousness (especially the consciousness radically explored by the new science of psychoanalysis); by an exploration of myth not as prescientific religion but as universal, instinctive truth; and, in varying degrees, by an engagement with the politics of history. The disarray in which the Great War left European civilization made for an understandable nostalgia for some orderly status quo ante (that of classical antiquity, for example). Thus the moderns, however formally radical, often proved politically conservative, even reactionary. For every Robert Graves or Ernest Hemingway or George Orwell who sympathized with the Spanish Republicans, an Ezra Pound or a W. B. Yeats or a Robert Frost or a Wyndham Lewis or a Louis-Ferdinand Céline or a Paul Claudel "wanted," like F. Scott Fitzgerald's Nick Carraway, "the world to be in uniform and at a sort of moral attention forever."[1] T. S. Eliot's 1927 credo ("I am an Anglo-Catholic in religion, a classicist in literature and a royalist in politics") was the definitive expression of this proclivity.[2] These writers, mostly born in the last years of the nineteenth century, came to prominence in the 1920s and reigned as the literary elite until midcentury (which saw Nobel Prizes for Hemingway, William Faulkner, and T. S. Eliot). Along with contemporaneous composers, painters, sculptors, filmmakers, architects, and choreographers, they fashioned modern art.

The emergence of the postmodern was heralded by a handful of writers – Jorge Luis Borges, Nabokov, Samuel Beckett – born at or shortly after the turn of the century. They had relatively little in common. Borges and Nabokov (both born in 1899) would die in Switzerland after long literary odysseys. Beckett (born in 1906) would, like Nabokov, witness a revolution before becoming a lifelong exile. Having served a literary apprenticeship as amanuensis to James Joyce, twenty-four years his elder, Beckett would in 1961 share the Prix International with Borges. Slightly too young to have had a hand in the creation of modernism, these writers signaled their artistic impatience in various quirky fictions that had, early on, no convenient label. But all three, arriving late to the modernist pub, began to think beyond closing time.

Each of these writers qualifies as a Janus of the modern–postmodern divide, but Nabokov offers the ideal example. The author most famous for his daring midcentury novel of pedophilia (or what purported to be pedophilia) came to maturity as a subversive re-fashioner of the modernism all around him in his formative years. By the time he began to make of himself an English-language author (subsequent to his flight from France to America in 1940), the literary writing was, as it were, on the wall. A Daniel rather than a Belshazzar, he knew its meaning: the day of the modern was passing. Thus the new aesthetic, still unnamed, began to manifest itself in the fictions of this Russian émigré. Nabokov's narrators – the "V." of *The Real Life of Sebastian Knight* (1941), the Humbert Humbert of *Lolita* (1955), the smug "litterateur" of *Pnin* (1957), the addled Kinbote of *Pale Fire* (1962) – prove always to mock our notions of identity and our expectations of identity's representation. Indeed, dismissing "reality" as "one of the few words which mean nothing without quotes," Nabokov tends always to problematize representation.[3] For all the precision with which he observes American mores and landscape, he takes little interest in mimesis per se, in the representation of the world. Rather, he devises worlds of his own (and again he reconfigures a Joycean conceit: the idea, articulated by Stephen Dedalus in *Portrait of the Artist as a Young Man*, that "[t]he artist, like the God of the creation, remains within or behind or beyond or above his handiwork, invisible, refined out of existence, indifferent, paring his fingernails").[4] The narrator of Nabokov's first novel in English, *The Real Life of Sebastian Knight*, depicts the title character at one point "lying spread-eagled on the floor of his study." The fatigued novelist explains: "I have finished building a world, and this is my Sabbath rest."[5] Thus Nabokov's novels exemplify what Brian McHale calls the "ontological" tendency of postmodern fiction.[6] A more radical artifice displaces the old mirror held up to nature: artists begin holding the mirror up to artifice itself.

30

This backing away from mimetic expectation ("I want to try to create a world, not represent it," declares John Hawkes) has its complement in new ways of thinking about the referentiality of words – the very medium of literary representation.[7] Indeed, the sharpest distinction between modernists and postmodernists lies in their respective conceptualization of language. From Stéphane Mallarmé to Eliot and from Hemingway to Orwell, modern writers subscribed to an ideal of language purified, made serviceable to the recording of the real and true. But writers after midcentury came more and more to think of language as a fluid, shifting, arbitrary, and self-referring medium. Grappling with the never-to-be-closed gap between signifier (word) and signified (thing), they began the quixotic yet brilliant project of "representing the unrepresentable," as another noted theorist observes, "in representation itself."[8] Honing the medium even as they drew attention to its unreliability as a reality-labeling instrument, postmodern writers – John Barth, Donald Barthelme, Tom Stoppard, and Richard Powers are exemplary – embraced an almost precious performativity. When Tom Robbins writes, "This sentence may be pregnant, it missed its period," the punctuation punctures the expected predication.[9] Perennially playful or "ludic" in this way, postmodern discourse tends to foreground its own status as discourse.

Challenging the shibboleth of originality, the postmoderns transform simple pastiche (the imitation of a famous style) into something rich and strange indeed. Borges's Pierre Menard leads the way: he undertakes to write a version of Cervantes's *Don Quixote* that will be the same, word for word, as the original. Succeeding in a handful of pages, he manages a style, Borges's narrator gravely observes, superior to that of Cervantes himself. First published in 1939, the story introduces in its title character the patron saint of pastiche, his vision presently realized in the proliferation of texts appropriated, cloned, recycled, reinscribed: from that "eighteenth-century novel in quotation marks," Barth's *The Sot-Weed Factor* (1960), to Jean Rhys's *Wide Sargasso Sea* and Tom Stoppard's *Rosencrantz and Guildenstern Are Dead* (both 1966), such works shared the cultural moment with the Pop Art images of Andy Warhol and Roy Lichtenstein. Thus Pynchon devotes a chapter of *V.* (1963) to the disastrous performance of a ballet modeled on Stravinsky's *Rite of Spring; The Crying of Lot 49* (1966) is leavened with parodies of thirties cinema (*Cashiered*) and seventeenth-century revenge drama (*The Courier's Tragedy*). Presently, too, John Gardner rewrites *Beowulf* as *Grendel* (1971), and Kathy Acker publishes her own *Don Quixote* (1986). In the capable hands of David Henry Huang, *Madama Butterfly* becomes *M. Butterfly* (1988). By the time Valerie Martin transforms *The Strange Case of Dr. Jekyll and Mr. Hyde* into *Mary Reilly* (1990) and Jane Smiley *King Lear* into *A Thousand Acres* (1991), readers had grown accustomed to what I have elsewhere called "literary symbiosis."[10]

Other markers of the postmodern present themselves as reversal after reversal, subversion after subversion, of features prominent in the aesthetic forged by the moderns. Myth is now conceptualized as local, not universal – it is invoked only to be deconstructed. The distinction between story and history (etymologically the same word) evaporates – neither is less subject to narrational shaping than the other. (New genres appear: nonfiction novels are written by John Hersey, Truman Capote, Norman Mailer, and Tom Wicker; "historiographic metafiction" by Barth, Pynchon, Robert Coover, and E. L. Doctorow, not to mention such European authors as John Fowles and Umberto Eco.)[11] Although the moderns saw the collapse of religious faith, they could still seek and affirm the truths of history, consciousness, language. Their successors saw the evisceration of such "depth models," as Fredric Jameson calls them, along with the foundational ideologies or "meta-narratives" they once supported and validated, including ancient hierarchies of race, gender, class, and political legitimacy. Meanwhile, the image reigns supreme; with no diminution of legitimacy, the simulacrum displaces what it once copied or imitated.[12]

But where does all of this begin? Seeking the womb in which postmodern American fiction gestated, one should remember the long travail of the Great Depression and World War II, which issued, in the 1950s, in the curious mix of prosperity, McCarthyite red baiting, the Cold War, the fear of automation, and the truculence, the scarcely disguised potential for violence, of Norman Mailer's hipster or "White Negro," who channeled the more genuinely seismic anger of America's black underclass (the Emmett Till murder took place in 1955). Pinning down postmodernism's inauguration on a calendar, however, remains tricky. The postmodern episteme proves uncongenial to the very concept of linear, divisible historical time. By the same token, one discerns in work dating from the eighteenth century (Laurence Sterne's *Tristram Shandy*), the sixteenth century (*Don Quixote*), and even antiquity (the *Satyricon* of Petronius Arbiter) many of the fictive elements that critics and theorists flag as postmodern.

One can get around this relativism by stipulating that the times must themselves be postmodern, along with the supposedly exemplary works. For their disruptiveness in these years, some would nominate the Beats – proto-hippies, an augury of the societal phenomenon that burgeoned in the 1960s – as literary postmodernism's shock troops. Others tend to see the Beats as modernism's mannerists – that is, those who turn a once fresh aesthetic into "mannered" predictability. Even William S. Burroughs's embrace of aleatory art – that of the "cut up" – looks a lot like warmed-over Dadaism.

Jack Kerouac, Allen Ginsberg, Burroughs, and their fellows exemplified modernism's *épatez le bourgeois* ethos; they pushed the boundaries of obscenity and, as candid as their contemporary, James Baldwin, about what dared not speak its name elsewhere in the culture, undertook in other ways to represent, as the modernists did, the unrepresentable. They stopped short, however, of the postmodern problematizing of representation itself. Their mythography of exuberance and saintly suffering and madness, however disruptive, never became self-interrogating. Thus Kerouac's Dean Moriarty (Neal Cassady in real life) was the mythic American Adam in his twilight phase – he would be displaced by such myth-pithing figures as Joseph Heller's Yossarian, Barth's Ebenezer Cooke, Ken Kesey's Randall Patrick McMurphy, and Kurt Vonnegut's Billy Pilgrim. Pynchon, by the same token, would present the American Eve, at once archetypal and postmodern, in Oedipa Maas and Frenesi Gates.

Those who do not trace annunciation of the postmodern to the Beats find likelier 1950s candidates in William Gaddis and Flannery O'Connor, who in 1955 published *The Recognitions* and the important collection *A Good Man Is Hard to Find*, respectively. James Baldwin's first novel, the autobiographical *Go Tell It on the Mountain*, came out in 1953; Grace Paley's first collection, *The Little Disturbances of Man*, in 1959. John Hawkes, who would become an iconic postmodernist, saw into print *The Cannibal* in 1949 and *The Beetle Leg* in 1951. John Barth published, in rapid succession, *The Floating Opera* (1956), *The End of the Road* (1958), and *The Sot-Weed Factor* (1960). Kurt Vonnegut's first stories and novels appeared in the 1950s as well. Producing important fiction in the 1950s and early 1960s, these writers, presently joined by such slower-blooming contemporaries as Joseph Heller, Gilbert Sorrentino, and David Markson (as well as the slightly younger Ken Kesey, Philip Roth, Thomas Pynchon, Don DeLillo, John Updike, Toni Morrison, Cormac McCarthy, John Gardner, Ishmael Reed, Donald Barthelme, Robert Coover, and Joan Didion), represent the first postmodern generation, which came of age (artistically) at a time in which events – from the bombing of Hiroshima to the assassination of John Fitzgerald Kennedy – seemed once again to challenge representational adequacy. Moreover, they quickly saw the possibilities adumbrated by the mold-breaking work of emergent writers disinclined to accept the role of modernist rear guard. John Barth, saluting Borges in a 1967 essay ("The Literature of Exhaustion"), gets credit for being among the first to see (and opt for) the literary future. As Barth implied, the displacement of modernism as cultural dominant began with writers who saw their future in some radically fresh relationship with artifice.

Those seeking a point of origin for both postmodernity (the cultural environment) and postmodernism (its artistic reflection) sometimes adduce the assassination of the American president in 1963.[13] Dealey Plaza saw, in DeLillo's memorable phrase, "the seven seconds that broke the back of the American century."[14] It was also the year of the American novel *V.*, in which Thomas Pynchon, seminal postmodernist, established himself overnight as the definitive instantiation of trends gathering momentum, as previously noted, in the early work of Gaddis, Barth, Heller, and Kesey. With *V.* and its successors (especially *Gravity's Rainbow* in 1973, the year that saw the World Trade Center dedicated), Pynchon identified as Zeitgeist the widespread, paranoid conviction of conspiracy that seemed to manifest itself everywhere, fed by the maturation of cinematic and televisual media in which the image took on a disturbingly coercive ontological authority. In 1966, the publication of his second novel, *The Crying of Lot 49*, coincided with the "Languages of Criticism and the Sciences" conference at Johns Hopkins, at which Jacques Derrida presented "Structure, Sign and Play in the Discourse of the Human Sciences," the paper that would establish poststructuralist theory as postmodernism's ideational complement.

One notes in passing that the postmodern tide, however engorged, never quite swept away its various rivals for aesthetic legitimacy, whether modernism, naturalism, or realism. In fact, the postmodern (especially in architecture) is endlessly eclectic: it incorporates or subsumes recognizable elements of all that precedes it. Nor does it, like some invasive species, drive other forms to extinction. Its emergence does not gainsay the artistic power of, say, Norman Mailer's naturalist 1948 fiction of World War II, *The Naked and the Dead* – or, for that matter, the novels of Joyce Carol Oates, which critics often characterize as latter-day naturalism as well. Meanwhile, the postwar realists – J. D. Salinger, John Cheever, John Updike, various *New Yorker* School alumni – were read and honored alongside the more iconoclastic Austers, Ackers, and Antrims.

As the 1950s ended and the 1960s began, in fact, authors seemed to be engaged in a cerebral game of literary *rayuela* or hopscotch (a figure made memorable as the title of a 1963 novel by another early postmodernist, Julio Cortázar). In 1959, Philip Roth's National Book Award–winning *Goodbye, Columbus* collection seemed to signal no diminution of realism's legitimacy. This from an author who would presently remark that the contemporary novelist "has his hands full in trying to understand, describe, and then make credible" an "American reality" that so "stupifies," "sickens," and "infuriates" that it becomes "a kind of embarrassment to one's meager imagination."[15] Of course, every age thinks itself uniquely beset by public folly and the attenuation of that "ancient virtue" Gibbon speaks of it in the opening paragraph of his monumental *Decline and Fall of the Roman Empire*. But Roth apes Gibbon in 1961, before the assassinations of

Martin Luther King Jr. and the Kennedy brothers, before Vietnam, before Civil Rights, before the Long Hot Summer of 1967, before Watergate, before Iran – Contra, before the vice presidency of Dan Quayle (not to mention the threatened vice presidency of Sarah Palin), before 9/11, before Iraq I and II, before Afghanistan, before the Islamic State Caliphate, and one could enumerate further the terrible passages of life in late-twentieth- and early twenty-first-century America and the proliferating *bêtises* of her politicians. Indeed, so appalling was the half century following Roth's famous observation that one wonders what might previously have merited such an extravagant lament.

Roth's own career would, in any event, illustrate the hopscotch art of the age. As he would by turns write realist fiction, Juvenalian satire (*Our Gang*, 1971), stories of vexed postmodern identity (*Operation Shylock*, 1993), and alternate history (*The Plot Against America*, 2004), so would the literary times devolve into alternating currents of traditional and experimental storytelling. In 1960, Updike began what would become a series of realist fictions about the sensualist, upwardly mobile heel Harry "Rabbit" Angstrom; in 1961, critics and readers delighted in the thoroughly postmodernist *Catch-22*, by Joseph Heller. In 1963, the literary sensation was Pynchon's *V.*, but in 1964 the naturalist *Last Exit to Brooklyn* by Hubert Selby Jr. struck no one as artistically antique. Indeed, Pynchon's celebrated 1966 *New York Times Magazine* article, "A Journey into the Mind of Watts," was steeped in the same outrage that characterized the work of muckrakers at the beginning of the twentieth century – the raw material for Frank Norris, Upton Sinclair, and company.[16] In the later fictions, *Against the Day* (2006), *Inherent Vice* (2009), and *Bleeding Edge* (2013), savage indignation would threaten to overwhelm Pynchon's every comedic premise. Roth, meanwhile, would become more and more moralistic in such late fictions as *American Pastoral* (1997) and *The Human Stain* (2000). Thus a variety of styles checker the literary landscape of the twentieth century's last decades – and the supposed shifting of artistic gears in the first decades of the twenty-first may well prove to be little more than another in the periodic resurfacing (in both senses of the word) of the realist–naturalist–modernist continuum. One suspects that for some decades yet, contemporary letters will have to be assessed as stylistic congeries, aging aesthetic sans-culottes playing Whac-A-Mole, perhaps, with belated naturalists, realists, and modernists.

The Widening Gyre

Different concerns – often less immediately recognizable as reflections of any modern–postmodern split – present themselves when one turns to the ethnic writers who figure so prominently in the period. Once relegated to the cultural margin, these writers have effectively "migrated" to the center – or so one interprets the enormous popular and critical response to the many fictive engagements with ethnic identity on the part of African Americans, Native Americans, and various immigrants and their children. Immigrant literati of the modern period – Abraham Cahan (1860–1951), say, or Ayn Rand (1905–1982), or Carlos Bulosan (1913–1956) – exemplified the old model of assimilationist accommodation. Unlike the last, who was never actually allowed to become a citizen, the Québec-born Saul Bellow (1915–2005) was swiftly Americanized when, speaking only Yiddish and French, he came to Chicago from Québec with his parents (Russian Jews) at the age of nine. But within Bellow's lifetime, immigrants began to take pride in their ethnic difference. Richard Rodriguez plausibly dates this shift to the 1970s, "that decade when middle-class ethnics began to resist the process of assimilation – the American melting pot."[17] The shift manifested itself in a turn to various proud affirmations of ethnic origin – Maxine Hong Kingston's 1976 *Woman Warrior* being an important example, presently followed by a spate of fictions devoted to parsing the experience of immigrants and their children: Theresa Hak Kyung Cha's *Dictee* (1982), Wendy Law-Yone's *The Coffin Tree* (1983), Bharati Mukherjee's *Jasmine* (1989), Oscar Hijuelos's *The Mambo Kings Play Songs of Love* (1989), Julia Alvarez's *How the García Girls Lost Their Accents* (1991), Cristina García's *Dreaming in Cuban* (1992), Edwidge Danticat's *Breath, Eyes, Memory* (1994), Chang-Rae Lee's *Native Speaker* (1995), and many more.

African American writing, on the other hand, had its own recognizable modernist phase, as seen in the work of Jean Toomer, Nella Larsen, James Weldon Johnson, Langston Hughes, Ralph Ellison, Richard Wright, and Zora Neale Hurston. Indeed, some have argued that much of modernism's energy can be traced to the appropriation of African and African American forms (one thinks of the African mask in the imagination of a Picasso or a Lawrence, or the musical idioms of black America in the hands of the Gershwins and subsequent generations of jazz musicians). But the aesthetic assumptions of the black modernists also had to undergo revision or reassessment as their literary children and grandchildren undertook to hold some kind of mirror up to the post–Jim Crow era. African American literature, according to the celebrated "Signifying Monkey" thesis of Henry Louis Gates Jr., proceeds by a concatenation of texts that play ironically with prior texts.[18] As Zora Neale Hurston, in the opening sentences of *Their Eyes Were Watching God*, rewrites or "Signifies on" or – as the vernacular has it – "plays the dozens with" a famous passage in Frederick Douglass's 1845 autobiography, so does the shift into the more pervasive ironies of postmodernism come easily to the African American literary imagination.[19] Though Gates emphasizes the intertextual relations of a strictly African American literary tradition, it is not hard to see black writers playing the Signifying Monkey with a variety of white literary lions: Ralph Ellison rewrites Joyce in much the same parodic spirit as Nabokov does. In *Playing in the Dark* (1992), her revisionist reading of American literature, Toni Morrison Signifies on – or reconceptualizes – Ellison's invisibility conceit, but in the earlier *Song of Solomon* (1977) she rewrites Faulkner.[20] Alice Walker in turn plays the dozens with her Georgia neighbor Flannery O'Connor. The postmodern migration of the margins to the center, seen in Morrison's success as the first African American to win the Nobel Prize for Literature, is not something her successors would want to challenge or reverse. Thus she provides more inspiration than challenge to the originality of younger African American novelists.

Gloria Naylor, born at midcentury, exemplifies middle-generation African American postmodernism. While respectful of the aesthetic she inherits from Toni Morrison and Ishmael Reed, she devotes less energy than they do to deconstructing whiteness and white privilege. Like Alice Walker, in fact, she refuses to deny herself the rich resources of world literature – however dominated it might be by the much maligned "dead white males." In *Linden Hills* (1985), for example, she rewrites Dante's *Inferno*, and in *Mama Day* (1988), she rewrites Shakespeare every bit as much as she Signifies on Zora Neale Hurston (I am thinking of the doomed love and the great hurricane that the younger writer borrows from *Their Eyes Were Watching God*).

Attempting to demarcate succeeding generations in the postmodern apostolic succession, however, one risks ending up like the character in Nabokov who studies seventeenth-century pastoral, as opposed to the eighteenth-century variety (the sheep are a bit cleaner and fluffier in the earlier period). One ought rather to differentiate a convulsive, deck-clearing first phase from the sustained wave of consolidation over the last decades of the twentieth century and into the twenty-first. This wave builds in the work of writers born in the 1940s and 1950s – writers who began to publish important fiction in the 1980s: *Mrs. Caliban* (1982), by Rachel Ingalls (born 1940); *The Color Purple* (1982), by Alice Walker (born 1944); *The Women of Brewster Place* (1982), by Gloria Naylor (born 1950); *Three Farmers on Their Way to a Dance* (1985), by Richard Powers (born 1957); and *You Bright and Risen Angels* (1987), by William T. Vollmann (born 1959). Other writers of this generation would include Maxine Hong Kingston (born 1940); Tim O'Brien (1946); Paul Auster, Kathy Acker, and Octavia Butler (1947); Art

Spiegelman and William Gibson (1948); Mark Leyner (1956); and Donald Antrim, Ben Fountain, and George Saunders (1958).

Nor does this chronology represent any prospect of creative enervation. The 1960s, 1970s, and 1980s saw the birth of another generation, its members destined to be the face of the postmodern millennium, their work its index. Here readers find Marisa Silver (born 1960); Jennifer Egan, Chuck Palahniuk, and David Foster Wallace (1962); Jonathan Lethem (1964); Mark Z. Danielewski and Adam Johnson (1967); Dave Eggers and Nathan Englander (1970); ZZ Packer (1974); Garth Risk Hallberg (1978); Ben Lerner (1979); Nathaniel Rich (1980); and Karen Russell (1981). Complicating this schema, of course, is the undiminished vitality of the first postmodernists, continuing to publish important work in their advanced years (if postmodernism were a fugue, this feature would be the countersubject, with which the first voice continues as later voices enter). To be sure, the numbers of the postmodern pioneers have dwindled: Donald Barthelme dies in 1989, William S. Burroughs in 1997, William Gaddis in 1998, Joseph Heller in 1999, Ken Kesey in 2001, Ronald Sukenick in 2004, Gilbert Sorrentino in 2006, Grace Paley and Kurt Vonnegut in 2007, Raymond Federman in 2009, Robert Stone and E. L. Doctorow in 2015. But even after these deaths, the still-productive survivors of the old guard (Barth, Pynchon, DeLillo, McCarthy, and Morrison) have insured that younger writers have not had the postmodern field to themselves in the late twentieth and early twenty-first centuries.

Among the most important of these younger postmoderns is Richard Powers, a kind of Beckett to Pynchon's Joyce. Twenty years younger than Pynchon, Powers has often expressed his admiration for this elder statesman of postmodern letters. An exemplary second-generation postmodernist, the younger writer actually matches the polymathic range of the master. Like Pynchon, that is, he repeatedly contrives to unite the Two Cultures. Powers's fifth novel, *Galatea 2.2* (1995), concerns the attempts of a research scientist and "Richard Powers," a novelist experiencing vocational anxiety, to teach an advanced computer program to function as a neural net that can pass a kind of millennial Turing test by successfully negotiating a master's-level comprehensive exam in literature. The author's giving the protagonist his own name is of a piece with postmodern practice – one encounters the same calculated cloning of authorial identity in works by John Barth, Philip Roth, Paul Auster, Kathy Acker, Steve Erickson, and David Foster Wallace. Nor does this gesture exhaust the reflexivity of *Galatea 2.2*. In the course of his narrative, Powers recapitulates his own previous career as a novelist. Described but not named, the novels of "Richard Powers" are clearly those of his creator, and he speaks of them in terms that emphasize their postmodern aesthetics. "[M]aking worlds," *Galatea*'s narrator announces his allegiance to what has previously been flagged as the ontological imperative of postmodern fiction: representation having entered crisis, postmodern novelists problematize mimesis – or dispense with it altogether.[21]

Part of the richness of *Galatea 2.2* lies in its clever juxtaposition of two kinds of literary valuation. On the one hand, as the narrator, himself a one-time master's-level student of English, feeds the increasingly humanized, even conscious neural net a vast body of canonical literature, the book becomes the very metastasis of modernist allusion and nostalgia. On the other hand, without overt judgment, he presents the poststructural and postcolonial views of literature that have come to hold sway in academe. The agon between old-school humanist and the scorched-earth hermeneutic of cultural studies (canonical babies thrown out with patriarchal or Eurocentric bathwater) reifies and complicates the simultaneous development of postmodern literature and poststructuralist theory.

As I have noted previously, the attempt to divide literary postmodernism into phases corresponding to each succeeding generation may miscarry. If postmodernism has undergone change, one sees it, rather, in the attenuation, on the part of younger practitioners, of the need to break with (or stay broken with) their *modernist* predecessors. Where a Pynchon or a Barth (or even a John Gardner) was at pains to subvert the modernist valuation of myth as universal, instinctive truth – think of how elaborately the author of *V.* builds up, then demolishes, the myth that structures his novel – younger writers seem not to worry that their postmodern credentials will be called into question if they engage with the moderns in a more friendly or less tendentious way. Ironically, they repeat the veneration of the moderns that made the real extent of the first postmodernists' iconoclasm hard to spot at first. Unlike Nabokov, whose creative autonomy needed freeing from the powerful and temporally proximate Joycean example, today's younger writers feel no need to slay the modernist father. Indeed, they may venerate him – not to mention his consort, the modernist mother. Thus Ann Patchett, author of the engaging 2001 novel *Bel Canto*, cheerfully admits to a perennial desire to rewrite Mann's *Magic Mountain*.[22] Thus Michael Cunningham, in *The Hours* (1998), reconceptualizes Woolf's *Mrs. Dalloway*. Thus Jennifer Egan, in her 2010 novel *A Visit from the Goon Squad*, rewrites at least two modernist monuments: Proust's *In Search of Lost Time* and Eliot's *The Waste Land* (the novel features failed desire, a Fisher King, a death by water, auguries of a global warming apocalypse, and a host of allusions to the culture of the past, from the Orpheus and Eurydice story to Chaucer's *Canterbury Tales*). Egan even dallies with what Eliot called "Mr. Joyce's mythic method" – though she does not recuperate myth to its modernist cachet. Her Orpheus loses one Eurydice whom he does not recognize (his wife) while actually rescuing another (his niece) from infernal Naples (nor does he seem aware of that city's proximity to Avernus and the entrance to the Kingdom of the Dead). This effete art lover (as much Proust's Swann as mythic swain) admires the famous *Orpheus and Eurydice* sculpture in Naples's Museo Nationale, little realizing that he is as much a copy as it is. He is Orpheus as postmodern simulacrum, nor does the mythic identity signal much in the way of those larger constructs of cultural continuity so often evoked by the modernists.

Mark Z. Danielewski is another of the younger writers who play with the very rupture instantiated in the work of the first-generation postmodernists. In his monumental 2000 novel *House of Leaves*, he devises a vast labyrinth, its intricacy seeming to dwarf even Borges's Library of Babel or Garden of Forking Paths. In its scale and ambition, *House of Leaves* vies, withal, with the great encyclopedic narratives of Joyce and Pynchon. Danielewski introduces dual narrators, both decidedly postmodern in their storytelling, except that the younger one, who is still living, subtly implies that the older, now dead, remained beholden to a modernist aesthetic. This is of course ludic eclecticism, not nervousness about Danielewski's own legitimacy as a postmodernist.

Many of these younger writers (those born, say, thirty and more years after the postmodern masters, the Hellers, Barths, O'Connors, Gaddises, and Vonneguts born in the 1920s, as well as the Pynchons, DeLillos, Roths, Updikes, and Morrisons born in the 1930s) may play with and interrogate the aesthetics of both modernism and postmodernism, but they seem disinclined really to repudiate either. Latter-day Pierre Menards, such writers fine-tune the pastiche of Nabokov, Barth, Pynchon, Stoppard, and Gardner. Without becoming epigones or mannerists, they are still, most emphatically, "doing postmodernism." They also give the lie to models of creative anxiety developed by Walter Jackson Bate and Harold Bloom – or, more comically, Thomas Pynchon. Bate studied writers' handling of what he called "the burden of the past."[23] Bloom characterizes the intergenerational dynamic among writers (he speaks chiefly of poets, in fact) as grounded in the "anxiety of influence."[24] The "ephebe" or younger writer must neutralize the fear that the older writer has exhausted the tropes, the language, the very well of original expression. Reading the work of the younger writer as creative misprision of some proximate predecessor, Bloom devises a sixfold typology of strategies whereby the respected, even canonized, work of an older, established writer can be reconfigured, undermined, made to seem dissimilar. According to Bloom's schema, the younger postmodernists ought to be showing signs of worry. Yet none writhes, so far as one can see, with creative envy, anxiety, and dread. Rather, one sees variations on what Pynchon, in *Gravity's Rainbow*, imagines as the witty interplay of the Kenosha Kid and his upshot rival, the Smartass Youth, personages conjured, via sodium pentothal drip, from the idling preconscious of Lt. Tyrone Slothrop:

(2) Smartass youth: Aw, I did all them old-fashioned dances, I did the "Charleston," a-and the "Big Apple," too!
Old veteran hoofer: Bet you never did the "Kenosha," kid!
(2.1) S.Y.: Shucks, I did all them dances, I did the "Castle Walk," and I did the "Lindy," too!
O.V.H.: Bet you never did the "Kenosha Kid."
(3) Minor employee: Well, he has been avoiding me, and I thought it might be because of the Slothrop Affair. If he somehow held me responsible –
Superior (haughtily): You! never did the Kenosha Kid think for one instant that *you* ...
(3.1) Superior (incredulously): You? Never! Did the Kenosha Kid think for one instant that *you* ... ?
(4) And at the end of the mighty day in which he gave us in fiery letters across the sky all the words we'd ever need, words we enjoy today, and fill our dictionaries with, the meek voice of little Tyrone Slothrop, celebrated ever after in tradition and song, ventured to filter upward to the Kid's attention: "You never did '*the*,' Kenosha Kid!"[25]

Pynchon, who was well under forty when he wrote this, captures the funny side of any such apostolic succession. In the fullness of time, of course, he is himself the Old Veteran Hoofer presiding over generational revels at once terpsichorean and verbal.

Among the few to articulate anything like resentment of Pynchon are David Foster Wallace (tentatively) and Jonathan Franzen (somewhat more forcefully). Such writers articulate a dread that they are being epistemically coerced, obliged by the weight of postmodernity and the success of its literary hierophants to fit into a mold they find uncongenial. Both Wallace and Franzen express considerable anxiety about Thomas Pynchon's daunting preeminence in the world of contemporary American letters. Their sentiments resemble those of Cassius in Shakespeare's *Julius Caesar*:

> Why, man, he doth bestride the narrow world
> Like a Colossus, and we petty men
> Walk under his huge legs and peep about
> To find ourselves dishonorable graves.
>
> (I.ii.136–139)[26]

Sadly, Wallace would in fact hie him to an untimely grave – though one in which he enjoys not dishonor but the respect of those who have belatedly come to know the magnitude of the mental and emotional afflictions under which he labored. And if one asks who, among the post-Pynchon literati, wrote the most ambitiously encyclopedic novel, the answer turns out to be not Powers, not Danielewski, not Hallberg, not Adam Levin (author of a 2010 fiction, *The Instructions*, running to 1030 pages). It is, of course, the author of *Infinite Jest* (1996).

But Wallace flirted – I think that is the right word – with some contemporary version of *la trahison des clercs*, the treason of the intellectuals. Though he called, indeed, for a return to the literature of sincerity, any such appeal begs the question of just how committed he was to the "single-entendre principles" he seemed to endorse in a widely read 1993 essay, "I Unibus Pluram."[27] After all, none of Wallace's fiction really strikes one as anything other than the most thoroughgoing postmodernism, however leavened, at times, with sentiment. The same goes for Jonathan Lethem, Junot Díaz, George Saunders, Dave Eggers, and other writers of the putative post-postmodern. Jonathan Franzen is perhaps another matter – and he is, I would argue, the least convincing of the contemporary practitioners that we are asked to take seriously. He belongs, rather, to that class of writers whose novels are less compelling than their nonfiction. (Even confirmed admirers of David Foster Wallace will hesitate when asked: which would you rather re-read – one of his novels or one of his essays?) What Wallace actually deplores in his contentious essay is not some cowardly flight from honest feeling on the part of the American intelligentsia, nor does he repudiate literary irony as somehow precluding legitimate political outrage. Rather, he speculates on some future emergence of literati less married to ironic distance. Yet nowhere does he suggest that the political conviction of a Vonnegut, a Pynchon, a Barth, or a DeLillo is difficult to spot (ironically, Wallace was never particularly transparent about his own politics).

After World War I, as Paul Fussell has suggested, the survivors repudiated the dishonest rhetoric that had justified it. They embraced, with passionate intensity, irony as an all-purpose corrective to cultural ills. Nor, in the succeeding century, has the world recovered the moral clarity that licenses – indeed, demands – the suspension of irony. Even the stark contrast between good and evil in World War II could not lay irony to rest. The greatest novels to come out of that conflict – Mailer's *The Naked and the Dead*, Heller's *Catch-22*, Vonnegut's *Slaughterhouse-Five* – turn on ironic exposure of dark political and economic forces (one thinks of General Cummings's fascism, of

Milo Minderbinder's mercantile rapacity, of Howard W. Campbell's moral confusion) that years of patriotic purpose never quite suppressed.

Both world wars, then, fostered aesthetic transformations, and one wonders, in retrospect, at those few diehards who insisted (and still insist) that there is no such thing as postmodernism – that the creative energy seen in the latter part of the twentieth century somehow represents the continuation of what began with Joyce and Eliot and Picasso and Alban Berg. "Late" modernism, as it were, complement to that "late capitalism" about which one hears so much. But most of those who read across the long twentieth century concur that some kind of epistemic rupture took place after World War II. The question remains: Have the aesthetic energies released thereby exhausted themselves? Is the future of letters contested now between postmodern mannerism and some as yet inchoate literary force? What rough beast slouches toward Knopf or Scribner's to be born?

Inevitably, after half a century of postmodernism, the logic of periodicity reasserts itself – the same logic, ironically, that came eventually to affirm modernism's displacement. Thus a number of literary and cultural historians have speculated about the emergence of Something New. Jeffrey T. Nealon speaks for a minority when he affirms epistemic continuance – but wholly in terms of an "intensification of postmodern capitalism over the past decades."[28] Meanwhile, the observations of critics such as Andrew Hoberek, Rachel Adams, and Josh Toth range from variously modulated anticipation to outright elegy for the presumed passing of an era.[29] Adam Kelly, in his 2013 study *American Fiction in Transition: Observer-Hero Narrative, the 1990s, and Postmodernism*, speaks of an "eclipse" of the twentieth century's last great literary movement and ponders "the idea that the 1990s witnessed the signs of a transition beyond postmodernism."[30] But other critics, notably Mary K. Holland in her 2013 study *Succeeding Postmodernism: Language and Humanism in Contemporary American Literature*, resist this tide. I, too, resist it, mindful of that medieval bring-out-your-dead Monty Python sketch in which the hapless plague victim keeps protesting: "I'm not dead yet!" More seriously, I would suggest that what strikes many as a fading or attenuation of postmodernism, prologue to the birth of a new aesthetic, might better be understood as its "routinization" (as Max Weber's term *Veralltäglichung* is clumsily translated). That is, the culture is so supersaturated with postmodernity that its stylistic reflection becomes invisible. Like Molière's would-be gentleman who is surprised to learn that he has been speaking prose all his life, the person on the street eats and sleeps postmodernity in her cartoons and television programs, movies, advertisements, politics – everything ironic, everything fraught with an awareness that all is

43

text, all simulacra, that "depths" and foundations and metanarratives are illusions.

Like the novel or Mark Twain, then, postmodernism gives the lie to those who would pronounce over its grave. Intellectual historians, after all, have always recognized modernism as merely the last phase of a modernity that began with the Enlightenment, if not the Renaissance. Thus may postmodernity one day denote rather more than a handful of decades. The confusion of the times notwithstanding, one can imagine worse eventualities, for the cultural order that displaces it may prove, as an Orwell character prophesies, totalitarian: "If you want a picture of the future, imagine a boot stamping on a human face – forever" (this in 1949, the very dawn of the postmodern era).[31] On that day (irony whipped to its corner at the cultural periphery, there to subsist in some samizdat twilight), we may find ourselves nostalgic for postmodernism's honest "incredulity towards metanarratives," its reflexivity, its ludic relationship with language and artifice, its interrogations of hierarchy and political legitimacy.

Further Reading

Coale, Samuel Chase. *Quirks of the Quantum: Postmodern and Contemporary American Fiction*. Charlottesville: University of Virginia Press, 2012.

Cowart, David. *Trailing Clouds: Immigrant Fiction in Contemporary America*. Ithaca, NY: Cornell University Press, 2006.

Cowart, David. *Tribe of Pyn: Literary Generations in the Postmodern Period*. Ann Arbor: University of Michigan Press, 2015.

Entzminger, Bettina. *Contemporary Reconfigurations of American Literary Classics: The Origin and Evolution of American Stories*. New York: Routledge, 2013.

Fujii, Hikaru. *Outside, America: The Temporal Turn in Contemporary American Fiction*. New York: Bloomsbury, 2013.

Holland, Mary K. *Succeeding Postmodernism: Language and Humanism in Contemporary American Literature*. London: Bloomsbury, 2013.

Hume, Kathryn. *Aggressive Fictions: Reading the Contemporary American Novel*. Ithaca, NY: Cornell University Press, 2011.

Hume, Kathryn. *American Dream, American Nightmare: Fiction since 1960*. Champaign-Urbana: University of Illinois Press, 2000.

Hutcheon, Linda. *A Poetics of Postmodernism: History, Theory, Fiction*. New York: Routledge Kegan & Paul, 1988.

Hutcheon, Linda. *The Politics of Postmodernism*. London & New York: Routledge, 1989.

McClure, John A. *Partial Faiths: Postsecular Fiction in the Age of Pynchon and Morrison*. Athens: University of Georgia Press, 2007.

McHale, Brian. *The Cambridge Introduction to Postmodernism*. New York: Cambridge University Press, 2015.

McHale, Brian. *Constructing Postmodernism*. New York: Routledge, 1992.

McHale, Brian. *Postmodernist Fiction*. New York: Routledge, 1987.

McHale, Brian. "What was postmodernism?" *Electronic Book Review*, last modified December 20, 2007, www.electronicbookreview.com/thread/fictionspresent/ tense.

Moraru, Christian. *Memorious Discourse: Reprise and Representation in Postmodernism*. Madison, NJ: Fairleigh Dickinson University Press, 2005.

Moraru, Christian. *Rewriting: Postmodern Narrative and Cultural Critique in the Age of Cloning*. Albany: SUNY Press, 2001.

NOTES

1 F. Scott Fitzgerald, *The Great Gatsby*, ed. Matthew J. Bruccoli (Cambridge: Cambridge University Press, 1991), 2.

2 T. S. Eliot, "Preface," in *For Lancelot Andrewes: Essays on Style and Order* (Garden City, NY: Doubleday, Doran and Company, 1929), vii.

3 Vladimir Nabokov, "On a Book Entitled *Lolita*," in *Lolita* (New York: Putnam's, 1955), 314.

4 James Joyce, *Portrait of the Artist As a Young Man* (1916, New York: Viking Compass, 1968), 215.

5 Vladimir Nabokov, *The Real Life of Sebastian Knight* (New York: New Directions, 1941), 90.

6 McHale observes, in *Postmodernist Fiction* (New York: Routledge, 1987), that where the moderns sought to capture an epistemological (i.e., knowable) reality, their successors opted to create realities of their own: separate, non-mimetic worlds with their own "ontological" standing, their own independent claim to being.

7 John Enck, "John Hawkes: An Interview," *Wisconsin Studies in Contemporary Literature* 6 (1965): 154.

8 Jean-François Lyotard, *The Postmodern Condition: A Report on Knowledge*, trans. Geoff Bennington and Brian Massumi (Minneapolis: University of Minnesota Press, 1984), 81.

9 Tom Robbins, *Even Cowgirls Get the Blues* (Boston: Houghton Mifflin, 1976), 108.

10 See David Cowart, *Literary Symbiosis: The Reconfigured Text in Twentieth-Century Writing*, rev. ed. (Athens: University of Georgia Press, 2012).

11 Introduced and defined in Linda Hutcheon's *A Poetics of Postmodernism: History, Theory, Fiction* (New York: Routledge Kegan & Paul, 1988), historiographic metafiction blurs the boundaries between "story" and "history," revealing that history is always fictive – and not necessarily less fictive than historical fiction.

12 Jameson's observation about "depth models" frames the argument that the postmodern is characterized by a radical superficiality. See *Postmodernism, or, The Cultural Logic of Late Capitalism* (Durham: Duke University Press, 1991), 9, 12. The term "metanarrative" (*grand récit*) originates with Lyotard. On the simulacrum, see Jean Baudrillard, The Precession of the Simulacra," *in* Simulations, trans. Paul Foss, Paul Patton, and Philip Bleitchman (New York: Semiotext[e], 1983).

13 Thomas Docherty, "Postmodernism: An Introduction," in *Postmodernism: A Reader*, ed. Thomas Docherty (New York: Columbia University Press, 1993), 3.

14 Don DeLillo, *Libra* (New York: Viking, 1988), 181.

15 Philip Roth, "Writing American Fiction," *Commentary* 31 (1961): 224.

16 See Thomas Pynchon, "A Journey into the Mind of Watts," *New York Times Magazine*, 12 June, 1966, 34–35, 78, 80–82, 84.

17 Richard Rodriguez, *An Autobiography: Hunger of Memory: The Education of Richard Rodriguez* (Boston: D.R. Godine, 1982), 26.

18 Henry Louis Gates Jr., *The Signifying Monkey: A Theory of African-American Literary Criticism* (New York: Oxford University Press, 1988).

19 For a full account, see Chapter 5 of *The Signifying Monkey*, especially 184–186.

20 Toni Morrison, *Playing in the Dark: Whiteness and the Literary Imagination* (Cambridge, MA: Harvard University Press, 1992).

21 Richard Powers, *Galatea 2.2* (New York: Farrar, Straus and Giroux, 1995), 202.

22 See Ann Patchett, "Constantly Plagiarizing Myself," in *Conversations with American Women Writers*, cond. and ed. Sarah Anne Johnson (Hanover, NH: University Press of New England, 2004), 172.

23 See Walter Jackson Bate, *The Burden of the Past and the English Poet* (Cambridge, MA: Harvard University Press, 1970).

24 Harold Bloom, *The Anxiety of Influence: A Theory of Poetry* (New York: Oxford University Press, 1973).

25 Thomas Pynchon, *Gravity's Rainbow* (New York: Viking, 1973), 60–61.

26 William Shakespeare, *The Tragedy of Julius Caesar*, in *The Complete Works of Shakespeare*, ed. Hardin Craig (Chicago: Scott Foresman, 1961).

27 David Foster Wallace, "I Unibus Pluram: Television and U.S. Fiction," in *A Supposedly Fun Thing I'll Never Do Again: Essays and Arguments* (New York: Little, Brown, 1997), 81.

28 Jeffrey T. Nealon, *Post-Postmodernism, or, The Cultural Logic of Just-In-Time Capitalism* (Stanford, CA: Stanford University Press, 2012), 228. Nealon sustains the Jamesonian argument for thinking of postmodernism in Marxist terms, which leads Thomas Docherty to observe "that aesthetic postmodernism is always intimately imbricated with the issue of a political postmodernity" (228). As the reader may have noticed, I am rather more formalist than political in my thinking about postmodern aesthetics.

29 See Andrew Hoberek, "Introduction: After Postmodernism," *Twentieth-Century Literature* 53, no. 3 (2007): 233–247; Rachel Adams, "The Ends of America, the Ends of Postmodernism," *Twentieth-Century Literature* 53, no. 3 (2007): 248–272; and Josh Toth, *The Passing of Postmodernism: A Spectroanalysis of the Present* (Albany: State University of New York Press, 2010).

30 Adam Kelly, *American Fiction in Transition: Observer-Hero Narrative, the 1990s, and Postmodernism* (London: Bloomsbury, 2013), 4, 5.

31 George Orwell, *1984* (New York: Plume, 1983), 277.

3

CAREN IRR

Postmodern American Fiction and Global Literature

Since 1992, postmodern American fiction has established a distinctive relationship to world literature. This period – which we might call "late postmodernism" – is readily distinguished from European modernism before World War II. Writers of that moment arguably expressed the organization and priorities of a world system reliant on imperialism; the literature of the early twentieth century gathered writers and writings of current and former colonies (including the United States) into the European metropolis. The aesthetics of shock, fragmentation, and radical novelty that resulted from this center–periphery encounter then rippled out again in the immediate postwar period to influence a generation of writers who were either thrown into exile by the war or affiliated with the anticolonial nationalisms of the day. This circuit of absorption, accumulation, disruption, and redistribution established the literary patterns of the modernist period. Landmark works of modernism – say, James Joyce's *Ulysses* (1922) – were animated by this cycle, seeking to rewrite classical motifs such as the hero's odyssey in their own new idiom.[1] Modernists in the Joycean mold could imagine their world as a single vibrant organism, and they attempted to create a single book-of-the-world, a work that would speak from their sense of inhabiting a new stage in world civilization. Modernists portrayed in the content and form of their writing a world order about to implode.

The modernist vision of a world in crisis found expression in the epic – from Ezra Pound's *Cantos* (1925–1968) to Robert Musil's *The Man Without Qualities* (1930–1943) and Marcel Proust's *In Search of Lost Time* (1913–1927). Like *Ulysses*, many of these epics had a metropolitan setting. Modernist literary cities condensed an entire world into a specific site, sensibility, and ideology. The modernist epic, in short, presented itself as the summation of world literature, a literature that embraced its imagined predecessors and recombined their elements into a new whole, a singular modernity. Figured by crisis, the vortex, or a blast (all titles of little magazines of the period), this world featured an accelerating explosive momentum. Not without reason was T. S. Eliot's refrain in *The Waste Land* (1922), "HURRY UP PLEASE ITS TIME."[2]

After the massive implosion of this Eurocentric vision of a unified modern world during World War II and its anticolonial aftermath, however, the center of political, military, and economic power shifted further westward to the United States, and a new pattern of cultural hegemony took hold. New York and Los Angeles became hubs of the postwar culture industries, especially in the visual media, and after an interregnum of protectionist-fueled accumulation of wealth by the manufacturing sector, US dominance over the global economy came to be exerted largely through control over the financial and technology sectors. Direct imperial rule over colonies and extraction of primary resources were replaced by proxy wars and control of the circuits of investment and lending. The roles of metropolitan centers and cultural authority were simultaneously redefined. In the postwar US-dominated world system, industrial and political authorities attempted to manage relations among a globally distributed set of cultural centers. They exported American mass culture around the world (altering tastes among newly cosmopolitan postcolonial middle classes), while US immigration laws were rewritten to allow for the entrance of a new wave of "global" subjects from previously excluded areas, especially Asia, Latin America, and (to a lesser extent) Africa. These carefully screened migrants brought with them a host of literary and material cultures that soon came to influence the postwar American novel. Rather than the top-down or center – periphery models of cultural diffusion more characteristic of prewar European modernism, however, American fiction since the mid-twentieth century has often reflected on the global networks and multinational genealogies that grounded its development. At the height of this new cycle of capital accumulation and cultural innovation, as Fredric Jameson has influentially argued, a distinctive cultural logic solidified: postmodernism.

Interest in postmodernism has not been limited to the United States, but the movement is nonetheless strongly associated with American culture. In literature, postmodernism had an especially strong impact on the novel. Like the most influential modernists, many "high" postmodernists of the American 1960s, 1970s, and 1980s were also fascinated by the prose epic, and several produced their own doorstop masterworks to sit side by side with the monuments of modernism. These would include William Gaddis's *The Recognitions* (1955), Robert Coover's *The Public Burning* (1977), William H. Gass's *The Tunnel* (1995), and Don DeLillo's *Underworld* (1997). Of these postmodern epics, however, Thomas Pynchon's *Gravity's Rainbow* (1973) is certainly the best known and probably the most innovative.[3] Traversing the zones of post–World War II Germany during the period of

its provisional control by various victors but before the Cold War ossifi-
cation into East and West, Pynchon's novel condenses a vast array of cultural and literary references into a single unstable territory. In this vortex,
the old Goethian notion of world literature as the pinnacle of (European)
cultural achievement soon gives way to an anarchic host of impulses and
desires. The novel's putative hero – the lustful comic American pseudo-
tourist Tyrone Slothrop – accelerates the urban wanderings of a Joycean
pedestrian to ridiculous degrees, and the novel's map soon reaches out to
encompass many other locations. It reaches outward to colonial Namibia,
the Central Asian steppes, Puritan New England, and the subarctic, as well as
making a climactic launch into the stratosphere and a plunge into a missile
production facility deep underground. Pynchon's hero then vanishes from
the novel roughly two-thirds of the way through the narrative, while the
surreal antics of his companions escalate. Consequently, there is no central
metropolis and no single story to which the novel's manic activity might
finally be anchored. Its voracious appetite for cultural references ranges
from the classic to the esoteric and trivial; Pynchon fuses a depiction of a
Faustian Walpurgisnacht, for example, with parodies of popular music and
intricate conspiracy theories. In full-blown postmodern fashion, Pynchon
assembles a story that either delights or frustrates its readers by endlessly
multiplying their opportunities for finding their worlds intertwined with
his.

As the arguably final gasp of an allusive highbrow artistic project premised
on a common literary culture, *Gravity's Rainbow* is a momentous and force-
ful achievement. It rivals metropolitan modernisms on their own territory,
imploding the very project of writing a new civilizational epic at its ground
zero: the chaotic interregnum of the immediate postwar period. Out of
those ruins, the novel suggests, no new single world literature can arise.
The postwar world system is premised instead on a decentralized and provisional set of relationships among global cultures. In *Gravity's Rainbow*
and several of his subsequent novels (especially *Mason & Dixon* [1997],
Vineland [1990], and *Inherent Vice* [2009]), Pynchon points toward a new
dynamic of interlocking highly mobile conspiracies propagated from above,
a process opposed (although perhaps only fantasmatically) by a persistent
"preterite" Counterforce expressing countercultural and populist sensibilities. Pynchon's worldview, in short, centers on new forms of repressive power
and anarchistic resistance – both of which syncretically combine diverse cultural sources. For this reason, although Pynchon has had many imitators at
the level of the sentence and paragraph, among those seeking a less ironic
relation to global literary influences, authors such as Ishmael Reed are more
typical.

In *Mumbo Jumbo* (1972) and his related essays on the NeoHoodoo Aesthetic, rather than focusing solely on undermining a Eurocentrism on the verge of collapse (although that is one part of his project), Reed creates his own alternative literary genealogy.[4] Ostensibly set in Harlem in the 1920s, *Mumbo Jumbo* spools out a long mythological prehistory stretching back to ancient Egypt and forward into the 1960s. The core of this alternate history is a battle between Jes Grew (a musical and kinetic pleasure principle) and the Atonists (puritanical worshipers of discipline). These two forces are kept in balance by the hoodoo practices officiated by Papa LaBas, a protean detective figure who stitches the novel's many set pieces together. A specialist who "clung to the ways of the old school," LaBas proselytizes for the *loas* by means of "techniques and therapy."[5] Anchoring his historical novel in midcentury hip diction, Reed's novel adds a new strain to the works of Zora Neale Hurston, Alejo Carpentier, Jean Rhys, and other postcolonial authors inspired by the Vodun tradition of possession. Being "ridden" by the *loa* (or personified spiritual force) brings the spirit world into the practitioner's multidimensional present. Rather than remaining faithful to a singular world-changing event, such as the Judeo-Christian fall of the temple or crucifixion, Papa LaBas physically becomes an instantiation of Papa Legba, and other characters embody *loas* such as Erzulie, Madame Charlotte, and so on. The tradition lives in and through them. While Reed's novel shares with Pynchon's an interest in satirizing cultural hegemony, his version of countercultural postmodernism does not spin off into an anarchic abyss. Instead, it uncovers in the present a living and alternate sensibility in which to anchor itself. Reed's hoodoo detective proposes a revisionist worldview on the basis of his discovered affinities with long-extant but often underappreciated sites in global literature and culture.

Reed's project of examining alternative genealogies became particularly attractive to postmodern American writers around 1992, the 500th anniversary of Christopher Columbus's arrival in the Caribbean. Largely discarding mythologies of the United States as a melting pot that boils down its migrants into the abstract equivalents of modern European subjects, no matter their origins, American authors of this moment became particularly interested in "roots" and "routes" narratives that trace not only the paths of physical migration but also the many varied intellectual and literary legacies shaping contemporary American writing. Leslie Marmon Silko's masterful *Almanac of the Dead* (1991) is a particularly compelling work of this type.[6] Set largely in and around the borderland city of Tucson, Arizona, Silko's novel folds the story of the city into a multiethnic and multinational narrative of revolution and counterrevolution, tracking back to Apache wars and Yaqui resistance as well as forward and outward to a proto-Zapatista and cyberwarrior future. This movement toward multistranded and ethnically grounded narrative has been called post-postmodern, modern, and cosmomodern[7], but it is perhaps simplest to designate the entire constellation of writing that continues pieces of the postmodern conversation and rebuilds its links to a multitude of sites in global literature as "late postmodernism."

The term "late" recalls Fredric Jameson's influential argument in "Postmodernism, or the Cultural Logic of Late Capitalism."[8] In his landmark essay (reprinted in a book of the same title in 1991), Jameson asserts that the defining feature of postmodernism is not a particular style or aesthetic, but rather a relation to changing material conditions. According to Jameson, the ahistorical and hyperspatial forms of the postmodern literary labyrinth transpose features of the information economy emerging during the 1970s and 1980s. With the acceleration of neoliberal political agendas, the consolidation of economic control into a smaller set of multinational corporations, the concentration of financial resources in the hands of a global super-elite, and the redistribution of labor on a global scale, post–Cold War economic globalization has increased global interdependence without deepening cross-cultural understanding. Following Jameson, then, one way to understand late postmodern literary culture is as an effort to recognize and map the interwovenness of culture and economy around the world through the metaphor of genealogy. A quest for affiliations and affinities scattered across a global landscape unifies late postmodern writing, as its practitioners work to make sense on the human scale of transformations wrought by global capital.

In late postmodern fiction, the quest for international connections expresses itself in a set of frequently recurring narrative features. These works often take as their protagonists characters who encounter large and well-established institutions; the protagonists tour and compare these institutions in the context of border-crossing plots. Their adventures commonly culminate in an attitude of skepticism about received national narratives. They typically turn instead to counter- or alternative histories collected firsthand from a variety of authorities. This multiplicity of sources sits comfortably with a taste for multistranded narrative, but it also involves a manifest exhaustion with the reflexive irony and paranoia characteristic of Pynchon's generation of postmodernists. Rather than concentrating their energy on provoking animus toward the perceived national other and its literary voice, late postmodernists dedicate themselves more fully to deepening the authority of the new voices they include; they more often honor than excoriate. Their relation to a diverse global literature is largely – though not exclusively – affirmative.

The late postmodernists' swerve away from a text's immediate progenitors within a domestic tradition might suggest a taste for the *sui generis* autobiographical narrative or oral histories, and examples of that tendency definitely come readily to mind. McSweeney's Voice of Witness series, for instance, collects oral histories from exiles, immigrants, prisoners, and other populations. The founder and sponsor of McSweeney's, the celebrated memoirist and novelist Dave Eggers, has written two narratives based in large part on this material – *What is the What* (2006) and *Zeitoun* (2009).[9] The result of a collaboration that took place "by way of tape recording, by electronic mailings, by telephone conversations and by many personal meetings and visitations," Valentino Achak Deng's story in *What is the What* is a personal narrative that is transformed in the telling.[10] Employing fictional techniques for documentary purposes, both of Eggers's well-received and influential works of creative nonfiction not only create new narrative opportunities along the uneasy border between fiction and nonfiction in a classically postmodern fashion; they also extend the author's sensibility well beyond national borders – beginning as they do with carefully retold memories of Sudan and Syria, respectively. Domestic crises from the robbery and integration issues at the heart of *What is the What* to the policing and disaster management questions in *Zeitoun* acquire meaning when they are set in the context of each migrant's multinational story.

Similarly, though in a more clearly fictional vein, the first two novels by Japanese-American author Karen Tei Yamashita, *Through the Arc of the Rainforest* (1990) and *Brazil-Maru* (1993), grew out of her collection of oral histories of Japanese migrants in Brazil.[11] The former imagines the effects that the discovery of a remarkable polymer has on an isolated but increasingly multiracial community in the Amazon, while the latter describes the inner workings of a utopian community founded by Japanese Christian socialists. In composing these works, both Eggers and Yamashita participated in a quasi-anthropological collection of stories that complicate and triangulate national narratives, usually by documenting the perspectives of migrants.

Both Eggers and Yamashita, however, also rely on literary predecessors. Yamashita fuses telenovela tropes with magical realist narration in *Through the Arc of the Rainforest*, granting orality to a bouncing ball with supernatural powers, for instance. In *Brazil-Maru*, Yamashita employs conventions of the historical novel, and both the setting and the ecological and left-of-center political concerns of her work suggest comparisons with influential Brazilian authors, especially the widely translated modernist Jorge Amado. Eggers's influences would certainly include not only the acclaimed American oral historian Studs Terkel but also, in *What is the What*, works such as the Sudanese classic by Tayeb Salih, *Season of Migration to the North* (1969).[12] Salih's story of the disenchanted migrant's return to his country of origin after a European sojourn and his recounting of his adventures not only presents a complicated exilic version of orality comparable to Eggers's collaboration with Valentino Achak Deng; it also complements the hackneyed American story of the immigrant's troubled assimilation with an increasingly common tale of return and reconsideration. Deng's narrative opens, after all, with an imagined return, as he and other Sudanese refugees remain indoors feeling "watched, pursued ... recognizable ... [worrying] not only about predatory young men but also that the US Immigration officials would change their minds."[13] Other important contemporary novels with an autobiographical bent such as the Nigerian writer Chimamanda Ngozi Adichie's *Americanah* (2013) also mine this vein, although Adichie is most explicitly concerned with "writing back" to touchstone texts such as Chinua Achebe's *Things Fall Apart* (1958) and V. S. Naipaul's *A Bend in the River* (1979).[14] Her heroine borrows a pseudonym from the hero of the former, while the narrative stance of the latter (a bemused exile observing curious local customs) informs her Nigerian protagonist's relation to American race relations. What all of these authors share, though, is an interest in autogenealogies or self-constructed networks of influential texts, networks that bring major international authors into conversation with source material collected firsthand in order to revise dominant American conventions for depicting migration. They redirect postmodern skepticism toward dominant narratives by calling up predecessors from outside the American canon.

Autogenealogical lineages sometimes reflect the author's personal linguistic or cultural tradition, and sometimes they do not. The Soviet-era Russian émigré Gary Shteyngart, for example, draws masterfully on classics of nineteenth-century Russian literature, making many allusions to Ivan Goncharov's Oblomov and Fyodor Dostoevsky's Prince Myshkin in *The Idiot* as well as contemporary Russian satires of consumerism such as Viktor Pelevin's *Generation P* (1999), in his broad satire of the post-Communist economic conditions in Russia and the Caucasus, *Absurdistan* (2006).[15] Similarly, in the gender-bending *Middlesex* (2002), Jeffrey Eugenides incorporates popular culture from Greece, most prominently the once-banned urban musical narratives of *rembetika*, as well as slyly commenting on some Greek classics familiar to American readers – most notably the folksy, manly hero of Nikos Kazantsis's *Zorba the Greek* (1946).[16] Similarly, Junot Díaz "writes back" to the Nobel Laureate Mario Vargas Llosa's dictator novel *The Feast of the Goat* (2000) in his account of a modest family's departure from and return to the Dominican Republic, *The Brief Wondrous Life of Oscar Wao*

(2007).[17] Wrestling with monumental works in a linguistically and ethnically marked heritage is clearly an important project for late postmodern authors. It is not, however, their only self-appointed task.

After all, Shteyngart, Eugenides, and Díaz – like Adichie and, somewhat differently, the Korean American author Chang-Rae Lee – also multiply their allusions many times over. Their fiction sets works originating within a recognizable ethnic, linguistic, or national tradition in dialogue with influences from contemporary music, science, and genre fiction, as well as a multitude of literary influences beyond those that might be imagined to belong to the author's identity. With his over-the-top consumer desires and exaggeratedly pathos-ridden erotic imagination, for example, Shteyngart's obese protagonist Misha clearly recalls Rabelais's Gargantua, at the same time that his self-soothing use of gangster rap lyrics and his mock-heroic nickname (Snack Daddy) require comparison to hip-hop artists such as Biggie Smalls, the Notorious B.I.G., and Heavy D. Swerving regularly from lowbrow to highbrow, *Absurdistan* also directly satirizes academic multiculturalism and the conventions governing group affiliation in a complicated subplot involving the voracious Misha's application for a foundation-sponsored grant administered by the American Jewish community; in a self-parodying shout-out to Jonathan Swift, the chapter describing Misha's initiative is titled "A Modest Proposal."

Eugenides's heroes in *Middlesex* are also invested in African American popular culture, especially the writings of Nation of Islam leader Wallace Fard Muhammad, though the nature of his allusions differs substantially from Shteyngart's. Following the influence, arguably, of politicized African diaspora writers such as Frantz Fanon, Shteyngart treats black urban culture as a portable and malleable sign of dispossession; his Afro-Latina heroine Rouenna feels at home once she and Misha visit the "real niggaz" of post-Soviet Russia, for instance, and Misha's rapping allows him to bond with American-born Russian Jews; together, they call themselves "The Gentlemen Who Like to Rap." In contrast, for Eugenides, the separatist ethic of black nationalism is a central concern. In one of the several multinational and transracial passing plots that complicate *Middlesex*, the Nation of Islam leader is revealed to be Turkish, thus complicating the racial antagonisms that organize conflicts in scenes set during the Depression and the Civil Rights struggle. Eugenides's novel grounds separatist traditions in a middling, mediatory set of exchanges. The narrating heroine-turned-hero of the novel appreciatively observes a street corner dude in "space funk goggles" and a "velvet maroon hat," and finds in his exotic outfit the "peculiar creative energies of [her] hometown."[18] In cross-cultural exchanges like the one launched with this description, *Middlesex* pulls away from the ethnic particularism of American immigrant fiction and moves toward a cosmopolitan sensibility, associated in the novel with postmodern Berlin, the city from which its narration originates. In tone and setting, then, Eugenides affiliates himself less with ethnic tradition and more with the decontextualized and aestheticized exile culture of an ironist like Vladimir Nabokov.

Meanwhile, Junot Díaz's recurring narrator Yunior also reaches beyond an ethnically specific tradition to invoke J. R. R. Tolkien's *Lord of the Rings* (1954), *The Watchmen* comic-book series, and many other texts central to geek culture. Like Eugenides and Shteyngart, Díaz intermixes influences from several different transnational traditions to create his "fuku americanus" or New World curse. Similarly, in *Americanah*, Adichie's range of influences includes not only Africans writing in English but also *Huckleberry Finn* (1885) and, most persistently, Graham Greene's tale of English expatriates in West Africa, *The Heart of the Matter* (1948). Adichie also makes repeated allusions to an international tradition of exile writing. At the conclusion of the novel, her heroine writes about Nigerian scenes, describing with the returned exile's alien eye street fashion, turns of phrase, and the views from her window: "a white egret drooped on the compound wall, exhausted from heat."[19] Reminiscent of late colonial motifs, these scenes place the narrator's perspective in proximity to the contemplative moral universe of Greene's fiction.

Along the same lines, in his dystopian satire *On Such a Full Sea* (2014), Lee blends influences from several origins.[20] Narrated in the first person plural, his novel repeatedly raises questions of group identity and incorporates this material into its form in a reflexively postmodern fashion. It describes the we-narrator's cultivation of a legend about two young people who have left the walled city of B-Mor, a near-future version of Baltimore resettled and reorganized as an urban fish farm by migrants from New China. Opening with oblique self-referentiality, in sentences such as "It is known where we come from, but no one much cares about things like that any more," this Asian-American collective voice employs an elaborately formal and evasive diction reminiscent of the formulations of the immigrant father in Lee's first novel, *Native Speaker* (1995).[21] The novel's suspenseful road narrative also employs motifs familiar from European folk tales – especially Hansel and Gretel, a story repeatedly invoked when the heroine and the boyfriend she pursues discover their entrapment in a sequence of fanciful houses. Yet, the conclusion to the novel withholds the triumphant reunion and return so common in the Grimm Brothers' tales. Maintaining tension and keeping the lovers separated and their story legendary, Lee's narrator insists on a kind of poetic irresolution one might associate equally with the domestic lyricism favored in American creative writing programs and classic tales in

Chinese folklore, such as the story of the cowherd and the weaving damsel, a pair of lovers eternally separated by the Milky Way. Lee's novel continues its project of multiplying and cross-fertilizing its traditions by wedding its treatment of genre predecessors – from Aldous Huxley's *Brave New World* (1932) and George Orwell's *1984* (1949) – to reworkings of iconic texts in popular culture, from anime to *The Hunger Games* (2008). In Lee's novel, both ethnic and genre lineages branch off in several directions because, like Adichie, Díaz, Shteyngart, and Eugenides, he writes from within a matrix of situation-specific influences. All of these influential late postmodernists recognize a single immigrant or national tradition with which they have intimate familiarity, while also turning repeatedly farther afield to other literary influences. Their work shares not a single movement or influence, but rather a commitment to constructing global autogenealogies – provisional family trees that intermingle ethnic, political, and generic influences from around the world.

At the same time, these autogenealogies are not infinitely eclectic. Postmodern American fiction consistently draws more frequently from some wells than others. Its attention is not evenly distributed across the globe, and its preoccupations are largely limited to the sensibilities of the educated literary classes. Consequently, its world is lopsided and pockmarked; it does not mirror the globe so much as model certain sectors of the globe. Other than the tales of Scheherazade, for instance, very few references to either classic Arabic writing or the modern Arab novel appear in postmodern American fiction (though the work of Laila Lalami and Teju Cole provides important exceptions). Turkish and Central Asian literature is also almost unrecognized as an influence on American writers. Scandinavian writing has little influence, nor do Australian writers have much of a presence in contemporary American postmodernism (apart from émigrés such as Peter Carey). Individual authors from Latin American literature have been very important (especially Jorge Luis Borges and most recently Roberto Bolaño), but their American reception is often delayed and extremely partial even when they are widely translated. The response to global literature by American writers is not primarily governed by the accessibility of texts, nor does it correlate directly to the size or cultural influence of migrant populations. Latinos are, after all, widely recognized as the most numerous immigrants in the United States.

Instead, the figures and traditions that are most prominent in the autogenealogies created by postmodern American authors reflect their suitability for specific projects undertaken by these authors. The most common project is a mapping of lines of influence and cross-cultural rivalry that situates the cultural authority of the United States in a network of partial influences. Late postmodernists typically create a genealogy by reworking conventions established by Anglophone predecessors in their genre, borrowing characterization and thematic elements from established authors in a legacy ethnic tradition, incorporating passing allusions to widely disseminated popular culture (often but not always Anglophone), and basing events on episodes recounted in firsthand oral histories or autobiography. In other words, to recall Franco Moretti's classic essay "Conjectures on World Literature," contemporary American authors influenced by postmodernism continue in several respects the high postmodernist project of disrupting established metanarratives of the mid-twentieth century, but they do so by injecting new regional content.[22] American postmodernists turn to those works in global literature that most forcefully engage and disturb the still-dominant traditions of Anglophone literary realism. They turn to influential works that offer rapid access to a larger, older, and often (but not always) more highly valued cultural tradition in order to provincialize and reformulate the modern American novel. Whether it is Chinese folklore, Russian existentialist writing, or the pop culture of a multinational geek sensibility, the exotic "global" material pulls the postmodern American novel into a context in which it is one among several rival forms; its capacity to define a world on its own terms need not be dissipated entirely, but it is routinely minimized and relativized.

To some extent, this gesture of overleaping the most proximate American predecessors in a particular genre in order to tap international sources reveals the enormous influence exerted during the 1980s by magical realism – especially the versions of this varied aesthetic expressed by Gabriel García Márquez in *One Hundred Years of Solitude* (1967) and Salman Rushdie in *Midnight's Children* (1981).[23] Magical realists like Márquez and Rushdie dove into cultural reservoirs of folklore and mythology to develop alternatives to imperialist writing that self-interestedly figured the colonies as culturally impoverished and in need of tutelage. Magical realists also wrestled with the nationalist politics and social realist styles of the first generation of postcolonial writers, many of whom they found dated, overly serious, and/or unduly preoccupied with catering to European and American audiences. *Midnight's Children*, for instance, opens its distinctive retelling of modern Indian history by making a distinctly profane and embodied comparison between the narrator's prominent nose and the outline of the subcontinent as it appears on world maps. The novel is riddled with bad smells, minor ailments, and folk remedies – making little attempt to dress up or romanticize its heroes according to the dictates of an earlier generation's realist sensibilities. Unlike *One Hundred Years of Solitude* (with its heavenly ascensions and green blood), Rushdie's novel is rarely "magical" in the fairy tale sense; it draws instead on folklore, humor, and other antirealist narrative devices.

In the American context, magical realism most directly influenced writers such as Toni Morrison and Philip Roth, both of whom – as children of the 1930s – are rough contemporaries of Rushdie (b. 1947) and Márquez (b. 1927). Morrison's most widely read novel, *Beloved* (1987), famously shares Márquez's fascination with Faulkner and the power of interlocking, unreliable legends.[24] While Roth's writing is more corrosive and satirical, several of his later novels – especially *American Pastoral* (1997) – echo Rushdie in their bawdy comedy, their complex narration, and their disproportionate exaggerations of individual physical features.[25] Influenced by the magical realists' folkloristic tendencies, both Roth and Morrison exploit the narrative resources of their own ethnic communities (Jewish American and African American) to tell the story of that community and contest its falsification in dominant accounts.

Other late postmodernists share Roth and Morrison's skepticism toward a rationality that falsely universalizes the perspective of the dominant social group, but it is not always magic or folklore that serves as their primary tool for disturbing that perspective. In fact, at times, an explicit rejection of the most classic gestures of magical realism marks their work. In *The Brief Wondrous Life of Oscar Wao*, for instance, Díaz refuses the lure of magical realism. His Dominican immigrant hero and his narrator are both transformed by with stories of a mythic mongoose, and the mongoose carries with it an African spirit of resistance and tricksterish surprise. Yet, despite its almost textbook appearance as a source of wisdom and spiritual sustenance in a degraded modern world, the mongoose is only comprehensible in Díaz's novel when it is linked to the gaming and comic book subculture of the self-professed ghetto nerds. "Many watchers suspect that the Mongoose arrived to our world from another," the narrator remarks in a quasi-anthropological footnote.[26] This would-be folk motif becomes a game piece, a power boost, and a special effect, because Díaz's impulse is not ethnically particularist so much as it is textually promiscuous.

Still other late postmoderns do draw more fully on selected elements of magical realism, though, mingling its effects with features inspired by European avant-garde writing. The surrealist Rikki Ducornet, for instance, explores classic early twentieth-century motifs – such as dreams, erotic liberation, toys, and uncanny objects – in her tetralogy based on the elements. In the water volume, *The Fountains of Neptune* (1989), the European hero Nicolas melts plastic soldiers to create figurines who will help him grapple with the strangeness of a world whose transformations he does not fully understand, having slept through two world wars.[27] The same lyrical intensity characterizes Ducornet's ecologically themed novel set in the Caribbean – *Phosphor in Dreamland* (1995) – as well as her revisioning of the life of the Marquis de Sade in *The Fan-Maker's Inquisition* (1999) and her portrait of a girl's sexual awakening in Egypt in *Gazelle* (2004). Simultaneously sensual and visionary, Ducornet's writing mines the vein of magical excess that we can also recognize, in a very different form, in Márquez in particular, though she has laced her magic with strains of Salvador Dalí and André Breton. Some related concerns animate the fiction of Robert Coover, Donald Barthelme, and Margaret Atwood and more recently Sarah Shun-Lien Bynum, all of whom also retell stories from fairy tales and children's literature, usually with the aim of probing their subliminal eroticism.[28]

Lydia Davis's ironic antirealism, by contrast, turns to the French avant-garde, especially Maurice Blanchot and Marcel Proust (both of whom she has translated), adapting their methods of metafiction and fabulation to contemporary American settings. Davis's very short fictions reveal the influence of the former's allergy to genre in particular. Several single-sentence stories in *Samuel Johnson Is Indignant* (2001), for example, compress the observational meanderings of psychological realism into perfectly formed dilemmas.[29] The story "Double Negative" consists entirely of this: "At a certain point in her life, she realizes it is not so much that she wants to have a child as that she does not want not to have a child, or not to have had a child."[30] In fictions such as these, Davis's writing is fascinated by the sort of magical double-thinking that characterizes upper-middle-class American lives. She brilliantly exposes the subtexts of contemporary fantasies – the folklore of professionals in the suburbs – in her postmodern fables.

Among postmodernists concerned, like Davis, with the professional managerial class, European modernism has a particularly strong continuing influence. The hugely influential Jonathan Franzen – widely appreciated for his novels dissecting the fantasies of prosperous residents of housing developments and second-tier cities such as St. Louis, Philadelphia, and Saint Paul in *The Corrections* (2001) and *Freedom* (2010) – has made his fascination with German-language satire quite clear in *The Kraus Project* (2013), a translation and extended annotation of the works of the Austrian writer Karl Kraus.[31] Similarly, Franz Kafka's fascination with labyrinths and entrapment has clearly been a hugely important influence on any number of contemporary postmodernist satirists – from Bret Easton Ellis's *American Psycho* (1991) to Michael Chabon's *The Amazing Adventures of Kavalier & Clay* (2000).[32] In all of these cases, however, the classic modernist treatment of psychic life as a register of social (usually urban and bureaucratic) irrationality has mutated into new forms. For Franzen, Ellis, and Chabon's heroes, psychic life is largely occupied by and organized around commercial forms – from the addictive psychotropic drugs secretly consumed by Alfred, the father in the family saga of *The Corrections*, to the cocaine, schlock television, banal pop songs, dime-store gimmicks, and comic-book heroism of Ellis and Chabon's fiction. The European modernism invoked consistently by these authors is reworked, its concern for the abyss of self-consciousness in particular being redirected toward institutional and economic forces that shape whatever selves emerge in the postmodern context. Like William Gaddis, these authors come to German-language modernism largely by way of the merciless bleakness of Thomas Bernhard – the Austrian author whose novel *The Loser* (1983) has been claimed as an influence by everyone from Franzen to the experimentalist Ben Marcus.

In their rethinking of the meaning and shape of modernism, a few late postmodernists have also turned toward East Asia for inspiration. Although his own work is heavily influenced by American writers – especially Raymond Carver, whom he has translated – the Japanese novelist Haruki Murakami has arguably exerted an even greater impact on contemporary US fiction than he has absorbed. His weightless, disaffected hipsters inhabit a transnational, media-inflected underworld of which we also see glimpses in Tao Lin's semi-autobiographical *Shoplifting from American Apparel* (2009) and Aleksandar Hemon's *Nowhere Man* (2002).[33] Shot through with brand names and a pervasive refusal of interiority, *Shoplifting* begins with a late-rising hero whose waking ritual involves a smoothie, email, cereal, and eBay. His poetry is stored in Microsoft Word files, and his friendships take place in Gmail chats. Hemon's titular Nowhere Man is similarly disaffected as he drifts through Chicago, renaming and rebranding himself as needed in the shallow ethnic stew that city provides. The figure of an emotionally depleted hero traversing a largely commercial, physically damaged cultural wasteland does not of course belong to any single author or cultural tradition, but the enormous influence in American creative writing programs of strains of Buddhism suggests that there may well be a stronger drift toward Buddhist-influenced Asian literature in years to come.

Overall, then, among the late postmodernists publishing in the United States since the 1990s, no single influence from global literature predominates. What these authors share instead is an affirmative relationship to the ideology of the global, rather than a specific or consistent instantiation of it. Perhaps this tendency to choose one's own progenitors by combining influences from multiple sources reflects a trend in contemporary assertions of taste more generally – a hipster fascination with eclectic juxtapositions of classic and obscure. More than any single author or work, a selectively cosmopolitan hipsterism itself seems to have become an international cultural phenomenon of such significance that it might be thought to constitute a literary movement. Wherever it takes root, this sensibility erodes the continuity of purely national, linguistic, or ethnic traditions in favor of a purportedly global sensibility. Constructing their own genealogies on a provisional basis as needed for each project, late postmoderns continue asking without firmly answering the question posed by Thomas Pynchon's heroine Oedipa Maas in *The Crying of Lot 49* (1966): "Shall I project a world?"[34] In so doing, they point toward a diverse, unevenly developed contemporary world without claiming to know or encapsulate it. Late postmodern fiction in this sense can be understood as expressing an American uncertainty about its role in governing or extracting value from contemporary global relations.

Further Reading

Casanova, Pascale. *The World Republic of Letters.* Translated by M. B. DeBevoise. Cambridge, MA: Harvard University Press, 2007.

Gladstone, Jason, Andrew Hoberek, and Daniel Worden, eds. *Postwar/Postmodern – and After.* Iowa City: University of Iowa Press, 2016.

Jameson, Fredric. *Postmodernism, or, The Cultural Logic of Late Modernism.* Durham, NC: Duke University Press, 1991.

Irr, Caren. *Toward the Geopolitical Novel: U.S. Fiction in the 21ˢᵗ Century.* New York: Columbia University Press, 2013.

McGurl, Mark. *The Program Era: Postwar Fiction and the Rise of Creative Writing.* Cambridge, MA: Harvard University Press, 2011.

NOTES

1 James Joyce, *Ulysses: the corrected text*, ed. Hans Walter Gabler with Wolfhard Steppe and Claus Melchior (New York: Vintage, 1986).

2 T. S. Eliot, *The Waste Land and Other Poems* (New York: Harcourt, Brace & World, 1934), 34–35, 141, 152, 165, 168, 169.

3 Thomas Pynchon, *Gravity's Rainbow* (New York: Viking, 1973).

4 Ishmael Reed, *Mumbo Jumbo* (New York: Scribner, 1996).

5 Ibid., 16.

6 Leslie Marmon Silko, *Almanac of the Dead* (New York: Simon & Schuster, 1991).

7 A helpful overview of the debate over post-postmodernism appears in the introduction to Jason Gladstone, Andrew Hoberek, and Daniel Worden's collection, *Postwar/Postmodern – and After* (Iowa City: University of Iowa Press, 2016).

8 Fredric Jameson, "The Cultural Logic of Late Capitalism" in *Postmodernism, or, The Cultural Logic of Late Capitalism* (Durham, NC: Duke University Press, 1991).

9 Dave Eggers, *What is the What: The Autobiography of Valentino Achak Deng* (New York: Vintage, 2007); and Dave Eggers, *Zeitoun* (San Francisco: McSweeney's Books, 2009).

10 Eggers, *What is the What*, xiv.

11 Karen Yamashita, *Through the Arc of the Rainforest* (Minneapolis: Coffee House Press, 1990); and Karen Yamashita, *Brazil-Maru* (Minneapolis: Coffee House Press, 1992).

12 Tayeb Salih, *Season of Migration to the North*, trans. Denys Johnson-Davies (New York: NYRB Classics, 2009).

13 Eggers, *What is the What*, 17.

14 Chimamanda Ngozi Adichie, *Americanah* (New York: Anchor, 2014).

15 Gary Shteyngart, *Absurdistan* (New York: Random House, 2006).

16 Jeffrey Eugenides, *Middlesex* (New York: Farrar, Straus and Giroux, 2002).

17 Junot Díaz, *The Brief Wondrous Life of Oscar Wao* (New York: Riverhead, 2007).

18 Eugenides, *Middlesex*, 516.

19 Adichie, *Americanah*, 585.

20 Chang-Rae Lee, *On Such a Full Sea* (New York: Riverhead, 2014).

21 Ibid., 1.

22 Franco Moretti, "Conjectures on World Literature," *New Left Review* (January-February 2000): 54–68.

23 Salman Rushdie, *Midnight's Children* (London: Jonathan Cape, 1981); and Gabriel García Márquez, *One Hundred Years of Solitude*, trans. Gregory Rabassa (New York: Harper & Row, 1970).

24 Toni Morrison, *Beloved* (New York: Knopf, 1987).

25 Philip Roth, *American Pastoral* (New York: Houghton Mifflin, 1997).

26 Díaz, *The Brief Wondrous Life of Oscar Wao*, 141.

27 Rikki Ducornet, *The Fountains of Neptune* (Normal, IL: Dalkey Archive, 1993).

28 See, for example, Robert Coover, *Pricksongs and Descants: Fictions* (New York: Grove, 1969); Donald Barthelme, *Snow White* (New York: Athenaeum, 1967); Margaret Atwood, *The Robber Bride* (Toronto: McClelland & Stewart, 1993); and Sarah Shun-Lien Bynum, *Madeleine is Sleeping* (New York: Harcourt, 2004).

29 Lydia Davis, *Samuel Johnson is Indignant* (San Francisco: McSweeney's, 2001).

30 Ibid., 66

31 Jonathan Franzen, *The Corrections* (New York: Farrar, Straus and Giroux, 2001); *Freedom* (New York: Farrar, Straus and Giroux, 2010); and *The Kraus Project: Essays by Karl Kraus* (New York: Farrar, Straus and Giroux, 2013).

32 Michael Chabon, *The Amazing Adventures of Kavalier & Clay* (New York: Random House, 2000); and Bret Easton Ellis, *American Psycho* (New York: Vintage, 1991).

33 Tao Lin, *Shoplifting from American Apparel* (New York: Melville House, 2007); and Aleksandar Hemon, *Nowhere Man* (New York: Vintage, 2002).

34 Thomas Pynchon, *The Crying of Lot 49* (Philadelphia: J.B. Lippincott, 1966; reprint, New York: Harper Perennial, 2006), 82.

4

ARKADY PLOTNITSKY

Philosophical Skepticism and Narrative Incredulity

Postmodern Theory and Postmodern American Fiction

Taking as its point of departure Jean-François Lyotard's inaugural argument in *The Postmodern Condition: A Report on Knowledge* (1979),[1] this chapter considers the nature of postmodern theoretical thinking (at least a sufficiently representative spectrum of it), including that found in literature and specifically postmodern American fiction, and the nature of resistance to this thinking. Postmodern theoretical thinking arises against a certain type of preceding theoretical thinking, which has been dominant throughout the history of modernity, roughly, from the fifteenth century on, until our own time (although Lyotard focuses on its roots in the eighteenth-century Enlightenment). This thinking has a much longer history, extending even to the pre-Socratics, and as such it may be called *classical* thinking, a concept that I shall explain below, merely noting here that it should not be identified with ancient Greek thinking. It acquires a particular, *modern* form with modernity, although other forms of classical thinking continue to subsist alongside modern thinking. Classical and modern thinking were the dominant and nearly the only forms of thinking, at least in theoretical fields, until the end of the nineteenth century, and their dominance has continued into our own time, which in part accounts for the resistance to postmodern thinking, especially to postmodern *theory*. Literature is better able to avoid this resistance. By a "theory," I mean an organized assemblage of concepts defined by a given form of theoretical thinking, including in literature, although literature exceeds whatever theory it might contain.

Apart from a few inconsequential exceptions, however, the postmodern critique of classical or modern thinking is not a critique of literature, whether postmodern or earlier. Instead, beginning even with the ancient Greek literature, but especially with *modernist* (not the same as modern!) literature, literature has been an instrument, rather than a target, of postmodern theoretical critique. Indeed, literature has been an active constitutive part of postmodern theory and its avatars, such as poststructuralism, deconstruction, gender theory, or postmodern reincarnations of psychoanalytic theory.

Accordingly, one can speak of postmodern theoretical thinking (hereafter postmodern thinking) in postmodern theory and postmodern literature alike, although literature, again, always exceeds theory. This excess is one of the reasons why postmodern literature is able to avoid the kind of resistance encountered by postmodern theory.

As I said, classical and then modern thinking continue to shape our thinking and culture. Both are also found in postmodern thinking, which, however, gives classical and modern thinking limited and differently delimited roles, determined by their postmodern underpinnings. Either thinking is, thus, not a problem for postmodern thinking: only claims concerning its unlimited validity are. On the other hand, postmodern thinking is a problem for classical or modern thinking, because postmodern thinking and theories are incompatible with some of the imperatives of classical and modern thinking. One might, however, question whether the imperatives of classical and modern theory are sustainable even within the limits either envisions for itself. Indeed, both, *especially classical thinking*, envision themselves as having a nearly unlimited range, at least in principle (practical limitations are acknowledged), something that postmodern thinking in principle precludes, including for itself. I qualify because modern thinking contains elements of skepticism concerning its limits and power, and allows that postmodern thinking is logically possible. Classical or modern thinking only admits practical limitations upon its power. Postmodern thinking advances thinking and knowledge, while accepting insuperable limits upon how far they could in principle reach. The presence of these limits need not mean that we cannot advance thought and knowledge; quite the contrary, working with these limits leads to new thought and knowledge that would not be possible otherwise.

I shall now define the terms "classical," "modern," and "postmodern," as they are understood here, because they are subject to significant fluctuations. Lyotard's primary category in *The Postmodern Condition: A Report on Knowledge* is "knowledge" rather than "thinking." However, his concept of knowledge is broad and contains or entails the concepts of theoretical thinking and theory adopted here, and for the sake of economy, I shall primarily speak of postmodern thinking. At stake are also social, including political, determinations of thinking and knowledge, and their ultimately irreducible multiplicity and heterogeneity. By invoking "a subject constituted by various [heterogeneous] areas of competence composing it," Lyotard indicates the postmodern deconstruction of the Enlightenment concept of subjectivity, as defined by the concept of unity and the possibility of consensus among such subjects.[2] Lyotard sees this Enlightenment ideal, championed by Jürgen Habermas, as "outmoded" and unrealizable, and he defines postmodern thinking and knowledge in juxtaposition to this ideal. Postmodern theory, also by means of literature, is both a product and a theory of this thinking, which makes metatheoretical and self-reflexive considerations part of postmodern theory.

"*Postmodern* thinking" is defined by grounding its understanding in: (1) *irreducible* multiplicity; (2) the *irreducibly unthinkable* in thought; and (3) *irreducible* chance. The irreducible nature of each is crucial because the multiple, the unthinkable, and chance are also considered by classical and modern thinking, but there they are seen as ultimately reducible, at least in principle, to, respectively, unity, accessibility to thought, and causality. It is this reducibility that most essentially defines classical and modern thinking. As indicated above, the difference between them is that modern thinking accepts the logical possibility of postmodern thinking, but rejects it and searches for classical-like alternatives. Indeed, sometimes modern thinking even admits that such alternatives might be impossible, but still nonetheless desires them, nostalgically. Could one trace the modern earlier in the classical? This is possible, at least to some degree. I would argue, however, that in theoretical fields, modern thinking emerges only around the time of the Enlightenment.

This is, it is true, a particular concept of postmodern thinking. I would contend, however, that it encompasses or strongly relates to the thinking of most key postmodernist figures at stake in the debates concerning postmodern theory. This concept also implies a particular view of postmodernism and postmodernity, the one that is equally essentially at stake in these debates. By "postmodernism" I mean the set of practices (philosophical, scientific, artistic, cultural, or political) that involve postmodern thinking; and by "postmodernity" I refer to the culture or rather, given its multicultural character, the cultural landscape of the last fifty years or so. "Postmodern" is a kind of umbrella term, the meaning of which may depend on how one understands the phenomena just mentioned. First, this understanding always reflects an emphasis on certain specific aspects of the multifaceted postmodern landscape. Secondly, insofar as one deals with particular postmodern phenomena, ideas, and authors, one can only offer *an* interpretation of each of them, one among several possible interpretations.

I would like to comment on several alternative, if related, conceptions of the postmodern. It would be impossible to give a comprehensive account of such conceptions here, or to do justice to those that I will briefly discuss. My aim is to help the reader have a better image of the landscape of postmodern theory and culture, and to more firmly situate the present analysis, which addresses arguably the most radical and the most vehemently resisted forms of postmodern thinking. It might be fitting to begin with Fredric Jameson's concept of postmodernism as "the cultural logic of late capitalism"

65

developed in *Postmodernism, or, The Cultural Logic of Late Capitalism* and other works.[3] Jameson's argument has been prominent in literary studies. While indebted to that of Lyotard (Jameson wrote a foreword to *The Postmodern Condition*), Jameson's Marxist argument is different, especially by virtue of being grounded in the base–superstructure relationships between capitalism and postmodernism. The role of these relationships would not be denied by Lyotard, but they are not seen by him (or here) as *defining* "the cultural logic" of postmodernity. They would need to be considered differently, for example, along more Foucauldian lines of new technologies of power. Another Marxist legacy, the dialectical causality (correlative to the base–superstructure theory) governing Jameson's scheme, by way of a certain grand narrative, is also a problem in the present view, which precludes all strict causality and grand narratives (a concept explained below). Jameson's argument is about the same postmodern world and, thus, shares some of its points with Lyotard's or the present argument. Overall, however, Jameson's dialectical understanding of the postmodern world is different from the one advocated here, which is based in the architecture of postmodern thinking defined above.

While both Lyotard's and Jameson's work have been influential in literary studies from the 1980s on, the term "postmodern literature" was already in circulation by the early 1970s.[4] Historically, the term has been used to refer to certain, more innovative, works of contemporary literature, roughly from the 1960s on. Most of the postmodern American fiction considered in this chapter also belongs to this period, while the (modernist) literature and art considered by Lyotard as postmodern generally do not, because Lyotard focuses on literature and art, mostly from the first third of the twentieth century, which is usually (including here) defined as modernist. Either way, however, such literary works or their interpretations are usually associated with conceptions of the postmodern developed to accommodate literature, either in accordance with Lyotard's or Jameson's view or moving in other directions. By now, these conceptions form a spectrum of their own, too broad to address here, beyond noting a few prominent theorists, which I shall do as I proceed. By virtue of the same terminological dissemination, thinking that I define as "postmodern" may also be and has been called differently, for example and in particular "poststructuralist." This term, always used more narrowly, has receded in recent years and has been largely supplanted by "postmodern."

The type of thinking or knowledge at stake in Lyotard's *The Postmodern Condition* emerged, he argued, as a result of the transformation (also referred to as the second industrial revolution) of culture defined by the rise of new, especially digital, information and telecommunication technologies.

While at the time of Lyotard's "report," these technologies (then in their early stages as well) were becoming dominant in the so-called industrialized societies, by now they have spread and become ubiquitous globally. In this respect, postmodernism may be seen *in relation* to the contemporary, "late" capitalism (economically responsible for the development and use of these technologies) and its cultural logic, which, however, is not the same as being *defined* by this logic.

Besides, while the postmodern world formed sometime in the 1960s, many key aspects of postmodern thinking had emerged in philosophy, art, and mathematics and science earlier, some of them in the 1900s, the historical juncture of (proto-)postmodern thought that, as will be seen, is captured by Thomas Pynchon's *Against the Day* (2006). There is an important difference as well, especially as concerns science. For most of Western intellectual history, the science that occupied the dominant position in culture was physics, and this was still true at the time of Lyotard's "report" in 1979. In recent decades, however, physics has been largely supplanted in this role by biological and informational sciences, sometimes in combination, as in modern genomics, neuroscience, or cognitive psychology. This shift is also felt in critical theory's engagement with science, for example in the prominent role of cognitive and neural sciences, or, again, digital and information sciences and technology in posthumanist theory and criticism.[5] Lyotard argues that twentieth-century mathematics and science direct us toward postmodern thinking and knowledge, as concerns both the fundamental aspects and the heterogeneity of their practice.[6]

They appear to tell us what literature and art, beginning at least with modernism, tell us. Lyotard does not consider works of literature and art from the late 1960s on, such as those considered here or those that attracted Jameson's attention as, in his view, postmodernist. This is not surprising. Some of the works from this period, such as those discussed here, exhibit postmodern features that concern Lyotard as well. Most, however, are characterized by different facets of the postmodern, such as their emphasis on "simulacra," à la Jean Baudrillard, and "appropriation," as in Kathy Acker's works, which, however, also engage with gender theory and deconstruction. As I noted, literature and art, such as that of Franz Kafka, James Joyce, the Cubists, Marcel Duchamp, and Barnett Newman, which Lyotard considers as "postmodern" are commonly defined as "modernist." For him and most other major postmodern theorists, such as Gilles Deleuze and Jacques Derrida, modernism is the main literary and artistic juncture in the genealogy of postmodern thinking, and its mathematical, scientific, and philosophical genealogy extends from roughly the 1900s as well. The postmodern American fiction to be primarily discussed here is, too, closer to modernist works.

For Lyotard or here, then, postmodern thinking is not only a matter of history, although history, specifically that of postmodern culture during the last fifty years, is important, not the least for our understanding of postmodern literature. At stake is the *character* of thinking – philosophical, scientific, literary and artistic, or other – as thinking of the *irreducible* multiplicity, the *irreducible* role of the unthinkable in thinking, and the *irreducible* role of randomness or chance. Some ingredients of postmodern thought could be traced as early as the pre-Socratics. Lyotard's analysis of the postmodern implies this longer history as well. However, his invocation of Michel de Montaigne notwithstanding, it would be difficult to speak of postmodern thinking in theoretical fields before the end of the nineteenth century. Literature may be a different matter. Thus, the works of some Romantic authors, such as Heinrich von Kleist, Friedrich Hölderlin, and Percy Bysshe Shelley, have been considered as instances of postmodern thought, but are usually still read through the optics of modernism.

Postmodern American fiction reveals new ways of postmodern thinking and poses new tasks for postmodern theory. It may, however, be argued that these new ways of thinking have as much or more to do with the way the postmodern *world* enters (it is not only a matter of representing it) postmodern literature, rather than with advancing the fundamentals of postmodern theory in the way literary modernism did. First, especially from the 1970s on, it is often already informed by or, in such authors as John Barth, plays upon these fundamentals (in Barth, in their poststructuralist incarnation). By contrast, modernism or even, again, some earlier literature "was there first," before postmodern theory, although some modernism, too, borrowed its postmodern aspects from contemporary philosophy and mathematics and science. Secondly, modernism was radically experimental in terms of literary or artistic *form*, through which it textually enacts postmodern theory, including that of literature itself. James Joyce's *Ulysses* and *Finnegans Wake*, Ezra Pound's *Cantos*, and William Faulkner's *The Sound and the Fury* are paradigmatic examples of such modernist experimentation. Some postmodern American fiction, including that which especially interests me here (fiction defined by the enactment of theoretical thinking or theories), continues this formal experimentation, or *form*-experimentation. However, there is a difference, which may be described in Thomas Kuhn's terms, not so much those of "paradigm change," which are pertinent too, but rather those of "revolutionary" versus "normal" practice, but with a twist, because usually a revolutionary practice is characterized by its experimental, innovative nature. While the form-experimentation was revolutionary literary and artistic practice, especially against realism, it becomes or continues to be considered a *normal* literary practice, inflected by the ways in which the postmodern world enters postmodern literature. The main and characteristically postmodern exception is digital fiction (or art), which expressly requires different forms of experimentation. Of course, even leaving aside transitional figures, such as William S. Burroughs, and different facets of literary experimentation (linguistic, visual, and so forth), how postmodern or, conversely, modern, or even how experimental, a given work is is a matter of interpretation. Indeed, how normal or how revolutionary a given form of literary experimentation is would be a matter of interpretation as well. Either way, my main concern here is the *experimental* enactment of the key postmodern features – the irreducibly multiple, the irreducibly unthinkable, and the irreducibly random – by literary works.

Consider multiplicity, a concept arguably most prominent in postmodern thinking and most reflecting the character of the postmodern world. There have been instances of denying the possibility of applying the idea of multiplicity to the ultimate level of existence, beginning with Parmenides's famous concept of the One, as defining the ultimate reality of things, a concept adopted by Plato. Difference, multiplicity, and change were in his view seen as illusions of the human senses to be overcome by philosophical thought. The idea has never died. However, throughout history, our understanding of nature and mind was much more commonly characterized by considering the role of difference, multiplicity, and change in their workings. From the pre-Socratics to Martin Heidegger and beyond, it is not so much the undifferentiated Oneness that was primarily at stake in classical and then modern thought, but instead how the play of difference, multiplicity, or chance is contained. The postmodern multiple is, in Badiou's language, the multiple-*without*-One or even the *multiple* of multiples-without-One, a form of multiplicity that cannot be subsumed by any unity or even containable multiplicity.[7] Luce Irigaray, especially in her earlier works, such as *This Sex Which Is Not One*, and Deleuze and Guattari, from *Anti-Oedipus: Capitalism and Schizophrenia* on, would be among the most uncompromising theorists of the multiple in, respectively, gender theory and philosophy.

Lyotard's argument concerning the postmodern and narrative in *The Postmodern Condition* is based in the concept of the narrative multiple-*without*-One, which cannot be governed by any single narrative, or in Lyotard's terms a grand narrative or metanarrative. Postmodern thinking, according to Lyotard, is characterized by its skepticism ("incredulity") toward grand narratives, in particular that of scientific progress, which has defined modernity from the Enlightenment on, or rather modernity's view of itself. Lyotard's famous contention that the postmodern "precedes" the modern similarly refers to the irreducibly multiple, unthinkable, and random that inhabits and inhibits the modern that refuses to accept it beyond, at most, being a logical possibility. The same view of the multiple defines Lyotard's argument, via Ludwig Wittgenstein, concerning the heteromorphous language games (actions into which language is woven), which cannot be governed by a single (meta) language game. Some of them cannot be positively related to each other at all: they are "incommensurable." These two multiplicities, that of narratives and that of language games, are interactive, and postmodern subjectivity is constituted by them and other multiplicities. Postmodern literature, from modernist to contemporary fiction, dramatizes, by form and content alike, this constitution. Classical or modern aspects of subjectivity do not disappear, but they become resituated as emerging from the postmodern multiple.

There is a question whether the postmodern multiplicity is only epistemological or also ontological, that is, whether it reflects the plurality of thinking and knowledge concerning a single world, or the plurality of worlds themselves, or whether it reflects both: multiple worlds and multiple ways of thinking and knowledge concerning each. The answer may depend on the given domain of the multiple. Thus, in physics and cosmology one tends to think of a single world, although various many-worlds views have been entertained in physics and beyond at least since Gottfried Leibniz. Such views have acquired new prominence in physics in the wake of the so-called "many-worlds interpretation" of quantum mechanics. This interpretation was introduced by Hugh Everett in 1957, intriguingly as a classical or modern response to the postmodern epistemology of quantum mechanics. Literature would be more open to experimentation with multiple worlds or ontologies. Brian McHale sees this experimentation as characterizing and even defining postmodern literature, with Pynchon's novels, especially *Gravity's Rainbow*, as paradigmatic examples, vis-à-vis modernist literature, defined by experimenting with epistemological pluralities of thinking concerning a single world.[8] The situation and the borderlines between postmodernism and modernism in this regard may be more complex, but this is secondary for the moment. The argument is justified as concerns at least some postmodernist fiction, such as Pynchon's novels, which have been impacted by Everett's theory, as well as science fiction, such that of Philip K. Dick (*The Man in the High Castle*), where Everett's theory and the many-worlds ontology figured prominently. Quantum mechanics is a persistent reference in Pynchon (who studied science and engineering at Cornell). Thus, by way of a play of the signifier, characteristic of Pynchon, the name of one of the main protagonists of *Vineland* (1990), Zoyd Wheeler, refers to John A. Wheeler, a major quantum theorist and the dissertation director of both Richard Feynman and Everett. (Z in Zoyd is likely standing for the Z-particle, discovered

just then, as well as "schiZoid.") One of the novel's key concepts, that of life–
death or life and non-life (the "Wawazumi Life&Non-Life" corporation),
is an allusion to another famous quantum paradox, that of the so-called
"Schrödinger's cat," one of the reasons for the many-worlds interpretations
of quantum mechanics.[9] The nature of the paradox is that, according to the
standard view of quantum mechanics, the cat is, at least for a while, both
dead and alive at once. The many-worlds interpretation resolves the paradox by maintaining that there are two cats in two different worlds, in one
of which it is alive and in the other dead. Actually there are many worlds,
with many dead or alive cats. Pynchon also alludes to a related concept,
"Wigner's friend," named after another famous quantum theorist and a col-
league of Wheeler, Eugene Wigner. The novel is populated by "alive-dead"
friends, the "Thanatoids." For quite a while by now, literary and theoretical
explorations of these conjoined, ontological and epistemological, multiplicities have been aided by bringing in the virtual worlds, more readily open to
ontological multiplicities. This problematic has been extensively explored in
postmodern literary works, often of a science-fictional nature or orientation
(such as novels by William Gibson and Neal Stephenson), and in posthumanist theory, a prominent postmodern trend.

Another crucial dimension of the multiple found in postmodern literature
should be stressed. This literature is not only a *representation* of the multiple but also an *enactment* of this multiple by its own multiplicity, sometimes within a single work, but especially by its overall decentered multiplicity – its many-worlds nature – psychological, cultural, ethical, and political.
This multiple posed new tasks and shaped postmodern theory, such as those
of defining more multiple and multiply interactive forms and practices of
subjectivity. Postmodern gender, postcolonial, and multicultural theories are
responses to these new tasks, jointly posed by the postmodern world and
postmodern literature, for example, by such authors as Joanna Russ, Toni
Morrison, Gerald Vizenor, and Junot Díaz. Each of these fields (which by
now include many important theorists and critics) and the literature itself
involved would require a separate discussion. Their contribution to the postmodern multiple affirms the uncontainable nature of this multiple, the multiple of multiples, with which postmodern literary authors and theorists are
compelled to engage in confronting the many-worlds character of the postmodern world.

The second defining aspect of postmodern thinking as defined here is that
it reveals the potentially insurmountable limits upon thinking and knowledge concerning the ultimate nature of phenomena considered, and, hence,
the irreducible *incompleteness* of both. Lyotard comes closest to this conception of the unthinkable in his definition of the postmodern, offered in the

context of literature and art in "Answering the Question: What is Postmodernism?" He says: "The postmodern would be that which, in the modern, puts forward the un-presentable in presentation itself; that denies itself the solace of good forms, the consensus of a taste which would make it possible to share collectively the nostalgia for the unattainable; [the postmodern is] that which searches for new presentations, not in order to enjoy them but in order to impart a stronger sense of the unpresentable."[10] This placing the postmodern *in* the modern becomes clearer if we recall that, as against other forms classical thinking, modern thinking considers the key postmodern features, such as the unthinkable and thus the un-presentable in presentation, as possible, but refuses to make them part of its theory building. Then, the nostalgia in question would not be unexpected either, and it could prevent one from pursuing postmodern theorizing, where the unthinkable is also responsible for what we think and know, which also means that postmodern thinking unavoidably involves classical or modern thinking. This is why Lyotard speaks of the postmodern *in* the modern and of the un-presentable *in* presentation: the un-presentable and ultimately the unthinkable has palpable effects on what is presented or thought.

Postmodern thinking and practice, literary or theoretical, may thus also exhibit their awareness of this loss in presentation, also as linked to the irreducibly multiple or the irreducibly random. It does not follow, however, as some commentators have argued, that the difference between the modern and the postmodern is defined *only* by the attitudinal (self-)awareness of this loss, in conjunction with the lack of nostalgia for it. A prominent example of this argument is Linda Hutcheon's works.[11] The difference between the modern and the postmodern is, as just explained, *structural* because the very nature of thought and knowledge changes. Postmodern thinking makes the un-presentable and ultimately the unthinkable part of thought and moreover, its efficacious part, responsible for what could be thought and known as its effects.

It does follow, however, that these effects do not have classical causes. As noted from the outset, the critique of causality and the roles of randomness or chance and probability are a major part of postmodern thinking in literature and theory. I use "causality" as an ontological category relating to the behavior of systems whose evolution is defined by the fact that the state of the system is determined at all points by its state at a given point. I use "determinism" as an epistemological category having to do with *our ability* to predict exactly the state of a system at any point once we know its state at a given point. There are causal theories where such predictions are not possible, for example chaos and complexity theories, prominent references in postmodern literature and theory.

I also need to define randomness or chance and probability. A random or chance event is an unpredictable event. It may or may not be possible to estimate whether it would occur, or often to anticipate it as an event. Probability, which measures our expectations concerning events whose occurrence (say, how a tossed coin will fall) cannot be predicted with certainty, introduces an element of order in our confrontations with randomness or chance and helps us to deal with them. The main question here is whether chance is a manifestation of causality, however hidden or remote, or not. These two alternatives define the two corresponding concepts of chance – classical and postmodern, with the modern, again, suspended between them, because it accepts the possibility of the second, postmodern, eventuality, but prefers or longs for the first, classical one. Classically, randomness or chance is seen as arising from our insufficient knowledge of the total configuration of the forces involved and of a lawful causality postulated behind an apparently random event. If this configuration becomes available, or if it could be made available, this randomness would disappear. It would reveal itself to be a product of the play of forces that is, at least in principle, calculable by man, or at least by God, who, in this view, "does not play dice," as Einstein famously said. It is worth keeping in mind that, while Einstein spoke of God (a brilliant rhetorical move, which immortalized the statement), he meant nature. All scientific and philosophical theories of randomness and probability prior to quantum theory or at least Darwin's evolutionary theory, and many beyond them, are of this classical type. Randomness of chance and probability result from insufficient information concerning systems that are at bottom causal. It is their mechanical complexity that prevents us from accessing their causal behavior and making deterministic predictions concerning it. Thus, classical mechanics deals deterministically with causal systems; classical statistical physics deals with causal systems, but only statistically; and chaos and complexity theories deal with systems that are causal, but whose behavior cannot be predicted exactly in view of its highly nonlinear character, known as the sensitivity to initial conditions.

By contrast, quantum mechanics deals with systems that may not be and, in most versions of the theory, cannot be considered as causal or, in the first place, represented by the theory. They are defined by the postmodern unpresentable in presentation, which makes automatic the absence of causality itself, rather than only determinism. Quantum mechanics predicts, probabilistically, the outcomes of quantum events, but does not explain the physical processes that make these events come about. These events are not merely random, and some of them exhibit *regularities*, for otherwise probabilistic predictions would not be possible. The recourse to probability, however, does not arise in view of our inability to access the underlying causal behavior of quantum systems. For technical reasons, which I cannot discuss here, it is difficult to assume quantum behavior to be causal or, to begin with, representable. The character of the existence of quantum objects is such that it precludes us from representing this existence.

It does not follow that in physics or elsewhere, we should abandon classical thinking and knowledge, because we infer the existence of that which cannot be presented or thought of, such as quantum objects, from its effects in the world we can represent and know. We might need to *resist* the resistance to postmodern thinking in modern thinking or classical thinking, where this resistance is even stronger, because it denies the postmodern even as possible. As noted, Einstein, whose attitude was modern, led the way to this resistance. Although he admitted that quantum epistemology is logically possible, he never accepted it or gave up hope for a classical-like theory of the ultimate constitution of nature. While Einstein's hope has not materialized thus far, the search for such classical alternatives continues and might yet succeed one day.

As Stephen J. Gould observes in the context of Darwin's evolutionary theory, "although contingency has been consistently underrated (or even unacknowledged) in stereotypical descriptions of scientific practice, the same subject remains a perennial favorite among literary folk, from the most snootily arcane to the most vigorously vernacular – and it behooves us to ask why."[12] Contingency (a concept that I haven't used thus far) is the interplay of randomness and causality, or more accurately regularity, which, as I noted, is not always causal. The question is, again, what is the nature of the law and the regularities contingency reflects, in particular, whether this law is causal or not, and those of evolution or human history or politics may not be, just as the regularities and laws of quantum mechanics are not.

Gould invokes nineteenth-century novels, such as Leo Tolstoy's *War and Peace* and Emily Brontë's *Wuthering Heights*, as his examples. These are great novels of contingency, which may even be seen as defining the novel as a genre, from Cervantes's *Don Quixote* on. Gould's answer to his question is that literature aims at the extraordinary, which is contingent, as the product of a singular, unique trajectory. This is true. Literature, beginning with the ancient Greek tragedy or Homer, explores the realm of the contingent, the particular, and the extraordinary. And yet, Gould's description of contingency still allows for a classical view, which Darwin's theory would question, as Gould knows. Modernist novels, such as those of Kafka, Joyce, and Woolf, and then, following these precursors, postmodern American novels present more nonclassical portrayals of contingency, in part by using, directly or allegorically, quantum theory.

Pynchon's and DeLillo's novels are paradigmatic examples of this kind of engagement with scientific theories of contingencies and mathematics and science in general, also in their postmodern aspects. Beginning with *The Crying of Lot 49* (1966), the relationships among chance, contingency, and probability are prominent in Pynchon, and they are often accompanied by depictions or allegories (beginning, as already noted, at the level of signifiers) of scientific theories involving them – thermodynamics, quantum theory, and, in later novels, chaos and complexity theory. *The Crying of Lot 49* may be seen as an exploration of possible laws of contingency, governing the singular trajectories of the characters' lives and their interactions. Some of these trajectories are causal (on the model of thermodynamics, expressly discussed in the novel); others are noncausal (in the model of quantum theory), which is, again, not the same as random, although randomness is found in the novel as well.[13] Contingency is staged by the novel as defining the characters' lives, or life itself. Its protagonist, Oedipa Mass, whose name suggests a causal law of fate (after Sophocles's *Oedipus the King*), *might* be set to discover this, but, if so, only after the novel ends. In the course of the novel, Oedipa assumes her quest to be governed by causal laws, which makes this quest continually go astray, because any assumed causal connections are subverted soon after they are assumed. A more quantum-mechanical understanding of life appears to be required. This nature of life is, again, not random, which may appear to be the only alternative to causality, an alternative that would, because it defeats probability, paralyze any strategy of action, which is always probabilistic. This absolute reversal of causality is found in *Oedipus the King*, and it may be called "the Jocasta ontology" because it was dramatically expressed by Jocasta, Oedipus' mother and wife: "Fear? What should a man fear? It's all chance, chance rules our lives. Not a man on earth can see a day ahead, groping through the dark. Better to live at random, best we can."[14] This view is proven illusory in the play because the lives of the characters are ultimately ruled by fate. By contrast, while it defeats a strictly causal reasoning, a quantum-mechanical-like contingency of life allows for a form of order and hence probabilistic thinking. The novel ends on an auction, a paradigmatic event of contingency defined by the interplay of contingent trajectories, of sellers and buyers, or those who set up the auction. The question is: What is the law of this contingency? The novel's answer may be not only that we cannot always count on causality and must sometimes reason in the quantum-mechanical way, but also that there is no single such law. Life's law of contingency is the multiplicity of such laws, which also includes the unlawful, whereby things are purely random. This complexity is helped by the detective dimensions of *The Crying of Lot 49*, again, recasting those of

Oedipus the King. These dimensions are found in all of Pynchon's novels, including *Inherent Vice* (2009), also a detective novel, and are something that he shares with Dostoyevsky. ("Inherent" may also be read as signifying heredity, another contingent phenomenon.) But this is only one part of this great game of contingency, and contingency also defines the very concept of game or play, multiply allegorized by Pynchon's novels as well.

This game becomes ever more complex from *Gravity's Rainbow* on.[15] The *improbable* coincidence of two statistical distributions – that of London locations where German V2 rockets hit and that of the protagonist Tyron Slothrop's sexual encounters – is the novel's setup, which alludes to some famous quantum experiments. As the novel proceeds, it becomes clear that its form and content allegorize conflicts of contrasting laws of causality and contingency, sometimes adopted and advocated by different characters – laws that are scientific (mathematical, physical, chemical, and biological), psychological (Freudian versus Pavlovian), or sociological. The novel even allegorically embodies the conflict now defining fundamental physics, that between Einstein's relativistic theory of gravity (a causal theory) and quantum mechanics. Each theory is true within its proper limits, but they are incompatible. This conflict is already implied by the signifying conjunction of the novel's title, combining gravity and rainbow. A rainbow is an optical and thus ultimately quantum phenomenon.

I have already mentioned the role of quantum mechanics in *Vineland*. Both *Mason & Dixon* and *Against the Day* are defined by equally complex landscapes of contingency, multiply related to mathematics and science. These landscapes are also actual landscapes, territories and escapes from territories or deterritorializations, as Deleuze and Guattari would have it. I would like to briefly comment on *Against the Day*, not only because the flight of the balloon, named "The Chums of Chance," around which the novel is organized, is subject to and is an allegory of contingency, multiplied by the trajectory of the balloon's journey. Even more remarkable is the landscape of modern mathematics and science depicted and allegorized by the novel. Virtually everything that came to define twentieth-century mathematics and science, and to some degree technology, is found there, from Cantor's set theory to quantum mechanics. Several chapters take place in the mathematics department of the University of Göttingen, the birthplace of several key developments of modern mathematics. Its arguably greatest figure, David Hilbert, and his French counterpart Henri Poincaré make their appearance in the novel. It was also the birthplace of quantum mechanics, discovered by Werner Heisenberg, there at the time, and much research on relativity was done at Göttingen as well. One of Pynchon's signature songs comically captures this landscape:

Her idea of banter
Likely isn't Cantor
Nor is she apt to murmur low
Axioms of Zermelo,
She's been kissed by geniuses,
Amateur Frobeniuses
One by one in swank array,
Bright as any Poincaré,
And ... though she
May not care for Cauchy,
Any more than Riemann,
We'll just have to dream on ... [16]

These are the names of some of the key figures of conceptually postmodern mathematics, specifically set theory, the foundation of the modern mathematical multiple. The novel becomes a portrayal, direct and allegorical, of mathematical and scientific developments that helped to define postmodern thinking and knowledge in Lyotard. These connections are also extended to politics and culture, or modernist literature and art, again, by way of a landscape of contingencies and interactive contingent trajectories – rhizomes. In this regard, the novel echoes Deleuze and Guattari's vision in *Anti-Oedipus* (Deleuze and Guattari are parodically mentioned in *Vineland*).[17] The novel, thus, embodies the *condition* of the postmodern condition, at one of the most decisive junctures of its history.

Don DeLillo's novels are also allegorical embodiments of the landscapes of contingency, often expressly in postmodern settings, as, for example, in *Cosmopolis* (2003), although the connections to science are most manifested and deliberate in *White Noise*. *Cosmopolis* is structured around the singular one-day/one-lifetime trajectory of the protagonist Eric Packer (a reader of Einstein and Freud in German), through, digitally, the global world of finance and, actually, the crowded (also with contingencies) world of New York, on his way to both his financial ruin and nearly certainly his actual death, murder, at the intersection with another contingent trajectory, that of his killer. One cannot be quite certain about Eric's ultimate fate, because the novel ends with Eric "waiting for the shot to sound."[18] This ending is peculiarly reminiscent of "Oedipa settled back, to await the crying of lot 49," the sentence that ends Pynchon's novel.[19]

Postmodern literature and theory explore the relationships between the contingent and the multiple, and of both with the unthinkable, and make the irreducibility of all three and their relationships their primary concern. The ultimate nature of this concern is, however, ethical and political. The main question is this: Are our aspirations for a more just society better served by the ideologies and grand narratives, such as those of the Enlightenment or, its perennial competition, theologically grounded ideologies and grand narratives, or are they better served by postmodern thinking defined by a deep skepticism concerning the reach of our thinking or knowledge and, correlatively, of grand narratives? I am willing to grant such aspirations to the proponents of the first, advocated by Habermas, whom Lyotard, too, credits with a good aspiration – a more just society – but not with a good argument concerning how to achieve it.[20] The question just stated is, actually, double. First, when it comes to a more just society, is the secular, scientific Enlightenment better than theologically grounded systems of ethics and justice? Perhaps, and perhaps even likely! In fairness, though, theological thinking has made its contributions to the advancement of knowledge and justice, while science and the ideology of scientific progress have sometimes been used without regard for justice and for purposes that are hardly just. Second, is the Enlightenment (thus conceived) better than postmodernism? While that it may be better cannot be excluded, it appears to be at best uncertain that it is. This brings me back to Lyotard and his case for justice under "the postmodern condition," the case that ultimately drives the argument of *The Postmodern Condition*. First, Lyotard argues that while the Enlightenment's cause for justice, advocated by Habermas, is good, Habermas's conceptions of consensus and of the unity of knowledge and culture, grounding the cause, are "*outmoded* and suspect values." They are unlikely to survive "that severe reexamination which postmodernity imposes on the thought of the Enlightenment, on the idea of a unitary end of history and of a subject."[21] "But," Lyotard says, "justice is a value that is neither outmoded nor suspect. We must thus arrive at an idea and practice of justice that is not linked to that of consensus."[22] Lyotard then offers a brief, manifesto-like outline of postmodern politics that would respect both "the desire for justice" and, this is crucial, "the desire for the unknown," and, I would add, the desire for and in any event acceptance of the unthinkable.[23] This is closer to Emmanuel Levinas's ethics of "the absolute Other," who is always beyond the reach of thought, but whom we must nevertheless welcome with hospitality, and to Derrida's elaboration of this problematic in a geopolitical context.[24] From *The Bluest Eye* to *Beloved* and beyond, Toni Morrison explored, arguably most deeply among postmodern American authors, the complexities of otherness and hospitality (or the inhospitable), especially, but far from exclusively, in the context of race relations.

Is this kind of justice possible? At least, it appears no more impossible and may even prove to be more likely to work than justice based on the idea of consensus or other Enlightenment (or theological) principles, defined by grand narratives, dominant and persistent as these principles remain. But, this justice could not be one justice for all or the same justice forever. I am not suggesting that we cannot or should not try to minimize injustice in our efforts to achieve a better justice, a justice to come, as Derrida might say and in effect did say in speaking of "a democracy *to come*" in *Specters of Marx*.[25] "We need some kind of tomorrow," Toni Morrison says, in closing *Beloved* or just about (a brief and darker epilogue follows), in the seemingly personal context of the future of two of its characters.[26] It would, however, be difficult to think that a much larger scale of tomorrow, a tomorrow of the world, is not at stake here, a tomorrow of a justice to come, and perhaps there is no other justice.

Further Reading

Hayles, Katharine N.. *Chaos Bound: Orderly Disorder in Contemporary Literature and Science*. Ithaca, NY: Cornell University Press, 1990.

Latour, Bruno. *We Have Never Been Modern*. Translated by Catherine Porter. Cambridge, MA: Harvard University Press, 1993.

Lyotard, Jean-François. *The Postmodern Condition: A Report on Knowledge*. Translated by Geoff Bennington and Brian Massumi. Minneapolis: University of Minnesota Press, 1984.

Plotnitsky, Arkady. *Reconfigurations: Critical Theory and General Economy*. Gainesville: University of Florida Press, 1993.

Wolfe, Cary. *What is Posthumanism?* Minneapolis: University of Minnesota Press, 2013.

NOTES

1 Jean-François Lyotard, *The Postmodern Condition: A Report on Knowledge*, trans. Geoff Bennington and Brian Massumi (Minneapolis: University of Minnesota Press, 1984).

2 Ibid., 18.

3 Fredric Jameson, *Postmodernism, or, The Cultural Logic of Late Capitalism* (Durham, NC: Duke University Press, 1990).

4 It appears, for example, in the title of Ihab Hassan's *The Dismemberment of Orpheus: Toward Postmodern Literature* (Oxford: Oxford University Press, 1971).

5 N. Katherine Hayles, *How We Became Posthuman: Virtual Bodies in Cybernetics, Literature, and Informatics* (Chicago: University of Chicago Press, 1999); and Cary Wolfe, *What is Posthumanism?* (Minneapolis: University of Minnesota Press, 2013).

6 Lyotard, *The Postmodern Condition*, 55–58.

7 Alain Badiou, *Being and Event*, trans. Oliver Feltman (New York: Continuum, 2007), 29.

8 Brian McHale, *Postmodern Fiction* (New York: Routledge, 1987).

9 Thomas Pynchon, *Vineland* (Boston: Little, Brown, 1990), 142.

10 Lyotard, "Answering the Question: What is Postmodernism?" in *The Postmodern Condition*, 81.

11 Linda Hutcheon, *A Poetics of Postmodernism: History, Theory, Fiction* (London: Routledge, 1990).

12 Stephen J. Gould, *The Structure of Evolutionary Theory* (Cambridge, MA: Harvard University Press, 2002), 1340.

13 Thomas Pynchon, *The Crying of Lot 49* (New York: Harper and Row, 1966).

14 Sophocles, *The Three Theban Plays: Antigone, Oedipus the King, and Oedipus at Colonus*, trans. Robert Fagles (New York: Penguin, 1984), 146.

15 Thomas Pynchon, *Gravity's Rainbow* (New York: Bantam, 1973).

16 Thomas Pynchon, *Against the Day* (New York: Penguin, 2006), 589.

17 Pynchon, *Vineland*, 97.

18 Don DeLillo, *Cosmopolis* (New York: Scribner, 2003), 205.

19 Pynchon, *The Crying of Lot 49*, 183.

20 Lyotard, *The Postmodern Condition*, 66–67.

21 Lyotard, "Answering the Question: What is Postmodernism?" in *The Postmodern Condition*, 73.

22 Lyotard, *The Postmodern Condition*, 66.

23 Ibid., 67.

24 Emmanuel Levinas, *Totality and Infinity: An Essay on Exteriority*, trans. Alfonso Lingis (Pittsburgh, PA: Duquesne University Press, 1969); and Jacques Derrida, *Adieu to Emmanuel Levinas*, trans. Pascale-Anne Brault and Michael Nass (Stanford, CA: Stanford University Press, 1999).

25 Jacques Derrida, *Specters of Marx: The State of Debt, the Work of Mourning, and the New International*, trans. Peggy Kamuf (London: Taylor & Francis, 1993), 81.

26 Toni Morrison, *Beloved* (New York: Plume, 1987), 286.

5

TIMOTHY PARRISH

History and Fiction

What do we mean when we use the word "history"? Nineteenth-century German historian Leopold von Ranke famously defined it as "wie es eigentlich gewesen," that is, "what actually happened."[1] If history is an event that has already occurred, it is over, and its essence can be known and its story told. But how do we know when the past is divided from the present, and who gets to tell the story of "what actually happened"? Peter Gay says simply that "the objects of the historian's inquiry are precisely that, objects, out there in a real and single past."[2] If history is an object, like a Roman coin or a nuclear laboratory in Los Alamos, New Mexico, then it is a fact to be known. But is a fact ever meaningful by itself, or does its meaning only come to light when a story exists to explain it? And does that story simply arise from the facts like the Lord from Moses' burning bush, or is it always the product of selection by a particular narrator? After all, not all objects exist to be known, and indeed not every object of history remains for us to contemplate.

According to R. K. Ankersmit, the work of historians since the nineteenth century has relied on two basic premises. First, "the historical text is considered 'transparent' with regard to the underlying historical reality," and, second, the historical text is "transparent with regard to the historian's judgment of the relevant part of the past."[3] Near the end of the nineteenth century, J. B. Bury insisted "history is a science, no less and no more and thus 'not a branch of literature.'"[4] Since modernism came to the novel in the form of James Joyce, Virginia Woolf, Marcel Proust, Robert Musil, and William Faulkner, though, we have come to understand that narrative is not so much a science as it is an art. A past exists, to be sure. Writers like Proust or Faulkner, though, would insist that the past is never past, which would mean that history is an ongoing event where the past bleeds into the present. History may consist of facts and documented events, but its story is uncertain until it is told – and even then, the story is subject to the demands of the teller and the teller's audience. Postmodernist critic Linda Hutcheon flatly states that "history does not exist except as text."[5]

Hutcheon's claim takes the practice of history through the "linguistic turn" characteristic of postmodern theorists such as Jacques Derrida, Jean-François Lyotard, and Hayden White, who in different ways have challenged the positivistic assumptions that have governed the discipline of history since the nineteenth century. The linguistic turn tells us that nothing exists outside the text or truly separate from the text. It threatens views of history that insist the past is over, set in stone like an object, and lies still waiting for a historian to come along and read the writing left on the stone. Questioning the assumption that history is as objective and knowable as a scientific premise is said to be, Jean-François Lyotard asks: can we "continue to organize the events which crowd in upon us from the human and nonhuman worlds with the help of the Idea of a universal history?"[6]

If we accept Lyotard's premise, we may well ask: how particular must history become to be true to the story it tells? For instance, can there be a single history of the United States that is coherent, objective, and complete? Do the stories of Native Americans, African Americans, and European Americans since 1492 coalesce into the same story, or does the history of America depend on who is telling it? In the past half century, historians have tried to address the concerns such a question implies by writing a variety of "histories from below" and "outside" (cf. histories of childhood, of the working class, of women, of different ethnic and racial groups), yet these approaches cannot fully dispense with Hutcheon's claim that history is at bottom a question of narrative. For even a history limited to the narrowest perspective, and the most rigorous "scientific" model, cannot dispense with the narrative imperative to cut, prune, and order the "facts" one presents as true. At the same time, history cannot dispense with the need to establish the meaning, relevance, and coherence that narrative provides.

Perhaps because fiction surrenders the claim to an Absolute Truth, postmodern American novelists have been able to explore the permeable nature of history in ways that historians have not. On the one hand, they have been intent on showing the ways in which any history, even when the facts are known and more or less agreed upon, may be understood as a form of narrative that shares the same tendencies as fiction. This group would include writers such as Walter Abish, Don DeLillo, Kurt Vonnegut, Thomas Pynchon, E. L. Doctorow, Joan Didion, Robert Coover, Donald Barthelme, and John Barth. These writers challenge the assumptions that history is a practice separable from fiction. On the other hand, many postmodern American novelists have tried to reclaim a version of history that recuperates a notion of truth that relies upon the shared belief between teller and audience. This group, which we might call the "rememory" group, after the word Toni Morrison invents in *Beloved* (1987), includes such writers as Alice Walker,

Toni Cade Bambara, Louise Erdrich, Leslie Marmon Silko, Maxine Hong Kingston, Philip Roth, and Ishmael Reed. In *Beloved*, the act of "rememory" involves putting together the severed pieces of the past to create a story that heals – that re-members broken bodies into one whole. The "rememory" novelists use fiction to tell versions of history that have been ignored or insufficiently represented by conventional historians in order to create a more livable present for the implied audiences of their narratives.

Perhaps no recent American work better exemplifies the challenge to telling an objectively true and coherently consistent "history" than Don DeLillo's *Libra* (1988).[7] In retelling the history of John F. Kennedy's assassination, *Libra* is both a novel and a critique of conventional historiography. Its protagonist, Lee Harvey Oswald, the reputed assassin of President Kennedy, is a version of the "patsy" he famously claimed he was shortly before his own murder. Also "patsies" are those who believe the "official" version of events, its so-called "history," sanctioned by the Warren Commission, wherein a single, disgruntled ex-marine kills the president through his own cunning and sharp shooting. The novel is less interested, though, in identifying who killed Kennedy than in showing how difficult it is to tell a history that is unambiguously true.

In DeLillo's "fictional" version, the plan to kill Kennedy is conceived in a basement at Texas Woman's University by a disgraced CIA officer who has been sent there to teach after his role in the failed Bay of Pigs operation meant to topple Fidel Castro. His basic idea is to set up a fictional plot to kill the president that is linked to Castro. The CIA officer does not actually want to kill the president: he wants to create a political context that forces Kennedy to commit to murdering Castro. Oswald becomes enmeshed in this plan and soon the plot takes on a life of its own, separate from its maker. Into this mélange of plots and counterplots, DeLillo mixes several well-known "conspiracy" theories with actual historical documents and conversations recorded by J. Edgar Hoover. In the novel, Oswald does fire at Kennedy, but he is not the lone gunman and he does not fire the fatal bullet. Neither the plotter – the CIA agent – nor the protagonist of his plot – Oswald – realize their roles as they were originally conceived. Yet, it becomes difficult for even the most well-informed reader to distinguish between fact and fiction. The only known truth is the end: the assassination of Kennedy. How it happened, who orchestrated it, and for what purposes are issues harder to settle without changing the story. The novel seems to suggest that, at best, history is something we make up to conceal all of the things we can never know. If history exists, it lies somewhere in the gap between intentions and effects.

DeLillo originally planned to call the novel *Texas Schoolbook*, a fitting title given that *Libra* is a virtual textbook for how novels in the postmodern era have persistently refashioned history as something contingent and subject to the endless fluidity of narrative. Novels such as E. L. Doctorow's *Ragtime* (1975), Robert Coover's *The Public Burning* (1977), John Barth's *The Sot-Weed Factor* (1960), Max Apple's *The Propheteers* (1987), and Thomas Pynchon's *Mason & Dixon* (1997) begin at least in the same place as do scholarly works of history, since to write them the writers have had to exhaustively research their fictions. Without a historical record, the novels could not exist. Still, they draw on and re-create historical figures and documents to convey how what we call history is often at its core simply a matter of calculated belief, since narrative re-enactments by definition repress some of what happened to tell the story they tell. To describe postmodern novels that blend history with fiction, Linda Hutcheon has invented the term "historiographic metafiction." According to Hutcheon, postmodernism's basic impulse is to make an "ironic dialogue" with the past; thus, postmodernist fiction insists that we consider how history is made, received, and understood. She distinguishes this postmodern gesture from the modernist impulse to break with the past and the realist tendency to understand the past as being divided from the present. Historiographic metafiction, for instance, differs from historical fiction (which dates back to Walter Scott) because it does not leave "what happened" intact as something that we already know and thus cannot be changed. Historiographic metafiction is distinguished by its "theoretical self-awareness of history and fiction as human constructs," and this self-awareness becomes the basis of how such fiction reimagines the past.[8] While theorists such as Fredric Jameson have argued that postmodernism is characterized by its complicity with the corporate structures of multinational capitalism, Hutcheon suggests that postmodern art situates itself "squarely within both economic capitalism and cultural humanism" and thus offers a "complicitous critique" of existing power structures through forms that are often "parodic, historical, and reflexive."[9] For this reason, postmodern fiction generally has been interested in locating the marginal and redefining how we understand history from marginalized perspectives, which often emphasize issues of race, class, and gender.

Hutcheon characterizes postmodernism as "fundamentally contradictory, resolutely historical, and inescapably political."[10] Consider Doctorow's *Book of Daniel* (1971) or Coover's *The Public Burning*. Both novels retell the story of Julius and Ethel Rosenberg, Americans executed as spies for the Soviet Union, until it becomes something quite different from newspaper accounts. It becomes a living event that cannot be contained by any single narrative. *The Book of Daniel* concludes with its narrator, the Rosenbergs' son, participating in a march to protest the Vietnam War and the course of history that killed his parents. Coover's Uncle Sam, not to mention his portrayals of Joe McCarthy and Richard Nixon, is a counterhistory to the exceptionalist one that justifies US exploitation of the resources of other nations as attempts to bring freedom and democracy to as many people as possible. These novels insist on the primacy of history and work to fashion a living version alternative to the reality the novels challenge.

Arguably, the postmodern novelist's choice to blur the line between history and fiction is merely an attempt to keep up with the mutability of reality in the media-driven postmodern age. If the official story of the Kennedy assassination, canonized in the Warren Commission Report, became for many a fiction fabulated by the US government to protect its citizens from knowing what happened, that is because its narrative representations were multiple and contradictory. The cause of this shift in perception regarding the Kennedy assassination was not a theory but a film taken by the amateur home movie-maker, Abraham Zapruder, who happened to be recording the presidential procession when Kennedy was shot. Once Zapruder's film reached the public consciousness, it yielded a reality and perspective different from the one previously presented to the American public. Alternative versions of the event began to surface, and suddenly history no longer seemed something knowable, verifiable, but something so hidden that it had to be invented to be understood.

In the 1960s, Philip Roth claimed that "the American writer in the middle of the twentieth century has his hands full in trying to understand, describe, and make *credible* much of American reality."[11] For Roth, contemporary American life outstripped the novelist's capacity to imagine it. Roth's claim makes sense not because history became more chaotic, but because its capacity to be reproduced had been multiplied exponentially through film, television, and now people's phones. How can we know what history is when its most prominent makers have access to the mechanisms of narrative reproductions and the means to distribute them during, after, and *before* an event happens? Works such as *Slaughterhouse-Five* (1969), *Gravity's Rainbow* (1973), and *The Book of Daniel* dramatize how rendering history as fiction was no longer just the province of novelists, but the official policy of the US government. During World War II, the US government hired filmmakers such as John Huston and Frank Capra to make documentary movies meant to enhance American patriotism, just as German filmmaker Leni Riefenstahl had filmed Hitler to such dramatic effect during his rise to power in the thirties. *Libra, Underworld, Gravity's Rainbow, The Public Burning*, and Ishmael Reed's *Mumbo Jumbo* (1972) depict contemporary history as a sort of hypertext whose meaning is always changing. In so doing, these writers portray the aestheticization of political power in the postmodern age. Major historical events after the Kennedy assassination – the Vietnam War,

Watergate, the wars against Iran and Afghanistan, even 9/11 – may be experienced as fictions written and performed by vague figures in the US government whose only concern with "the truth" is their ability to construct plausible, even fantastic, events that the majority of the intended audience believes are true.

As DeLillo portrays him in *Underworld* (1997), FBI director J. Edgar Hoover can be seen as a sort of Joycean master of narrative who wrote history before it happened through the vast yet intricate set of files he kept on the words and acts of American citizens.[12] In *Underworld*, Hoover's files, not unlike the Warren Commission Report, operate as an achievement that mimics Joyce's ambition in *Ulysses* (1922) or *Finnegan's Wake* (1939), in which the author knows every character's biography and every potential political plot.[13] The narrative power of DeLillo's Hoover is his recognition that no fact is fixed and no version is permanent. More facts can be found or fabricated to tell the story he needs to tell that day. Indeed, the story need not be consistent as long as he is the one telling it, and his files contain all the possible characters and plots needed for his historical fiction. DeLillo's Hoover connects the dots to political narratives that please him and enjoys more narrative power than even Joyce could have imagined.

Artists such as Hoover or actors such as Ronald Reagan achieve and preserve power through their capacity to create fictions that justify their often horrifying political actions. In Pynchon's *The Crying of Lot 49* (1966) or *Gravity's Rainbow*, for instance, characters experience history as a plot designed either to exclude or to deceive them. Pynchon's characters work against an unnamed and threatening "They," whom DeLillo or Coover simply portray as the living historical figures we already know. Postmodern characters often work to create counterplots, counternarratives, in which their lives make sense as something other than the necessary effect of the narratives of government or multinational corporations. In Reed's *Mumbo Jumbo*, for instance, a counterconspiracy of jazz, blues, and polytheistic religion rises up to challenge the Western tradition of monotheism and cultural repression. At stake in such postmodern works is a version of history that is not false, but knowable, true, and even morally acceptable when the official organs of history seem to have become so compromised.

Along with portraying how government officials create narratives to protect themselves, postmodernist novelists suggest that history is neither true nor false, but becomes believable only through acts of narrative. Vonnegut's novel about World War II, *Slaughterhouse-Five*, is a representative case in point.[14] Its opening section recounts the personal difficulties Vonnegut faced in writing the novel and reads if it were a preface appended to the actual novel, written, possibly, years after its first publication. But the novel, the fiction, begins with this seemingly authentic account from the author about his life. Vladimir Nabokov's *Lolita* (1955), by contrast, begins with a fictional preface from a fictional character, "John Ray, Ph.D.," that many readers may mistake for an authentic version of the kinds of prefaces that accompany scholarly editions of novels. In either case, the author is making a claim to reality based on fiction and is challenging the notion that history can be separated from fiction. *Lolita*, however, concludes with an "Afterword" written by Nabokov that reflects upon the historical reception of the novel the reader has just read. *Slaughterhouse-Five*, by contrast, never redraws the line that separates fiction from history because Vonnegut's novel specifically wants to challenge his readers' presumed understanding of World War II.

Hence, a key character in the novel shares the same name as the author, "Kurt Vonnegut," to affirm that the history being told is true, even where it is made up. In *Operation Shylock* (1993), Philip Roth uses a similar device, but the story he tells about the author Philip Roth and his double, also named Philip Roth, and the mission he performs for the Israeli Mossad cannot be found in any "history" book except *Operation Shylock*. In *Slaughterhouse-Five*, the author-narrator-character is a witness and a victim of the historically documented bombing of Dresden in 1944. To understand what happened, the novel turns the bombing into an incidental event in a larger plot that involves time travel, intergalactic aliens, and the sense that Dresden was more important for being an event in the history of human technology than it was as an event that changed or did not change World War II. The novel even includes a brief account of how the universe and everything in it ended – though its end, our end, apparently does not eradicate the possibility of it being narrated. You can read his account to mean that nothing that happens, no matter how climactic it may seem at the time – be it the destruction of a historic city, the death of a president, the murder of six million Jews, the existence of American slavery, or a bird chirping from a tree – is more important than anything else that happens, or that narration, however variable, is the only way we have of knowing and remembering this world we are each born into. Only narrative, not the events it describes, may survive its actors, regardless of whether anyone remains to apprehend it.

The end of the novel stages a confrontation between Billy Pilgrim and a military historian in which the historian mocks Pilgrim's ability to comprehend what has happened. Pilgrim is merely an actor in a story whose premises and permutations are beyond his capacity to control or even understand them. The "historian," Professor Rumfoord, claims to understand and in effect write the story of which Pilgrim was an incidental part. Pilgrim's task is to submit to the higher authority the historian claims in shaping his story. Rumfoord's twenty-seven-volume *Official History of the Army Air*

Force in World War Two does not mention the bombing of Dresden – in part because the government wanted to keep it secret from the American public. The sense that one may be a hapless victim of history subject to the wills of other tellers who have usurped *your* story as if it were an inconsequential adjunct to *their* story is precisely what many postmodernist writers have tried to combat through their work. Vonnegut's narrative decision to put the author into the narrative gives the lie to the premise that the historian is ever separate from the story being told. Although *Slaughterhouse-Five* is one of the most well-known postmodernist novels written after World War II in part because of its experimenting with time and science fiction, perhaps its most influential narrative move was to put the author into the story, since that device more than any other has become emblematic of postmodernist American fiction.

The "rememory" works of Maxine Hong Kingston, Gloria Anzaldúa, and Joan Didion, among others, also blend memoir with fiction to allow the silenced to speak back in ways that Vonnegut never allows Pilgrim. For these writers, simply telling stories from previously unrepresented cultural or historical perspectives constitutes a critique of mainstream history. In blending fact with fiction, the personal with the political, and prose with poetry, as Anzaldúa does in *Borderlands/La Frontera* (1987), these writers seem to suggest that when received history is made up of others' lies about you, then you are obligated to invent yourself as a version of that which you want to affirm. A key figure in Kingston's memoir *The Woman Warrior* (1976) is called "no-name woman," and the narrator's telling of her story brings to light a history otherwise lost. In *Democracy* (1984), Didion presents her fiction as a memoir. To begin the second chapter, she greets the reader with the command: "call me the author."[15] Her gesture at once suggests the arbitrariness of any narrative perspective and alerts the reader that the story she is telling is personal. *Borderlands/La Frontera* makes narrative hybridity an inescapable condition of existence and narrative by putting the author's "I" into history.[16] Anzaldúa's notion of "la frontera," or the border, challenges those who believe that categories such as sexuality, cultural identity, and language can ever be fixed. In articulating an identity that is a mixture of categories often opposed, Anzaldúa makes her own history out of other histories and in the process creates an identity that conventional history has not been able to tell. That the book was actually banned for a time from being taught in New Mexico public schools can only convey the need for some authors to challenge the premises of conventional history and the prejudices it often supports.

Hutcheon notes that historiographic metafiction "problematizes the very possibility of historical knowledge," but it does more than that.[17]

Historiographic metafiction also offers a different paradigm for understanding how history works and why people need to believe in history. Even a supremely parodic work such as *The Public Burning* or Ishmael Reed's *Flight to Canada* (1976), a postmodern slave narrative, does not eradicate history or question its knowability. In Reed's book, Abraham Lincoln, Harriet B. Stowe, the myth of the happy "ole South," and even the Civil Rights Movement are portrayed in terms alternatively comedic and horrifying. While the novel is mainly concerned with how black history has been distorted by competing understandings of the war itself, it shows how all versions of history are partial and exclusive. More importantly, the novel challenges us to understand how the Civil War in many ways has not ended because our representations of it have been inadequate to do justice to all of its participants and their descendants. In this context, "rememory" works such as Alice Walker's *The Color Purple* (1982), Toni Cade Bambara's *The Salt Eaters* (1980), Paule Marshall's *Praisesong for the Widow* (1983), and Toni Morrison's *Beloved* (1987) can be read as a continuous historical project that dramatizes through fiction "what actually happened" to African Americans since the Civil War that conventional histories have been unable to tell. Each of these books concerns how African Americans preserved a sense of identity and community despite and against the efforts of other Americans to deny them this power.

Again, in these works history lives as a form of myth, and the novelist is often the one who preserves and carries forward the myths sacred to the group whose story is being told. If these novels question history, it is to find a better one. As American literature has become atomized into the stories of different groups of people whose existence precedes and in some ways resists the invention of American identity, postmodern fiction has been the seeding ground for this transformation. One might be tempted to call them "postmodern histories," since the overtly technical term "historiographic metafiction" hardly does them justice. Works such as Kingston's *Woman Warrior* and *China Men* (1980), Cynthia Ozick's *The Shawl* (1988), Leslie Marmon Silko's *Almanac of the Dead* (1991), or Louise Erdrich's interconnected novels beginning with *Love Medicine* (1984) may even been seen as alternative histories for peoples whose stories have been repressed by totalizing "American" ones intent on telling a homogeneous story that excludes particular ones in favor of a unifying whole. In these novels, one encounters a Chinese American history, an African American history, and a Native American history at odds with histories that begin with the Founding Fathers. These novels serve as both a critique of typical exceptionalist American history and an affirmation of a way of being in a narrative that is alternative and opposed to the narrative it critiques. They obviously critique versions of history that justified their disenfranchisement and slavery, but just as importantly, they also compel faith in their readers to believe in their stories as ones worth telling.

These "postmodern histories" share a belief in the power of fiction to remake the world. They also share a skepticism concerning the ways in which a timeless, as it were, history, a history that is seen as fixed forever, can be a weapon used by people who hold social and political power to disenfranchise and demonize people whom they wish to keep powerless. Tayo, the scarred Army veteran of Leslie Marmon Silko's *Ceremony* (1977), struggles to find a balance between his Laguna ancestry and his American identity. In telling his story, Silko draws on tribal legends to weave a new history fashioned out of prior ones. On the other hand, the question of whose language can be used to tell such a story can be problematic. In Morrison's *Beloved*, a slave, Sixo, refuses to speak English because he does not want to be a part of that language's history. He dies, laughing, shouting the word "Seven-O," an allusion to his child growing in the womb of Thirty-Mile Woman.[18] "Seven-O" gestures to the possibility of a future history different from the one that enslaved him. In these works, narrative may seem disjointed and contingent, time frames may jump back and forth unexpectedly, and point of view may shift or seem unstable when compared to a traditional realist novel. However, at their core is the impulse to create a fiction in which communities can come together to affirm a history previously untold except perhaps in oral traditions. They are political because they imagine creating other histories alternative to the totalizing one of domination so often associated with existing histories of the United States.

Some postmodern fiction that mixes history and fiction can seem old fashioned and conservative, since it believes there is a single truth that will unite teller and audience. Whether the intended audience of *Beloved* or *Love Medicine* includes all readers, or only the readers who can claim to be part of the history of the story being told, depends on whether you view the novel as a book whose meaning is available for any reader to accept and claim. Can all readers of *Beloved* or *Song of Solomon* claim these novels in the same way that many African Americans can? Whatever the case, "history" is very much a living idea and open question in these works.

Thomas Pynchon's novel *Mason & Dixon*, however, asks what happens when one can no longer believe in history as a redeeming force.[19] In terms of American history, what story remains from a history that begins as an invention of "Founding Fathers" who happen to be white men who mostly own slaves and devise a republic where only property-owning white men vote? *Mason & Dixon* re-imagines American history through the lens of two real-life surveyors, Roger Mason and Jeremiah Dixon. They think they have been brought to America to settle a property dispute, but to the twenty-first-century reader there is something ominous in their every act since they drew the line that divided North from South, free from slave, and in a way marked the divide that became the Civil War. In Pynchon's version of the national story, the United States has never been more than a glorified real estate scam, abetted by scientific and technological discoveries that have enabled a few people to command vast amounts of resources unheard of in human history, for the enablement of the few and with the disenfranchisement of the many. The lands the Founding Fathers appropriate for themselves are not limited to the continental United States but are part of a global scheme, realized in the nineteenth and twentieth centuries, to extract and exploit the globe's natural assets to continually create their own power. They bring to the world not freedom and democracy, but a plague of destruction whose acts recall the smallpox-infested blankets that British soldiers passed on to the Indians in the eighteenth century. One could hardly imagine a more devastating, or coherent, version of American history than the one *Mason & Dixon* presents.

Although the novelists and theorists discussed so far have been influential in reorienting how literary critics conceive of history, they have not influenced historians. Is history conceived along postmodern narrative lines even possible except in works that have been designated fictions? One potential answer can be seen in novelist Nicholson Baker's work of history, *Human Smoke* (2008).[20] Baker is the author of such postmodern novels as *Vox* (1992) and *U and I* (1991), and understands how postmodern narrative has changed the way we think about how truth works in narrative. *Human Smoke* is not a novel pretending to be a history, though it effectively abolishes the line between the two disciplines. Baker's history is neither technical ("scientific") nor written, as best-selling histories often are, to portray their subjects as if they were the heroes of a nineteenth-century realist novel. Hutcheon speaks of the prevalence of irony in postmodern fiction and its function "to posit" a "critical distance and then undo it."[21] In *Human Smoke*, the usual markings of postmodern irony have been all but erased, since it works to eliminate the distance between the reader and the events of the period as they happened. Baker tries to enact what it would mean to achieve the familiar injunction of telling "what actually happened." Never is there any suggestion that World War II or the Holocaust could be avoided. In the process, Baker's history, more than any other novel so far discussed, portrays the risks – and even the appeal – of assuming history is something that can simply tell itself.

The book is mostly composed of accounts of primary documents and sources with no obvious commentary on the part of the recounter. The book contains very little narrative per se, and what narrative it possesses is as simple and straightforward as a book written for young adults. The reader is told in neutral language who said what to whom and when it was said. Mostly made up of primary documents, its form verges on collage – except a story is told. Letters, diaries, and news reports make up the majority of the book. As nearly as possible, Baker constructs a history composed only of the words and acts of the history's real-life players. The effect is to place the reader in history while it happens and then allow this living history to confront, challenge, and contradict what the reader "knows" to be true about the events being described. If postmodernist novelists generally collapse the line between past and present that historians insist allow us to define what history is, *Human Smoke* redraws that line by portraying the depth of the helplessness of those who tried to stop the war and the Holocaust. By adhering so closely to the primary documents of the time, Baker puts the reader inside history. Yet, the effect of each page depends on the reader's knowledge that the European Jews were not saved and Roosevelt and Churchill did little to stop Hitler. The war won. What actually happened, happened. There is no alternative history to be told since the dead died. Their only story is their dying. No Ishmael or Morrison or Silko or Reed or Kingston may rise from the ashes to make them live on in their tales except as a fantasy. History is final.

Like *Slaughterhouse-Five* or *Beloved*, Baker's narrative experiment in history disorients the reader from the lessons of conventional history precisely because there are no heroes except those whom history ran over. If the reader thinks that Churchill and Roosevelt were the "good guys" and "Hitler" the embodiment of evil that the "good guys" were obligated to destroy at any cost, then that reader may be flabbergasted by what he or she reads. *Human Smoke* challenges the premise that World War II constituted a moral victory for any of its combatants. When Churchill and Roosevelt decide to blockade Europe and in effect starve the entire continent, friends and enemies alike, into submission, they make it easier for Hitler to commit the Holocaust. As one reads document after document of Churchill and Roosevelt's refusing to do almost anything to help Jews escape, when they clearly might have, and one sees their awareness of how their food blockades were making it impossible for even well-intentioned leaders to feed their populations, it is possible to see Churchill and Roosevelt as collaborators in the execution of the death camps. Likewise, the documents Baker quotes reveal Churchill and Roosevelt to be as bloodthirsty for war as Hitler was. Baker's documents show us a Churchill who welcomes the war as an opportunity to advance his pet theory for an untried war tactic: the bombing of civilians. War can now openly be waged against everyone. No one's history makes them safe.

Baker chooses to arrest his history of World War II on the last day of 1941, or just after the United States entered the war. The hand of the historian – the fact that the historian must shape any story being told – is evident in the fact that Baker lets the dead speak to the living and does not bring them to imaginary life to do it. The heroes of the narrative are the slain, the maimed, and anyone naïve enough to think that what was happening did not have to happen and that a world committed to violence and the mass destruction of human life should be unimaginable. "History" silenced those voices, and Baker's radical narrative act is to let them speak again. Whatever looking back is done by the reader who wishes to project this or that interpretation on what happened – an interpretation that is almost certainly governed by previous versions of the story the reader has already assimilated. The only way to argue against any particular version is to choose different documents to rearrange in a different order, though the conclusion could be no different. The war happened, and the dead cannot be raised. *Human Smoke* is unlike any history previously discussed, since it removes from its narrative structure the sense of looking back from a secure narrative position.

Baker's book arguably reinforces the school of Pynchon, DeLillo, Coover, and so on, who treat history with linguistic skepticism, and it thus challenges the idea that history can ever be coherent or total except through the agreement of an agreed-upon fact. Kennedy was killed. Slavery happened. World War II was a real event, and many died. As we have seen, the "rememory" school of Morrison, Silko, and Kingston treats history as continuous and subject to reshaping through retelling. In collapsing the present into the past, they reimagine history as a form of healing rather than merely as a form of abuse. An alternative to these schools is "counterfactual" history. Like *Human Smoke* or historical fiction, counterfactual histories assume the reader knows what really happened. Instead of collapsing the present into the past, these works invite the reader to imagine a history radically different from the known one. Novels such as Philip K. Dick's *The Man in the High Castle* (1962) and Philip Roth's *The Plot Against America* (2004) reflect upon history by writing it as an alternative reality that oddly mirrors the one we know. Fundamental facts are changed, but the history we think we know remains discernible, if strangely slanted.

The Man in the High Castle is technically a science fiction novel, though it too is an attack on how history is conventionally understood.[22] Its basic premise is that the Allies lost World War II. Franklin Roosevelt was assassinated in 1933, and this touched off a series of events that led to the weakening of the United States so that England lacked the power to withstand Germany and Japan. The book opens in Japanese-occupied California. The conquered United States has been divided between Japan and Nazi Germany, so that Japan and Germany in effect become a version of the postwar United States and the Soviet Union, as each nation is paranoid about being destroyed by the other. Perhaps the most interesting feature of the book is the novel within the novel, *The Grasshopper Lies Heavy*, which postulates a world more or less like the one the 1962 American reader knows. In this version, though, England and the United States are enemies. The Nazis have banned *Grasshopper* from being read in the United States simply because it imagines a world different from the one the Nazis rule. At issue is the interpenetration of worlds – that point where fiction becomes history and history fiction. Which reality contains the others? It is a question the reader of *The Man in the High Castle* may ask too, since the descriptions of the Axis powers seem eerily similar to the description of the Allied powers in 1962.

Roth's *The Plot Against America* imagines what happened had Hitler and the United States been allies during World War II.[23] The protagonists are the Roth family and the narrator is the author, Philip, looking back on that remarkable period of history when American Jews were sent to detainment camps and feared their extermination. It is both a war book and a Jewish family memoir. The triggering episode occurs when the isolationist Charles Lindbergh defeats Franklin Roosevelt in the 1940 election. Lindbergh, who was sympathetic to Nazi Germany and whose disappointment over not being able to enlist on the Nazi side is quoted in Baker's book, forms a peaceful alliance with Germany. As in Dick's novel, Britain, without American support, seems unable to withstand Germany. Roth's family becomes involved in the war effort. An aunt seems to be a collaborator with the Lindbergh administration, while Roth's parents become resistance fighters. A cousin joins the Canadian military so he can fight against Hitler. Eventually, there is a revolt against Lindbergh. Roosevelt is installed as president, and then Roth sutures together his imagined history with the real one and the world we know today is as it has always been. "America's anti-Semitic fury" does not go "roaring through" America "and on up through our backstairs like the waters of a flood," and the Roth family, though tested, survives.[24] The boy Philip grows up to become the successful Jewish American novelist, Philip Roth, famous for writing postmodern books about Jewish American life.

Where Dick's novel defamiliarizes contemporary American history, Roth's novel arguably affirms its moral value. *The Plot Against America* frequently invokes Sinclair Lewis's *It Can't Happen Here* (1935), which also concerned fascists taking over America, and its title might well have been *It Didn't Happen Here*. Early in the novel, Roth's father invokes the Founding Fathers and the Declaration of Independence as guideposts that have kept this country from becoming what Nazi Germany was. Although many readers read it as a critique of the second Bush administration in the wake of 9/11 and the wars with Afghanistan and Iraq, the novel justifies the father's point of view. In the novel, a revolt is required to reaffirm the nation's original premises. Arguably, the novel, published the same year George W. Bush was re-elected, challenges Americans to revolt against their current leaders to restore their government, though Roth himself cautioned against such a reading.[25] The "America" of the title is something worth fighting for.

It may make more sense to read *The Plot Against America* in the same context as we read the works of Morrison, Kingston, or Silko. The book tells an ethnic story within an American story and presents America as a place where those within it struggle to tell "their" or "our" history as best they can. As a postmodern history, the novel frames America as a haven where Jews were not killed as they were in Europe. The main impulse of the genre, however, has not been to reinvent history, but to re-inhabit it so that its future iterations may become different from past ones.

In the "Author's Note" appended to the end of *Libra*, DeLillo notes that, because "this book makes no claim to literal truth" and "is only itself, apart and complete, readers may find refuge here."[26] DeLillo's formulation tacitly accepts the assumption that history's referents are presumed to be real and separate from their telling. His point seems to be that history is a space where lies and truth create each other, but art is a realm of deception that exists only to yield higher truth. For some postmodernist American novelists, history has been the higher truth they wish to discover. For others, history is just another story that the dead can no longer tell.

Further Reading

Berkhofer, Robert. *Beyond the Great Story*. Cambridge, MA: Harvard University Press, 1995.

Harlan, David. *The Degradation of History*. Chicago: University of Chicago Press, 1997.

Hobsbawm, Eric, J. *On History*. New York: Norton, 1997.

Hutcheon, Linda. *A Poetics of Postmodernism: History, Theory, Fiction*. New York: Routledge, 1988.

Hutcheon, Linda. *The Politics of Postmodernism*. New York: Routledge, 1989.

Jameson, Fredric. "Postmodernism, or The Cultural Logic of Late Capitalism," *New Left Review* 146 (1984): 53–92.

LaCapra, Dominick. *History in Transit: Experience, Identity, Critical Theory*. Ithaca, NY: Cornell University Press, 2004.

Parrish, Timothy. *From the Civil War to the Apocalypse: Postmodern History and American Fiction*. Amherst: University of Massachusetts Press, 2008.

Schama, Simon. *Dead Certainties: Unwarranted Speculations*. New York: Vintage Random, 1992.

White, Hayden. *Tropics of Discourse*. Baltimore: Johns Hopkins University Press, 1978.

NOTES

1 Quoted in Richard J. Evans, *In Defense of History* (New York: Norton, 1997), 14.
2 Quoted in Robert Berkhofer, *Beyond the Great Story* (Cambridge, MA: Harvard University Press, 1995), 48.
3 Quoted in Berkhofer, *Beyond the Great Story*, 28.
4 Quoted in Evans, *In Defense of History*, 19.
5 Linda Hutcheon, *A Poetics of Postmodernism: History, Theory, Fiction* (New York: Routledge, 1988), 16.
6 Quoted in Richard Rorty, *Objectivity, Relativism, and Truth: Philosophical Papers*, vol. 1 (Cambridge: Cambridge University Press, 1991), 212.
7 Don DeLillo, *Libra* (New York: Viking, 1988).
8 Hutcheon, *A Poetics of Postmodernism*, 4.
9 Linda Hutcheon, *The Politics of Postmodernism* (New York: Routledge, 1989), 13.
10 Ibid., 4.
11 Philip Roth, *Reading Myself and Others* (New York: Farrar, Straus and Giroux), 120.
12 Don DeLillo, *Underworld* (New York: Charles Scribner's Sons, 1997).
13 See Timothy L. Parrish, *From the Civil War to the Apocalypse: Postmodern History and American Fiction* (Amherst: University of Massachusetts Press, 2008), 209–231.
14 Kurt Vonnegut, *Slaughterhouse-Five* (New York: Dell, 1969).
15 Joan Didion, *Democracy* (New York: Simon, 1984), 16.
16 Gloria Anzaldúa, *Borderlands/La Frontera: The New Mestiza* (San Francisco: Aunt Lute Books, 1987).
17 Hutcheon, *A Poetics of Postmodernism*, 106.
18 Toni Morrison, *Beloved* (New York: Knopf, 1987), 226.
19 Thomas Pynchon, *Mason & Dixon* (New York: Picador, 1997).
20 Nicholson Baker, *Human Smoke: The Beginnings of World War II, the End of Civilization* (New York: Simon & Schuster, 2008).
21 Hutcheon, *A Poetics of Postmodernism*, 15.
22 Philip K. Dick, *The Man in the High Castle* (New York: Vintage, 1962).
23 Philip Roth, *The Plot Against America* (Boston: Houghton Mifflin, 2004).
24 Ibid., 343.
25 See "The Story Behind *The Plot Against America*," *New York Times Review of Books* 51, no. 18 (2004): 10–12.
26 DeLillo, *Libra*, n.p.

6

SALLY ROBINSON

Gender and Sexuality
Postmodern Constructions

In her influential book *The Politics of Postmodernism* (1988), Linda
Hutcheon argues that postmodern fiction decenters the "master narratives"
that cultures use to make sense of history and that individuals use to make
sense of identity.[1] These "master narratives" are perhaps nowhere more evident than in the realm of gender and sexuality, where what we know about
masculinity and femininity and what we understand as sexual norms and
sexual identities are framed and limited by familiar narratives. It is useful
to think of these narratives as prescribing certain "scripts" that individuals
follow and enact; as feminist theorist Judith Butler has taught us, gender
is a "doing" rather than a "being," and gender difference is produced and
perpetuated by our performance of it.[2] Performance, in this context, does
not mean conscious acting; it means that individuals, willingly or not, make
gender happen by reiterating widely recognizable social scripts, by insert-
ing ourselves into the narratives that make gender (and sexuality) culturally
intelligible. This way of thinking about identity signals a loss of faith in the
existence or even the possibility of a self-knowing, unified, autonomous self.
Even if we can imagine that we are unified selves who exist prior to or independent of ideology (such as gender ideology), we are, in fact, always subject
to the limits that discourses and institutions place on those selves and those
identities. Rethinking the subject or the self has opened up some possibilities
for challenging what have long been thought to be "masculine" notions of
identity that value boundedness, unity, singularity, and stability. The possibility that selves and identities might be more fluid, multiple, and open has been
embraced by feminist writers, particularly as these writers imagine ways to
unsettle oppressive long-standing ideas about gender and sexual identities.
In this chapter, I discuss how postmodern American fiction has challenged
ideas about gender and sexuality by interrogating the narratives that script
us as masculine or feminine.

Joanna Russ's *The Female Man* (1975) is one of several novels, including
Ursula K. Le Guin's *The Left Hand of Darkness* (1969) and Marge Piercy's

97

Woman on the Edge of Time (1976), that use the genre of science fiction to imagine alternatives to patriarchal narratives and their construction of gender and sexuality.[3] *The Female Man* suggests that, in order to upset ideas about gender, a writer must depart from linear narrative because that form has most often been used to sanctify man as the "hero" of the story and to position woman as either the obstacle he encounters on his quest or the prize awaiting him at the end of it. *The Female Man* disrupts nearly every conventional aspect of narrative, including coherent plot, identifiable chronology, and singular character. It is the story of Janet Evason, a time traveler from the all-female world of Whileaway who appears on Earth. Janet jumps from place to place, and era to era, seeking out an understanding of how gender works. She encounters three other Js along the way, including a Joanna who might or might not be the same as "me, the author." The narrative voice continually fluctuates, and it is not always clear which "I" is speaking. Because gender is a primary mode for grounding identity, Russ's strategy has the effect of making gender more fluid – so that, for example, one of the characters calls herself a "female man," and the Whileawayans have a completely nongendered way of organizing their society.

The Female Man literally and explicitly challenges the gender scripts men and women enact that keep male dominance in place. Joanna carries around a "little blue book" and a "little pink book," both composed of rules and observations about how men and women should relate to and treat each other.[4] The text reproduces conversations between men and women that reveal the dynamics of power required by a social system dependent on binary difference. Jeannine, the character with the most traditional views about gender, is constantly being hounded by friends and family who think her life will be over if she doesn't marry by the age of thirty. Laura Rose, whom the Js encounter when Janet (in her role as planetary emissary) lives with a "real" family, tells us that she's a "victim of penis envy," who, when five, said, "'I'm not a girl, I'm a genius.'"[5] Joanna, the "female man," explains that she had to turn into a woman before turning into a man, foregrounding how gender is performed through the iteration of certain scripts. Russ emphasizes how the use of language in speaking and writing not only *marks* the self as masculine or feminine, but actually *constructs* the self as masculine or feminine. "You will notice," Joanna says, "that even my diction is becoming feminine, thus revealing my true nature; I am not saying 'Damn' anymore, or 'Blast'; I am putting in lots of qualifiers like 'rather,' I am writing in these breathless little feminine tags … my thoughts seep out shapelessly like menstrual fluid, it is all very female and deep and full of essences, it is very primitive and full of 'and's,' it is called 'run-on sentences.'"[6] Later, "the author" reproduces excerpts from either real or imaginary reviews of her book, offering a hilarious but unfortunately realistic catalogue of dismissals and insults about "hysterical" feminine writing and "shrill" feminist critiques.[7]

The Female Man is a fantasy about female, and particularly lesbian, empowerment. Russ's novel embraces fragmentation and multiplicity, exploring the liberatory possibilities of an unbounded gender identity. Not all postmodern texts are quite this playful in their engagement with the master narratives governing our understanding of gender and sexuality, nor in their representation of decentered selves; other postmodern novels foreground the difficulties that come from being denied a coherent sense of identity. Gayl Jones's *Corregidora* (1975)[8] and Toni Morrison's *Beloved* (1987)[9], for example, focus on how master narratives about gender and sexuality are *literally* the master's narrative within the context of slavery. The protagonists of these novels, Ursa and Sethe, must battle against the racist and misogynist construction of them as mere objects to be used, while, at the same time, working to cobble together a self whose lack of clear boundaries is painful, rather than empowering. Nora Okja Keller's *Comfort Woman* (1997) presents a particularly complicated and compelling example of a novel that imagines the power of master narratives and their violent enforcement to constrain and even destroy identity, *and* possibilities for resisting those narratives, of finding ways to live with the incomplete, fluid, and boundaryless self.

Comfort Woman is the story of Soon Hyo, who is renamed Akiko by the soldiers who repeatedly rape her while she is confined in a "recreation camp" where kidnapped or sold Korean women are used to "service" the Japanese military during World War II. While Akiko is broken by this experience and will suffer a form of post-traumatic stress disorder for the remainder of her life, Keller takes pains to represent the enslaved women's resistance, not only to the master narratives that would deprive them of a sense of self and force them into shame, but also to the male figures who attempt to enforce those narratives. The women in the camps are conscious of the power of language to enforce ideologies of race and gender, and find "creative" ways to subvert that power. "Forbidden to speak any language at all," the women manage to communicate "through eye movements, body postures, tilts of the head"[10] – using the Japanese soldiers' dismissal of them to their advantage. Akiko tells us that "the Japanese say Koreans have an inherent gift for languages, proving that we are a natural colony, meant to be dominated. They delighted in their own ignorance, feeling they had nothing to fear or learn."[11] Akiko's account of the doctor who aborts her fetus in the camp foregrounds the ways in which the "comfort women" are made to embody constructions of gender and racial difference that serve the interests of the powerful: "As the doctor bound my legs and arms, gagged me, then reached for the stick he would use to hook and pull the baby, not quite a baby, into the world, he talked. He spoke of evolutionary differences between the races, biological quirks that made the women of one race so pure and the women of another so promiscuous. Base, really, almost like animals, he said."[12] The narrative into which this inhumane doctor inserts Akiko, "pinn[ing] her to the earth with his sticks and his words,"[13] paradoxically strips her of her gender even as it enforces her difference from other women. After escaping from the camp, Akiko finds herself among American missionaries who, while not constructing her merely as an object, nevertheless subject her to their own constructions of her gender and sexuality. Keller represents the missionary Richard as complicit in the construction of Akiko as an object of sexual interest who feeds his masculinist and orientalist fantasies about the "mysterious" and victimized Asian woman. While Akiko allows herself to be "saved" by Richard, who marries her and brings her to the United States, the novel makes it clear that she neither loves him nor accepts his construction of her.

Akiko's refusal to be assimilated to her husband's Christian and American worldview is coupled with her refusal to be defined by heteronormative constructions of female sexuality. Several scenes of sexual pleasure serve as a counterpoint to the scenes of rape. In a long, detailed description, Keller narrates a sexual encounter between Akiko and Induk, flesh and blood woman and immaterial spirit, suggesting that the trauma she has suffered has also enabled her to experience a pleasure in blurring the boundaries of the self: "I open myself to her and move in rhythm to the tug of her lips and fingers and the heat of her between my thighs. The steady buzzing that began at my fingertips shoots through my body, concentrates at the pulse point between my legs, then without warning explodes through the top of my head. I see only the blackness of my pleasure. My body sings in silence until emptied, and there is only her left. Induk."[14] Waking up one night and becoming excited by Akiko's unwonted sexual behavior, and not knowing that she is "with" Induk, Richard "thrusts" into her and attempts to take control over her body and her pleasure. Akiko tolerates Richard's interference because she has to, but when he accuses her of "self-fornication," she laughs at his ignorance. Attempting to place her as both a "child" in need of his rescue and a "succubus" who "exchanged natural relations for unnatural ones,"[15] Richard is terrified of Akiko in this moment because her behavior is not intelligible within the narrative he has constructed about her and about female sexuality.

Both *Comfort Woman* and *The Female Man* are interested in how master narratives about gender frame and even determine women's experiences and identities, and they suggest alternative frameworks that might disrupt the simplistic and binary construction of masculine *versus* feminine, and hetero-sexual *versus* lesbian. In Russ's novel, this exploration takes a comic form with the juxtaposition of the all-female Whileaway and Manland, and the representation of lesbian desire and sexuality as a way out of male dom-inance. Yet, Russ also complicates these binaries by challenging any and all efforts to understand gender and sexual identity as *essential*; the por-trayal of the women in the novel, particularly Janet and Jael, gestures toward something like a third gender. In *Comfort Woman*, Keller imagines a way out of the binary structures that justify the wartime "recreation" camps by drawing upon another epistemology entirely. This she finds in the mostly female tradition of shamanism and, also, and perhaps disturbingly, in what might be called Akiko's "madness." Keller's novel, like Russ's, is metafic-tional, foregrounding how meaning is constructed through the shaping of narrative, whether those narratives are "real" historical narratives or fic-tional, imaginative narratives. One of the hallmarks of postmodern fiction is its blurring of the boundaries between the historical and the fictional in what Hutcheon terms "historiographic metafiction." Margaret Atwood's *Alias Grace* (1996)[16] exemplifies this genre and tells the story of an actual historical figure, Grace Marks, who, in Atwood's retelling, becomes an enig-matic figure whom various male "experts" – doctors, lawyers, historians – try to interpret. Grace evades capture by the various narratives that attempt to explain her, and Atwood suggests that it is not possible to ever really "know" the *real* Grace Marks. E. L. Doctorow's *The Book of Daniel* (1971), also a textbook example of historiographic metafiction, is a fictionalized version of the Rosenberg case that draws on real and fictionalized historical doc-uments. Unlike the female novelists I've discussed thus far, Doctorow does not have a feminist agenda and is not particularly interested in challenging constructions of femininity or ameliorating female oppression. What he is interested in is how individuals and institutions *use* gender and sexuality to represent relations of power; Doctorow uses gender metaphorically and symbolically to expose the violence behind both public and private modes of domination. In the process, the novel indicts, but does not dismantle, an ideology of masculinity based on the arrogation of power.

The Book of Daniel foregrounds the ways in which gender and sexual-ity are implicated in the exercise of power by insisting that the story of the Isaacsons is the story of the state "fucking" Paul and Rochelle and, by exten-sion, their children, Susan and Daniel. Doctorow brings this point home by the persistent use of sexual metaphors to describe what happens to the Isaac-sons – not only by representing them as "screwed" by the state, but also in the pervasive connections the narrative makes between electricity/electrocution and sexual pleasure. Countless references to "currents," "jolts," and "connections" coalesce into the image of the Isaacsons "offering up their genitals" to the state.[17] While in the hospital, where she is confined after a failed suicide attempt, Susan tells Daniel, "They're still fucking us"[18] – a statement that Daniel finds slightly cryptic, but one that he repeats several pages later when, after mentioning the family history for the first time, he taunts the reader with a challenge: "This is the story of a fucking, right?"[19] Daniel is an aggressive storyteller who assaults the reader's sensibilities and uses the language of sexual domination to do it. The novel uses postmodern narrative techniques – fragmentation, shifting points of view, paratexts, rapid transitions, jarring juxtapositions – to alienate the reader and interrupt identification with Daniel, but also to express his uncertainty about the historical (or personal) truth about what happened to his parents. What makes the novel a powerful statement about the use and abuse of gendered and sexualized forms of power is that Doctorow often couples these "postmodern" moments with representations of Daniel's troubling objectification of, and his sadistic behavior toward, his wife Phyllis. This has the odd effect of forcing an acknowledgement that postmodern, metafictional techniques might challenge epistemological certainty, but they do not necessarily ensure a progressive politics.

Daniel's fascination with the sexual violence of the state permeates his narrative, and his treatment of Phyllis makes him complicit in the sexual relations of power revealed by the persecution of the Isaacsons. Like the state, Daniel embodies a masculinity founded on abuse of power and fear of feminization. Daniel's explanation of the anti-communist hysteria that greeted the labor movement at the end of World War I brings these fears to the foreground: "It was feared that as in Russia, they were about to take over the country and shove large cocks into everyone's mother."[20] As if he realizes the offense that he might cause with such a statement, Daniel takes it back by saying, "Strike that."[21] He is fascinated by the sexual violence of the state – particularly as that violence is directed against his mother. He calls Rochelle "a sexy woman" and narrates a primal scene; he imagines Paul to be a feminized man and Rochelle to be a sexual dynamo. When he narrates the execution – only after taunting the reader with "I suppose you think I can't do the execution"[22] – he notes that Rochelle required two "doses" of electrical current before her body "spasmed" in death. It is impossible to read this account of the execution without remembering an early scene in the novel where Daniel describes a faded advertisement posted in his father's radio repair shop that features a "slim, green woman for whom the act of turning on an orange radio is enormous pleasure. Maybe it was a defective radio and gave her a jolt."[23] The fact of the electrocution has clearly shaped

Daniel's perceptions and might function to inoculate him against our condemnation of his sexual obsessions or his unrepentant masculinity, but it can also work in the opposite way by highlighting the justificatory strategies of a man who himself "gets a charge" out of the circulation of power.

There is no question that Doctorow's primary interest is in the male Daniel's efforts to free himself from his historical legacy of violence and domination by an unfeeling state; the novel may invite us to judge Daniel's masculine domination of his wife as a product of that legacy, but it does not in any way displace that masculinity or suggest any blurring of the boundaries between masculinity and femininity. Power in *The Book of Daniel* is masculine, and we can lament but not change that. Like other postmodern male novelists – Thomas Pynchon, Charles Johnson, Ishmael Reed, and Bret Easton Ellis come to mind – Doctorow uses female characters primarily as reflections of male problems. These male authors do not focus on gender inequity and sexual persecution; they are more interested in how the postmodern challenges to epistemology (how we know what we know) and to liberal individualism (the self's freedom from social determination) have affected masculinity and male identity. Tim O'Brien's *The Things They Carried* (1990), a novel comprising twenty-two connected but free-standing stories about the American experience in Vietnam, goes beyond this theoretical conundrum to explore how the uncertainties of postmodern existence disrupt or unsettle traditional conceptions of masculinity.

The Things They Carried is a metanarrative; that is, like *The Book of Daniel*, it foregrounds the processes of fiction-making in order to comment on how knowledge and experience (of the self and of history) are constrained by the narratives we use to make sense of our worlds. O'Brien employs a number of narrative voices in the novel, all of which have a complicated relationship to the "truth" of the Vietnam experience and its effects on masculinity. Gender is never very far below the surface in this text; no matter what the circumstances, meaning is made through the language of gender. For example, in the story about a fictionalized "Tim O'Brien" confronting the decision of whether or not to go to war, what is at issue is the question of "courage" and how men's actions can mark them as either "heroes" or "pussies." He imagines his friends and family later telling stories about "how the damned sissy had taken off for Canada" and imagining him as a "treasonous pussy."[24] Masculinity means going to war; failure to do so feminizes a man, deprives him of his right to masculinity. The story appears to challenge this construction of masculinity through the narrator's conviction that the real act of courage would be resisting the draft, and the real act of cowardice acquiescing to it. However, he ends up making his decision based on his fear of embarrassment, not out of sincere conviction, and that embarrassment has everything to do with the ideology of gender that frames his decision. He decides to go to war because he's not brave enough to resist dominant constructions of masculinity. He imagines his actions judged, his manhood found wanting, and he, thus, abandons his desire to be "brave" and flee to Canada: "It was as if there were an audience to my life, that swirl of faces along the river, and in my head I could hear people screaming at me. Traitor! They yelled! Turncoat! Pussy! I felt myself blush. I couldn't tolerate it. I couldn't endure the mockery, or the disgrace, or the patriotic ridicule."[25]

In this story, O'Brien challenges, but does not displace, the gendered logic used to justify war, and in the stories that follow, he foregrounds, often without commentary, the centrality of a gendered discourse to the "grunts'" experience of war. There is a great deal of masculine posturing that goes on in these stories, and women and the feminine are often used to shore up the men's sense of masculinity. When the sister of a killed soldier fails to appreciate Rat Kiley's tribute to her brother's "stainless steel balls" in "How to Tell a True War Story," he calls her a "dumb cooze."[26] Later in the same story, "Tim O'Brien" talks about what happens when he gives a reading of his war stories, and someone, "always a woman," tells him that he should quit reliving his war experiences and move on. He tells us, "I won't say it but I'll think it. I'll picture Rat Kiley's face, his grief, and I'll think, *You dumb cooze.* Because she wasn't listening. It *wasn't* a war story. It was a *love* story."[27] Here, O'Brien expresses one of the most repeated narratives about gender and war: women are necessarily outside the masculine bond that cements the "brotherhood" of war experience. While "O'Brien" feels embarrassed enough not to call this woman a "dumb cooze" to her face, he nevertheless buys into the logic that differentiates those who fight (men) from those who do not (women or "pussies"). This rather complicated negotiation of the ideologies of gender characterizes this entire volume and makes its engagement with master narratives a good example of the postmodern.

The story called "Sweetheart of the Song Tra Bong" goes some distance in challenging the idea that women either facilitate or get in the way of the masculine bond during wartime, but they cannot be included within it. This story is about Mary Anne Bell, "import[ed]" into Vietnam by her boyfriend Mark Fossie as "personal poontang."[28] Rat Kiley tells the story of how this ordinary girl in white culottes and a pink sweater transforms into one of the "Greenies" – a unit of Green Berets that practices mysterious rituals and goes on secret ambushes. The story is framed as possibly true, possibly apocryphal, and the open-endedness suggests that it might be serving a narrative or ideological function, rather than describing an actual series of events. What is most interesting about this story is the way it works *both* to reinforce the exclusion of women from the masculine arena of war *and* to

suggest that the "mix of unnamed terror and unnamed pleasure" that constitutes the experience of the war in Vietnam goes beyond gender. On the one
hand, Rat identifies Mary Anne as the exception that proves the rule, the
anomalous case. "Mary Anne made you think about those girls back home,
how clear and innocent they all are, how they'll never understand any of
this, not in a billion years."[29] Yet, at the same time, Rat wants to entertain
the possibility that the difference between men and women, between masculinity and femininity, is merely conventional; in the face of his buddies'
disbelief, he says, "What's so impossible? She was a girl, that's all. I mean,
if it was a guy, everybody'd say, Hey, no big deal, he got caught up in the
Nam shit, he got seduced by the Greenies. See what I mean? You got these
blinders on about women. How gentle and peaceful they are."[30]

The Things They Carried represents the Vietnam War experience as both
a wound to traditional ideas about masculinity and a potential path toward
a more enlightened, less rigid understanding of gender difference. Throughout the stories, the narrative voice resists judging the men for their feelings
and their actions, staying far away from such gender rules as "men don't
cry." This is not to say that the men who people these stories are not stereo-
typically masculine, because they sometimes are: they objectify women, they
revel in violence, they dominate others. But O'Brien's narrative style and the
fragmented form the novel takes chip away at dominant narratives about
masculinity and war. Jessica Hagedorn's *Dogeaters* (1990) also focuses on
the relationship between war and masculinity, but foregrounds the ways in
which war allows men an arena in which to exercise, with impunity, the
violence that often defines masculine identity. The novel takes place in the
Philippines and tells the story of two large families whose lives are affected
by the long Marcos dictatorship. It also tells the stories of a number of satel-
lite characters – drug addicts, gay prostitutes, movie stars, corrupt generals,
beauty queens, painters, and guerillas. The novel is a collage of different
stories, all united by a sustained interrogation of master narratives about
gender and sexuality. Like *The Book of Daniel*, *Dogeaters* blurs the boundaries between history and fiction, juxtaposing historical with fictional characters, using both real and faked "historical" documents, and moving swiftly
and often chaotically between different years, different milieus, and different
discourses.

Dogeaters represents the Philippines as a brutally patriarchal culture
that poses an aggressive and violent masculinity against a sentimental and
masochistic femininity. The former is embodied in fantasies about rape and
torture, pornographic films, and the actual rape of a character who is captured by the military. The latter is represented by self-sacrificing women and
by the radio serial *Love Letters*, a serial "heavy with pure love, blood debts,

luscious revenge, the wisdom of mothers, and the enduring sorrow of Our Blessed Virgin Barbara Villanueva" – a Tagalog actress.[31] Leonor Ledesma, married to the general who is also involved with the actress Lolita Luna, embraces the ideology of feminine sacrifice and requests that her husband bring her an army cot to replace her luxurious bed in order to express her "devotion to an austere, forbidding God and her earnest struggles to earn sainthood through denial."[32] Lolita suffers the General's attentions in order to feed her hunger for drugs and money; in a chapter called "Surrender," we see Lolita "on her knees. She is trembling, trying hard not to scream. It is always more exciting when she restrains herself."[33] Hagedorn draws an extended analogy between the Philippines, colonized and recolonized by different foreign powers, and a suffering femininity. This is perhaps represented most forcefully in the novel's characterization of Baby Alacrán, daughter of the "King of Coconuts," Manila's leading businessman. Baby's body, afflicted with a "nonspecific tropical fungus," symbolizes the nation, whose geography is described in similar terms. "Think of your daughter's body as a landscape," the doctor tells her father, "a tropical jungle whose moistness breeds this fungus."[34]

Throughout the novel, we see how ideologies of gender get materialized through the characters' enactment of scripts of masculinity and femininity. Popular culture teaches both privileged and impoverished Filipinos how to act and what to desire. Rio Gonzaga refers to her mother as "My Mother, Rita Hayworth"; Trinidad Gamboa dreams Hollywood dreams of riches and romance; Romeo Rosales models himself after both Elvis Presley and Mabuhay Studios stars; and Joey Sands imagines himself as a disco-era celebrity known as "Mister Heartbreak." But Joey and Rio, the emotional centers of the novel, ultimately reject the scripts that enforce the difference between femininity and masculinity and serve to police sexual identity. Rio resists the normalizing force of "femininity," and Joey Sands, a self-involved gay prostitute and drug user, ends up joining the guerillas fighting against the military dictatorship.

Joey is savvy and street-smart, understanding that men are attracted to him because he is "Joey Taboo: my head of tight, kinky curls, my pretty hazel eyes, my sleek brown skin."[35] Unlike many of his compatriots, Joey resists seduction by Hollywood narratives. Expected to have sex with the famous but unappealing German film director Rainer (Fassbinder) during Manila's First International Film Festival, Joey fantasizes writing his own script:

> That's when I imagine I'm in my movie. I'm the strong young animal – I'm the panther. Or else I'm the statue of a magnificent young god in a beautiful

garden. The old man with elephant skin drools. Maybe he's God the Father, lost in paradise. He can't get over how perfect I am; he can't get over the perfection of his own creation. He falls in love with me. They always do. I'll admit, I can get off with some old man that way. I need my own movies, with their flexible endings.[36]

When, by a strange turn of events, Joey witnesses and is framed for the assassination of Senator Avila, his friend Boy Boy surprises Joey by his political consciousness and his connections with the rebel forces. He arranges for Joey to escape into the mountains, where he finds himself partnered up with Daisy Avila, who has rejected her life as a beauty pageant queen to join forces (politically and romantically) with Santos Tirador. Daisy has been gang-raped in a brutally explicit scene that Hagedorn frames with the plot and dialogue of a *Love Letters* episode – suggesting that scripts naturalizing aggressive masculinity and submissive femininity get literally played out in violence and the abuse of power. The unlikely pairing of the privileged daughter of one of Manila's leading politicians and the drug-addicted son of a prostitute is one example of how the novel challenges conventional narratives and reader expectations. It is similar to what happens in Manuel Puig's *Kiss of the Spider Woman* (1976),[37] where a gay transvestite partners up with, and performs a subversive act for, a macho political prisoner. The last we hear from Joey is that he has bonded deeply with Daisy and has made her cause his own: "She cries while Joey describes his mother, what he remembers of her. She reproaches herself, and apologizes for being sentimental. She will not cry when she describes how her lover was captured while she was in detention, or how her unnamed baby girl was born premature and dead. They are together all the time. She teaches him to use a gun."[38]

In comparison to Joey, Rio lives a completely sheltered life, in which politics, class inequities, and military abuse of power form only a shadowy backdrop. A figure whose story echoes Hagedorn's own, Rio eventually leaves the Philippines to go to the United States. Rio is a gender rebel who resists the force of normative femininity that leads to not only submission in marriage, but also, as Daisy's story makes clear, submission to violence. She identifies with the wrong characters in the American movies she watches with her cousin Pucha and finds the love stories "corny"; she balks at wearing a "ridiculous outfit with an itchy petticoat" to her birthday party.[39] She is attracted to Audrey Hepburn and tells us toward the end of the novel, "I have started menstruating. To celebrate, I cut off all my hair."[40] Rio's choice to "look like a boy" is a deliberate refusal of the sentimental narrative that requires girls to welcome "becoming a woman." Like Joey, Rio wants to make her own movies. Her story ends with a rejection of the religious, national, and familial expectations of femininity: "I am anxious and restless, at home only in airports. I travel whenever I can. My belief in God remains tentative. I have long ago stopped going to church. I never marry."[41]

Like Joey, Rio is a hybrid, a product of a complex social, cultural, and political situation: Hagedorn's representation of Manila stresses the often chaotic, contradictory, and unstable nature of a country formed by a history of imperialism, corruption, and class stratification. This representation is enhanced by the fragmented structure of the text, its mixing of fiction and history, and its use of a wide variety of discourses – real and imagined newspaper articles, excerpts from imperialist documents, and interviews with the president's wife. This postmodern technique foregrounds how narratives of all kinds structure reality and history. When an author juxtaposes seemingly contradictory pieces of texts and tracks ideologies of gender through a wide variety of narratives, the result is a decentering of one truth, one history, one narrative. Postmodern fiction *disrupts*, a process that can feel, to the reader, like a challenge or even an assault. Nowhere is this the case more than in Katherine Dunn's *Geek Love* (1983), a novel that shocks and surprises as it subverts conventional narrative plot, character, structure, and reader expectations. In the process, it deconstructs normative ideas about gender and sexuality, both antifeminist and feminist.

Geek Love traces the family history of the Binewskis, who own the Fabulon, a traveling carnival. Lampooning the rhetoric of reproductive engineering and of capitalist entrepreneurship, Dunn has Lil and Al, using "Yankee" self-determination and independence to "breed his own freak show,"[42] deliberately produce a family composed of children who will be successful as spectacles: Olympia, an albino, hunch-backed dwarf (who is the narrator and, to her chagrin, the least spectacular of the bunch); Electra and Iphigenia, a pair of conjoined twins who capitalize on their beauty and sexual allure; Chick, the seemingly normal last child, whose powers are mental, not physical; and Arturo, the older brother, a hybrid of human and amphibian, who starts a cult to reverse the opposition between "norm" and "freak," drawing thousands of followers who opt for surgeries that will render them "special." Add to this mix a woman outside the family, Miss Mary Lick, who, like Arty, works to turn "norms" into "freaks" – in her case, by paying beautiful and sexually attractive women to submit to disfiguring surgeries that render them less than fully feminine and, thus, "liberated" to pursue careers without fear of objectification by men. Through these various stories, the novel deconstructs narratives about women, sexuality, objectification, and (dis)empowerment.

Geek Love meditates on the classic feminist insight that women are constructed as the objects of the male gaze, but suggests that relations of power between the subjects and objects of the gaze are not always predictable or predictably gendered. Not only do the "freaks" in the Fabulon revel in producing themselves as "objects to be looked at," but also, in her post-Fabulon life, Olympia Binewski herself experiences triumph when she is placed on display on the stage at the Glass House – a strip club that specializes in female "freaks." Bald, hunchbacked, red-eyed, and with her "arrow tits flapping toward [her] knees," Oly also challenges the feminist insistence on the precedence of nurture over nature, the constructed over the essential, when she confesses, "How proud I am, dancing in the air full of eyes rubbing at me uncovered, unable to look away because of what I am. Those poor hop-toads behind me are silent. I've conquered them. They thought to use and shame me but I win out by nature, because a true freak cannot be made. A true freak must be born."[43] Dunn's riff on these feminist orthodoxies is part of the novel's reimagination of conventional narratives about gender, power, and subjectivity. This becomes clearest with the introduction of Miss Lick and her "projects."

Like Arty, whose "norm" followers allow themselves to be mutilated in order to transcend the body, Miss Lick aims to liberate women from essentialized femininity by de-eroticizing the female body and, thus, freeing women from their position as objects "to be looked at." Miss Lick's feminist project is eventually revealed to be just another form of self-replication; like Arty, she wants to turn her "subjects" into versions of herself, asexual, homely, and completely removed from norms of femininity. Because of her experience with Arty, Oly recognizes Miss Lick's project for what it is and exposes Lick's voyeuristic investment in these women: she videotapes and compulsively watches the "transformations." Dunn uses Miss Lick to comment on bodily practices of "self-improvement," like plastic surgery and other technological interventions; that Miss Lick's motivations are feminist does not essentially differentiate her actions from the actions of the others who set about "constructing" the body and the self – the Binewskis, who engineer pregnancies and births in order to produce the "perfect" family, or Arty, who convinces his followers that the route to peace is through transcending the body, literally, through amputation. All of these practices have the effect of actually further *reducing* the subject to the body, as the body comes to completely define the self. This is the paradox of what Susan Bordo refers to as "postmodern plasticity": the belief that technologies of the body "free" us from nature and from history, even as those technologies return us to the body again and again.[44]

Dunn's challenge to certain feminist narratives raises the following question: Do feminism and postmodernism work together? Must a fictional interrogation of the master narratives of gender and sexuality have a feminist aim or a feminist effect? Linda Hutcheon ends her book on *The Politics of Postmodernism* with a consideration of "Postmodernism and Feminisms," concluding that, while postmodern "representational strategies have offered feminist artists an effective way of working within yet challenging dominant patriarchal discourses," much postmodern fiction lacks the political agenda that drives feminist writing.[45] But Hutcheon, it seems to me, is setting up a false dichotomy because, as I've suggested here, any fictional interrogation of how dominant narratives about gender, sexuality, and identity force us to perform according to often-oppressive social scripts is *already* pursuing a political agenda. It makes sense that women writers are more invested in dismantling fictions of gender and sexuality than male writers; but American postmodern fiction, on the whole, succeeds in drawing critical attention to how narratives about gender and sexuality frame and limit the possibilities of identity, knowledge, and action – and some texts go even further in imagining alternative narratives and envisioning different gendered and sexual selves.

Further Reading

Alcoff, Linda. "Cultural Feminism vs. Post-Structuralism: The Identity Crisis in Feminist Theory." *Signs* 13, no. 3 (Spring): 405–436.
Butler, Judith. *Gender Trouble: Feminism and the Subversion of Identity*. New York and London: Routledge, 1990.
Butler, Judith, and Joan W. Scott, eds. *Feminists Theorize the Political*. New York and London: Routledge, 1992.
Hutcheon, Linda. *The Politics of Postmodernism*. New York and London: Routledge, 1988.
Modleski, Tania. *Feminism Without Women: Culture and Criticism in a "Postfeminist" Age*. New York and London: Routledge, 1991.
Nicholson, Linda, ed. *Feminism/Postmodernism*. New York and London: Routledge, 1989.
Waugh, Patricia. *Feminine Fictions: Revisiting the Postmodern*. New York and London: Routledge, 1989.

NOTES

1 Linda Hutcheon, *The Politics of Postmodernism* (New York and London: Routledge, 1988).
2 Judith Butler, *Gender Trouble* (New York and London: Routledge, 1990).
3 Joanna Russ, *The Female Man* (Boston: Beacon Press, 1975); and Ursula K. Le Guin, *The Left Hand of Darkness* (New York: Ace Books, 1969).
4 Russ, *The Female Man*, 47.
5 Ibid., 65.
6 Ibid., 137.
7 Ibid., 140–141.

8 Gayl Jones, *Corregidora* (Boston: Beacon Press, 1975).
9 Toni Morrison, *Beloved* (New York: Vintage, 1987).
10 Nora Okja Keller, *Comfort Woman* (New York: Penguin, 1998), 16.
11 Ibid., 16.
12 Ibid., 22.
13 Ibid., 22.
14 Ibid., 145.
15 Ibid., 146.
16 Margaret Atwood, *Alias Grace* (New York: Doubleday, 1996).
17 E. L. Doctorow, *The Book of Daniel* (New York: Random House, 1971, reprint 2007), 32.
18 Ibid., 9.
19 Ibid., 23.
20 Ibid., 24.
21 Ibid., 24.
22 Ibid., 295.
23 Ibid., 38.
24 Tim O'Brien, *The Things They Carried* (New York and London: Penguin Books, 1990), 48–49.
25 Ibid., 62–63.
26 Ibid., 75–76.
27 Ibid., 90.
28 Ibid., 102.
29 Ibid., 123.
30 Ibid., 117.
31 Jessica Hagedorn, *Dogeaters* (New York and London: Penguin Books, 1990), 12.
32 Ibid., 67.
33 Ibid., 95.
34 Ibid., 28–29.
35 Ibid., 72–73.
36 Ibid., 132.
37 Manuel Puig, *Kiss of the Spider Woman*, trans. Thomas Colchie (New York: Vintage, 1976).
38 Ibid., 233.
39 Ibid., 4, 83.
40 Ibid., 236.
41 Ibid., 247.
42 Katherine Dunn, *Geek Love* (New York: Warner Books, 1983), 7.
43 Ibid., 20.
44 Susan Bordo, "Material Girl: The Effacements of Postmodern Culture," in *The Female Body: Figures, Styles, Speculations*, ed. Lawrence Goldstein (Ann Arbor: University of Michigan Press, 1991), 106–130.
45 Hutcheon, *The Politics of Postmodernism*, 167–168.

7

DEAN FRANCO

Pluralism and Postmodernism

The Histories and Geographies of Ethnic American Literature

Introduction

Understanding the phrase "postmodern ethnic American literature" must begin by acknowledging that the subject is composed of critical terms of art and not of fixed categories. Postmodernism is an aesthetic, philosophical, and political engagement with undecidability, and likewise undecided are the consequences of the postmodern: alienating and destabilizing *and* pluralizing and proliferating multiple worlds. Harder to address are the meaning and the content of the category "ethnic American literature." "Ethnic" appears to have lost some of its critical salience in recent years, though it remains a constant catch-all for people and cultures that do not slot into a black–white binary. If "ethnic" is an easy catch-all and go-to, its fungibility – as opposed to the rigidity of reading for or according to race – is what allows for writers and critics to occupy multiple American subject positions, a maneuver that may be the starting point for critically examining the controlling power of normative regimes of identity in the United States. "Normative" refers to frames of knowledge, claims of truth, or practices of socialization that seek to establish and police the boundaries of normalcy and typicality, correct and incorrect. Postmodern ethnic American literature necessarily challenges and often renders moot that stable normality and typicality.

The etymology of "ethnic" signals artistic agendas and social itineraries that open up onto its companion term "American." In the early twentieth century, the term hued close to its Greek etymology, which resonates with its near homophone, the English "heathen." After World War II, "ethnic" referred to non-Protestant Americans, or white people from non-Anglophone countries. Only in the late 1960s did Americans previously regarded as fundamentally racially different – Mexican Americans, Asian Americans, and Native Americans – enter into the canon of ethnicity. The inclusion of Jews and African Americans under the banner of "ethnic" provokes some categorical trouble, insofar as Jews are largely regarded by

Americans as white, with a culture so thoroughly assimilated into the US mainstream as to be nearly unnoticeable. African Americans present quite the opposite problem for the category, partly because of intractable racism and cultural fetishism over blackness, and partly because "ethnicity" has always subtly signaled "different, but not 'black' different." Simply put, "ethnic" is a protean category, and no one's favorite designation. Rare as it is to find authors claiming to write literature about any given ethnicity, it is hard to imagine any author declaring that they write "ethnic American literature."[1]

In the end, "ethnic American literature" persists because it describes a common project: writers from a variety of social groups advancing their stories into the public sphere. Especially since the late 1960s, when a generation of Chicanos, African Americans, and Native Americans entered universities and helped found the first Ethnic Studies programs, "ethnic American literature" has designated an insurgent body of work that radically challenges social norms and stories of national formation. Often this challenge deconstructs binary identity positions (white and black, say), and demonstrates the way each position requires its opposite in order to have positive meaning. For instance, whiteness is an identity in part based on its negation of blackness – that is, whiteness contains the idea of blackness, a fact that necessarily renders the construct of whiteness incoherent to itself. We might think of Ralph Ellison's metaphor of white paint in his novel *Invisible Man* (1952), where a drop of black paint is added to cans of white paint in order for the whiteness to be visible. Ellison's sly metaphor ("If it's Optic White, It's the right white") doesn't undo the controlling power of whiteness, but it exposes the incoherence within the concept.[2]

Postmodernism and the Plurality of Identities

In his pathbreaking work of postcolonial criticism *The Location of Culture* (1991), Homi Bhabha argues that the postcolonial *is* the postmodern, and with a little critical imagination we can appropriate Bhabha's construct for post–Civil Rights era, ethnic American literature.[3] The "post" modifies but does not end either the legacies of colonialism or civil rights injustice. Instead, it indicates imaginative attempts by artists, writers, and intellectuals to establish a point of view and even a consciousness free from the perspectives cultivated under and imposed by colonial or racist subjugation. Especially after the Civil Rights movements of the 1960s and the bids for cultural recognition by quasi-nationalist groups representing African Americans, Native Americans, Asian Americans, and Chicanas/os in the 1970s and 1980s, ethnic American writers often understood their work as writing against the grain of American history, recalibrating aesthetics, as with the fiction of Sandra Cisneros or Percival Everett, for example, or turning the conventions of form against the presumption of the novel as the preeminent mode for narrating the nation, as in Toni Morrison's *Song of Solomon* (1977) and Michael Chabon's *The Yiddish Policemen's Union* (2007).[4] As Bhabha explains, the plurality of cultures, histories, and places – real or counterfactual – in the space of the nation questions the coherence of nationalism. On the one hand, with normative attempts at narrating the nation, "the political unity of the nation consists in a continual displacement of the anxiety of its irredeemably plural modern space – representing the nation's modern territoriality is turned into the archaic, atavistic temporality of Traditionalism."[5] Atavism is the present-time draw on the ancient past, the impulse of self-serving histories that justify the present as the natural destiny of the past. On the other hand, atavism masks an anxiety that comes back as haunting, as in Morrison's and Chabon's novels, which comprise "counter-narratives of the nation [that] continually evoke and erase its totalizing boundaries – both actual and conceptual – [and] disturb those ideological maneuvers through which 'imagined communities' are given essentialist identities."[6] "Imagined communities" is Benedict Anderson's phrase indicating how nations depend on widespread, everyday cultural practices – national flags and newspapers, broad time zones and weather forecasts, commonly sung songs, and widely viewed films and TV programs – to shore up and lend an "essence" to what would otherwise be a diverse population and a heterogeneous space.[7] The historical dimension of this sort of literature is clear enough, especially as African American and Native American writers assert their presence in or priority to American history, and Bhabha shows how national geographies erase an internal plurality of spaces. Writers of immigrant backgrounds or who are border-dwellers interrogate the spatial coherence of "America" and may literally turn the map of the United States inside out, prioritizing liminal spaces or even other nations, and highlighting the border as a conduit for flows of people and exchanges of cultures.

Within this context, we consider Michael Chabon's *The Yiddish Policemen's Union*, a counterfactual novel about Jewish refugees from Nazi Germany resettled in Sitka, Alaska. The novel dislodges the United States as a site of easy assimilation and disorients its frontier from the American mythos of Manifest Destiny. In Sitka, Jews and indigenous Alaskans compete for land and resources, jockeying for political power in advance of "reversion," the apocalyptic termination of the charter permitting Jewish settlement. The novel is written in *noir* style, with wise-cracking cops speaking translated Yiddish (including a treasury of Yiddish neologisms), so that dark realism is wedded to the fantastical counterfactual.

The Yiddish Policemen's Union, like other novels mentioned here, is a searching study of identities: an ethnic group is settled in the United States but is not remotely at home; they are haunted by a traumatic past (the Shoah, the Cultural Revolution, and Reconstruction-era white supremacy, respectively) that seems askew from or underrepresented in real life; and they yearn for a fulfilling form of belonging. In Chabon's novel, that belonging correlates with a messianic fantasy in the absence of any realistic possibility of national belonging. The Jews of Chabon's novel have created a baroque tapestry of culture, woven with wry Yiddish, subtle politics, and internecine sectarian competition; on the other hand, the culture's anticipated end resonates as an uncanny replay of Jewish trauma. Readers of *The Yiddish Policemen's Union* can't help but recognize and even admire this contingent Jewish culture, which stands as the "otherwise" to the real-life catastrophe perpetrated on Europe's Jews. Notably for this essay, the novel's innovations on identity can only occur as revisions of history and geography. Though the counterfactual is an extreme revision, all the literature discussed in this essay recalibrates causalities among history, geography, and identity.

Toni Morrison's novel *Paradise* (1997) likewise braids history, geography, and identity, though here the fantastic is not a messianic harbinger of an epistemic break (that is, a rupture of modes of knowing) from the present time; it is but a palliative otherwise that discovers possibilities beyond binaries of race and gender in a fantastical space that simultaneously and precariously signals a dream state, the afterlife, or a narrative fantasy of a world to come.[8] Morrison's novel is about Ruby, an all-black town in Oklahoma that insists on a "one-drop" logic of racial superiority, bestowing privilege on the town's founding families with the most undiluted African ancestry. Racial supremacy is twinned with violent patriarchy, with men protecting women's wombs from exogamous impurities, so when a colony of women (at least one of whom is white, though the race of none is specified) establishes a residence in a former convent near Ruby, the town's very reason for being is threatened. Set in the 1970s, *Paradise* explores a black nationalism that bears none of the political efficacy of the contemporaneous Black Panthers, since it literalizes the blood claims of "nation" and stakes its faith in American geography. Likewise, too, the town commits to its own peculiar historiography, retelling Ruby's founding narrative in a queer conflation with the Christian nativity story.

Paradise culminates with the town patriarchs killing the convent women, though the novel's epilogue suggests otherwise. In the closing chapter, women who were just murdered visit estranged family, travel freely, and haunt a reader's expectations. In its closing pages, the novel suggests that the ending may be wish fulfillment, as the leader of the convent women appears to have returned to her native Brazil, and whether she is alive or not, the reader can note that the novel's heretofore tightly contained geography and neatly mapped history are ruptured and realigned. The reappearance of the Brazilian Connie situates the novel's entire drama within a broader context of black Atlantic migration and cultural hybridity.

Chabon's and Morrison's novels are about trauma, and though that topic has received more critical and theoretical coverage than can be mentioned here, the traumatic may read as the postmodern. Insofar as traumatized texts are not only about melancholia, but may in fact *be* melancholic – deeply identified with loss, aestheticizing and repeating it through figural reiteration – the traumatized text eschews linearity, spatial stability, and the basic premise of a coherently dependable character. Cynthia Ozick's *The Messiah of Stockholm* (1987), for instance, is a novel whose protagonist, Lars, may or may not be the orphan son of the Polish author Bruno Schulz, infamously murdered by a Nazi at the beginning of the Holocaust.[9] That the novel never resolves Lars's identity, and that Lars himself melancholically identifies with Schulz and then melancholically *dis*-identifies with him, circles the novel back on itself, allowing no exterior reality to illuminate a reader's understanding. *The Messiah of Stockholm* apocalyptically ends as Lars burns what may or may not be "The Messiah," the rumored lost manuscript Schulz was working on when he died. The burning and the subsequent loss of identification for Lars draw the trauma of the Holocaust into the present, and the novel offers no palliative closure, only smoke and ashes.[10] As Idelber Avelar puts it, narratives of melancholy, then, "[loop] back around to engulf the mournful subject," not necessarily leading to resolution but at least to representation of the endless struggle for resolution.[11] Morrison's, Chabon's, and Ozick's novels all obsess over loss and all end in traumatic apocalypse, and Morrison's and Ozick's in particular suggest the inadequacy of literary realism for encountering the traumatic past.

Avelar suggests how Morrison's, Chabon's, and Ozick's novels interrupt linear time and recirculate the past. Similarly, Bhabha indicates how ethnic American literature produces new composites of history and geography, which are the axes of the nation itself. This essay continues by investigating that composite, beginning with "identity," and then the layering of "history" and "geography." Each layer is plied into the other, and so the selected critical concepts here will necessary bleed into one another.

Three Stances Toward Identity

As much as students may be stumped about what constitutes a historically enduring, geographically salient ethnic tradition ("Asian American," for instance), where that category would aggregate several linguistic, national, and artistic traditions, so too do literary writers struggle to make sense of and locate themselves within identities. Simply put, writers often demur when asked to identify according to ethnicity.[12] Consequently, we end up with perhaps three different (though not separable) stances in the literature reviewed here. One stance involves the recovery of identity, which may mean drawing forth neglected or censored stories from the past. Toni Morrison's body of literature, for example, charts the origins of black people in the United States (*A Mercy*), the experience of slavery and emancipation (*Beloved*), and black migration in the twentieth century amid the Civil Rights Movement (*Song of Solomon, Paradise*).[13] Interestingly, the social movements that most clearly demarcate black identity are largely absent from Morrison's fiction, though when she does depict them, say, at the margins of *Paradise*, we find not the unifying figure of a Martin Luther King Jr., but divisive black patriarchs who police black authenticity. Especially in Morrison's broadscale overviews of black history, we find internal diversity and opposing black worlds.

A second stance among writers involves exploding all myths of collective identity with straight-ahead satire. In Philip Roth's 2000 tour de force *The Human Stain*, Coleman Silk is a light-skinned black academic who lives out his adult life passing as white and Jewish.[14] Not about Jewishness per se, *The Human Stain*'s often-ambiguous narrative point of view and its consistently variable epistemology – "all that we don't know is astonishing. Even more astonishing is what passes for knowing," the narrator Nathan Zuckerman exclaims – expose "identity" for what it is: clunky, obsolete, yet indispensable for sustaining the fictions we depend upon in daily life.[15] If no one perceives Coleman to be black, what can blackness mean? If whiteness is so readily adopted, whence its controlling power? Is the identity "Jewish" in some way like the identity "black," or does it exist as some in-between thing, neither black, nor white, yet both, to cite Werner Sollors?[16] Even the fifty-year span of Coleman's academic ascension divides into different, incommensurate times when considered from the point of view of the black subject he left behind.

If the novel simply exposed all identities as empty signifiers, we might consider it a reactionary satire. Blackness materializes as the result of injury, however, and whiteness as the source of offense, yielding a legible dialectic that marks the return of the repressed – black identity for Coleman, and a broader history of racial subordination and white supremacism at large. Individually, we may be unknowable, but the novel demonstrates that we still presume to know the other; and despite their instability, social identities compose the turbulent reality wherein we live. As the novel proceeds, it is never clear what Nathan Zuckerman knows about Coleman and what he invents as fiction, though the fiction seems to deliver deeper, if not more fac-tual, truth than simple biography could. This extra layer of epistemic opac-ity – the narrative's blurring of truth and invention as part of the novel's fiction – sustains the tension between the deconstruction and endurance of racial identity.

The third stance toward identity looks toward the future. This is the stance taken up by those texts that either mine the past for the foundation stones of a new identity, or posit reading culture itself as the basis of identity. Américo Paredes's 1958 ethnography *With His Pistol in His Hand*, for instance, lays down a foundation for Chicana/o identity for generations of Chicana/o writers.[17] Paredes's study of turn-of-the-century Texas border ballads about the exploits of heroic men was among the first research studies by a Mexican American to identify how border Mexicans celebrated their own lives (in contrast to the preponderance of racist "scholarship" deriding the border dwellers of this period). For Paredes, the ballads are expressions of a rich folkway, in which he can discern the particular material and historical con-ditions constituting border life. Drawing on the work of Fredric Jameson, ethnographer José Limón argues that subsequent Chicana/o writers who interpolate Paredes's legendry express the cultural logic of late capitalism, which, in the Texas and California borderlands, means subsistence wage labor at *maquiladoras* (factories, often exempt from labor laws) and an emer-gent folk culture expressing the social dysfunction such work can engender.[18] *Machismo* is the underside to Paredes's folkloric, pistol-wielding heroes, and Limón considers it less an intrinsic condition of Mexican masculinity than a postmodern symptom of Mexican and Mexican American experience with neocolonialism. Sandra Cisneros's collection *Woman Hollering Creek* (1991), for instance, includes stories about heroic, border-crossing men who turn out to be opportunistic frauds and abandoners of women.[19] Cisneros's fiction explores the unaddressed patriarchal priorities at work in Chicano culture, and it offers a remedy, both through satire and through the recon-struction and re-gendering of myth. If Paredes's border-ballad hero mythol-ogizes a culture of resistance to US hegemony, Cisneros's female characters explore and appropriate feminine archetypes of the Aztec and Mexica, and locate themselves amid a canon of female saints. Paredes and Cisneros draw from popular culture – local informants and song for Paredes, gossip and *telenovelas* for Cisneros – and for both, the location of a countercultural borderlands folklore opens up the cultural wound that the border would otherwise suture over.

These three stances of ethnic American literature suggest that there is at least some ambivalence among writers about just what ethnic identity is – a stable resource, a social construct, or a site for renegotiating American belonging – and that the postmodern, however we define it, emerges from or expresses that ambivalence.

History

It should be clear, then, that "identity" is a composite, the result of retrieving, reconstructing, imagining, or critically reading history and geography. Beyond simply adding ethnic geographical itineraries and historical trajectories to traditional stories of American founding and development, ethnic American literature posits simultaneous yet incommensurate histories and geographies. As Bhabha might put it, when reading from the margins, the American center recedes from sight: Like the rainbow's plurality of colors that can only be viewed at a distance, the consolidating center of American belonging is an illusion underwritten by an irretrievable myth of consensus. Beyond celebrating difference, then, postmodern ethnic American literature distorts the otherwise clarion image of the nation presented on behalf of controlling nationalist regimes. In the phrase "ethnic American literature," we hear less an addition of the first term to the second and more of an ambivalent, mutual interrogation among the two terms, forming a hybridity that ramifies into all modes of belonging in and to the United States.

In African American literature, this ramification appears as a haunting, or the return of repressed history, as in Charles Johnson's *Middle Passage* (1990) or Toni Morrison's *Beloved* (1987), novels wherein buried history literally ruptures the surface of material reality.[20] In these novels, the uncanny past manifests as an ontological impossibility – an African god, a ghost – something that does not exist in Western reality, but that manifests as a consequence of Western colonialism and capture. Johnson's representation of the fantastic possibility of an African god stolen along with the people who worship him is startling and unsettling. Though the tone of the novel initially suggests a wry, almost urbane incredulity toward the fantastic, the very fact of the god in chains is eerie to the sailors on board the ship, it unsettles everyone who goes below decks to look at it, and it may be responsible for the slaver's destruction. By the end, the god prompts mystical visions that resolve several of the novel's plot conflicts.

Johnson's *Middle Passage* and Morrison's *Beloved* represent the traumatic or ghost-ridden past of black Atlantic slavery, and the novels' postmodernism exhibits the seam between ontology and epistemology – what we know to be true and what strikes us as beyond belief.[21] For some readers, the torture, trauma, and cruelty of enslavement may fall in that seam. Who can say, "I know what happened there," where knowledge presumes understanding the experience of enslavement? We are stopped at the border between fact and experience, the psychic geography of "limit events," Dominick LaCapra's term for traumatic events that exceed our capacity for comprehension.[22] In Johnson's and Morrison's novels, the fantastic suspends both ontological stability and the dependable frameworks of knowledge, installing belief as the affective response to the aporetic. Belief is the border dweller between fact and experience.

Beloved's ghosts appear as givens: as with Latin American magical realism, the fantastical dwells within the conventionally real. Radically estranging, and nearly impossible to grasp, is the moral choice Sethe makes to kill her family – an act that a reader may struggle to comprehend. Morrison has said that among her reasons for writing the novel, and for including Beloved as a flesh-and-blood character, was her need to understand how a mother could kill her daughter – such horrors really happened – in order to keep her out of slavery, and subsequently, what depths of pride, remorse, and resentment result from such a circumstance. Morrison's formula for comprehending the moral quandary of Sethe's act is that "it was the right thing to do, but she had no right to do it."[23] Haunting that paradox is the blank space between moral and political rights claims: In what world is murder the right thing to do? In what world does a slave boss have more claims on children than their own mother? The supernatural if material ghost is required in order to understand the haunting if brutal reality of plantation slavery. Reversing the stability of ontology and epistemology within the novel – where characters know all too well the conditions of their lives, but struggle to lay claim to those conditions – the writer herself is able to make claims on history, to draw out and redeploy this story, even though, in the novel's own words, it is "not a story to pass on."[24] Like the reader, Morrison has no privileged epistemic position, relying instead on the affective aesthetics of haunting to do the work of knowing.

The paradoxical unknowability of Beloved (and *Beloved*), the novel's insistence on plural stories that intersect but never wholly align, and the many opaque narrative passages (wherein it may be impossible to know for sure who is speaking, and from what ontological position) comprise the novel's aesthetic challenge to present-day attempts to know and thereby contain the past. The novel does not celebrate the play of multiple truths, or simply deconstruct the historical past. Rather, the novel requires the reader to consider how the present is haunted by the past, and this "hauntology," to borrow from Derrida, reveals how our present world relies on the bedrock of enslavement and white supremacy.[25]

Geography

Chicana writers Gloria Anzaldúa, Ana Castillo, Helena María Viramontes, and Sandra Cisneros write cartographic stories that transgress and are transposed upon American nationalist geography. Drawing on a history that precedes the division of the United States and Mexico, and plumbing ancient, pre-Colombian myths and archetypes, these authors trace the palimpsest of place, revealing how the United States is the site of plural, simultaneous, but incommensurate places. The mythical space of *Aztlán*, purportedly the original home of the Aztecs prior to their migration, is speculated to be somewhere in what is now the Southwestern United States. Archaeologists are unsure of the location, or if such a place in fact existed, but the idea of a lost home in the American Southwest has nourished the imagination of these literary writers, establishing a mythos of indigeneity and a wellspring of cultural belonging for Mexican Americans.

The myth of *Aztlán* informs the work of radical feminist poet and essayist Gloria Anzaldúa, whose collection *Borderlands/La Frontera* (1987) is a bracing, autobiographical manifesto asserting cultural belonging in the American Southwest.[26] The first, prose half of the book traces archaeological suppositions about *Aztlán* and appropriates *Mexica* deities who embody fluid or counter-stereotypical gender traits. Establishing proprietary rights to place, Anzaldúa next insists on the bilingualism of the American Southwest. Anzaldúa has said that she originally began the essay as a brief introduction to the poetry of the second half, believing her reader would need some context for the queer and bicultural poetics to come. The essay grounds poetic imagination in an enduring if suppressed material reality of the Americas. The essay keeps in check the tendency to read Anzaldúa's poetics as facile inventions that simply dismiss the past and invent some utopic, queer-Chicana future. Rather, Anzaldúa contends, the hybridity she imagines and forecasts is already in place, and has been the condition of the borderlands for generations.

Borderlands/La Frontera became a touchstone of Chicana identity and a prominent resource for emergent "border theory" in the 1980s and 1990s for historicizing and poeticizing the experience of living and even thriving between Anglo and Mexican worlds, and for deconstructing a series of intact oppositions between the categories Mexican and Anglo, male and female, lesbian and feminist, prose and poetry, and art and criticism. Being brown and of mixed parentage, a woman, and a lesbian, Anzaldúa named herself a "crossroads" of cultures, ideologies, and modes of being in the world, the product of the geographical borderlands between the United States and Mexico.[27]

Cultural borderlands and liminal spaces of belonging feature prominently in fiction by Sandra Cisneros and Helena María Viramontes. Cisneros's collection of stories, *Woman Hollering Creek* (1991), includes several women border crossers: one young woman is dispatched by her family from the United States to Mexico after she becomes pregnant by a fraudulent, self-professed Mexican poet-revolutionary. Another character crosses over from Mexico to Texas to start a family with her new husband, but returns home to her father and brothers after suffering years of domestic abuse. For these and other women, the border is a conduit into a new country as well as a passageway into a new way of being a woman. Crossing the border offers no real freedom from economic impoverishment or patriarchal domination, and it is only in the passage itself, the movement through the liminal space, that characters are liberated. Early in the title story, Cleófilas is tempted by *la Llorona*, the ghostly woman who haunts bodies of water, tempting mothers to drown themselves and their children. Rather than succumb, Cleófilas re-routes the temptation, finding in *la Llorana* inspiration to flee her violent history, and the story relays a watery death into an escape across the water. Cleófilas is assisted by a feminist Chicana in a pickup truck, who drives her on the first leg of her border crossing. The Chicana's embodied independence, her dismissal of gender norms, and her celebratory *grito* (holler) upon driving across "the woman hollering creek" prompts Cleófilas's own voice, a "gurgling out of her own throat, a long ribbon of laughter, like water."[28]

Helena María Viramontes draws on a similar stock of female archetypes as Cisneros, including the haunting *la Llorona* and the complex Mexica female deity *Coatlicue*. However, Viramontes's fiction takes a different trajectory through postmodern geographies than does Cisneros's. In contrast to Cisneros, Viramontes depicts geographies of containment determined by oppressive policing, neocolonial violence, and the invisibility that comes with being an undocumented border crosser. Still, Viramontes's stories frequently include what some have called "magical realist" elements amid depressing materialist conditions. In the widely anthologized story "The Moths," a young Chicana at odds with her family's restrictive expectation of traditional female quiescence bears witness to a flight of moths emerging from her grandmother as she dies – perhaps a physical correlative to the soul's release.[29] Viramontes has explained that she wrote the story under the influence of Gabriel García Márquez, with whom she was studying at the time. However, different from Márquez, the fantastic in Viramontes's fiction is neither knitted into the quotidian, nor does it allow for easy release from the everyday.[30] To the contrary, the fantastic is close kin to the delusional in Viramontes's fiction, engendering material realities to be navigated by vulnerable, precarious bodies. In the same collection as the "The Moths," Viramontes's story "The Cariboo Cafe" concludes with a grief-struck, delusional woman conflating the Los Angeles police with American-trained paramilitary operatives in her home country in Central America, resulting in her radical acts of resistance to several forms of constraint and oppression, and her violent death. Viramontes's novel *Their Dogs Came with Them* (2007) likewise ends with a killing and perhaps escape – the heroine may or may not fly away from the killing scene, depending on how one reads the closing line, "if she believed."[31] Different from Morrison's *Beloved*, where belief is anchored by the materialized ghost, in *Their Dogs Came with Them*, the materiality of a violent, industrial, toxic Los Angeles may – or may not – be the launching ground for some new, transcendent possibility.

Perhaps unsurprisingly, several other postmodern ethnic American authors are either from or live in Los Angeles, where they write about the instability of identity. In novels by Octavia Butler, Alejandro Morales, Karen Tei Yamashita, and Percival Everett, ethnic or racial identities exist more as part of a regime of social coercion, or a legacy (and a future, in the case of Butler and Morales) of neocolonialism.[32] Everett's often funny novel *Erasure* (2001), for instance, is about the frustration of a literary author named Thelonious Monk Ellison, whose fiction is regarded as not black enough to sell well.[33] Ellison does not attempt to escape his blackness, nor does he reify it as a would-be resource for plot and theme. In his growing frustration, he writes a satire (unpublishable, he believes, though it becomes a smash) of the trendy ghetto novel, which he provisionally titles "My Pafology," and which reads as a contemporary, even hyperbolized version of Richard Wright's *Native Son*.[34] Characteristic of Everett's fiction, the novel's point of view, a character's viewpoint, and the ostensible thrust of the plot converge in a vanishing point, leaving a tone of satire without a clear ground for assessing just what exactly has been dispatched and what, if anything, has been claimed.

Everett's novel *Watershed* (1996) takes a different tack, navigating a series of themes about identity and responding directly to American geography and history.[35] *Watershed's* protagonist is an African American geologist who lives in the mountains outside of Denver, and who becomes involved in a land- and water-rights dispute with a local (fictional) tribe of Indians, the Plata. In *Watershed*, the protagonist Robert's evasion of recent history, including his family's tragic involvement in Civil Rights activism in the 1960s, is clear enough: Robert wants to live alone, and he wants little or nothing to do with politics, least of all the politics of identity. This is not a novel where plural and aporetic (gapped) histories converge with postmodern effect. Rather, Robert's evasion of recent, personal history draws him into a postcolonial geography, and he literally becomes involved in remapping American space. It turns out cattle ranchers are diverting water from the Plata's rightful watershed, while a toxic waste site leaks downstream into their land. Robert's scientific curiosity leads him toward discovering the usurpation, but he drops the dispassionate, objective approach to the problem in response to a series of interpellations (or, moments of mutual recognition), when both the whites and Plata insist that Robert, the lone black man in the novel, declare his allegiance: are you with us, or them?

Typical of several of Everett's novels, *Watershed* includes textual threads that occasionally tie into the main narrative, but just as often seem to have only the slightest connection to it. Some of these threads include archival information on the region's geography or on federal law regarding Native Americans, while other threads are fabricated, occasionally absurdist mockeries of the same. In this way, the novel signals that history and geography are the salient structures of knowledge underwriting present-day racist and neocolonial practices, betraying the inadequacy of a positivist, revisionist history, as if to say, "Nope: going back in time to sort out right and wrong, legal and illegal, will not, in the end, be sufficient for sorting out today's regimes of power." Most efficacious in the novel are Robert's and his Plata acquaintances' mutual identifications as subjects of police surveillance and white supremacy, and as people struggling to define and defend claims of sovereignty over land. Counter to type, Everett's Plata have no mystical connection to their land and certainly have little or no working knowledge of its geology and ecology. Though they live on a stream, few have ever been fishing. Robert, in contrast, is a hydrologist and knows the land intimately, if scientifically. The novel's final lines are a feint toward closure: Robert photographs evidence of the water diversion and sets off to find some regulatory authority or perhaps media venue to set the record straight, though the preceding narrative renders this outcome entirely improbable.

Similarly without closure, and likewise evincing the plural histories and geographies of the Western United States, is Ana Castillo's body of work in general, and her 1993 novel *So Far from God* in particular, which amplifies the play with randomness to the point of absurdity.[36] But if the novel is absurd, its satiric aim must be directed at a reader's expectations of what ethnic literature should be, while eschewing teleologies of moral development and social progress that are the ostensible foundation of the novel form itself. The novel follows the story of the matriarch Sofi and her four daughters, living in New Mexico at a physical and spiritual crossroads of Spanish colonial, indigenous Mexican, and Anglo American cultures. The geography of the novel, like that of Silko's *Ceremony* discussed below, can be traced on a map of the United States, and it effectively remaps the American Southwest with languages, races, and spiritual folkways, not to mention local and low forms of popular culture prevailing over normative regimes of belief and belonging. The novel's "indigenous cosmologies and perspectives ... challenge Western conceptions of history as linear and teleological," according to Theresa Delgadillo.[37] Consequently, the presumed arc of historical development "from primitivism to modernity" is likewise upended by the novel's seeming anachronism.

Though deeply in the grain of magical realism, in contrast to Everett's skeptical novel, *So Far from God* likewise intertwines realist and absurdist narrative threads, without a clearly reliable narrative point of view. Indeed, the novel's magical realist elements, including characters returning from the dead, quotidian visits from *la Llorona*, and shamanistic spiritual channeling in and around Chimayo, are depicted with such an odd combination of hyperbole and litotes (understatement) as to suggest that the entire novel is a satire on the genre to which it seems indebted. Where Everett's novel presents several unnarrated sections, thereby challenging the reader to find coherence, Castillo's narrator speaks as if there is coherence where a reader may find none, offering love advice, culinary recipes, and a propulsive soap-operatic swing between love and loss. The melodrama of the bulk of the novel resolves into a political dénouement when Sofi forms a political coalition for Mothers of Martyrs and Saints (M.O.M.A.S) that becomes surprisingly adept at reconfiguring local politics. Nothing about it seems realistic, and it reads more like a mockery of the conclusion a reader desires than any sort of proper ending.[38]

History *is* Geography

Leslie Marmon Silko's American Book Award–winning novel *Ceremony* (1977) is likewise set in the American Southwest, on the Pueblo lands of New Mexico, in the years just following World War II and the return of disillusioned, traumatized Pueblo men from military service.[39] The novel's antihero is Tayo, namesake of the archetypal hero of Pueblo folklore. The folkloric Tayo is a quester, often on a difficult, lonely journey with high stakes for his people.[40] Silko's Tayo is presented as an inauspicious figure, suffering a mental breakdown and an addiction to alcohol, and living far from town, exiled by his shamed family. Still, in contrast to his peers, Tayo has an affective and intuitive grasp of indigenous Pueblo practices, and it is his peers' perception of him as antimodern and atavistic, more than his alcoholism, that shames him.

In *Ceremony*, Tayo makes a twofold journey, toward recovery of his own mental health and eventually toward combatting the evil force of "the witchery" – the entropic force of modern colonialism. The narrative weaves Tayo's story with a timeless folkloric story about animal forces questing to restore the rains, and Tayo intuits that his journey will bring rain to the parched Pueblo lands. The novel does not critique colonialism and modernity (in comparison to, say, *So Far from God*) so much as it shatters the frames of history and geography that organize those concepts and make them possible in the first place. With none of the irony of Castillo, and with dread delivery, the narrative explains that "white skin people like the belly of a fish, covered with hair" were created thousands of years ago by an evil witch.[41] White people were created deficient: alienated from and unable to appreciate their kinship with the earth, they migrate around the world satisfying their simple desire to propagate a sterile culture and destroy existing ecologies. Tayo, who is mixed race and possibly half-white (much remarked upon by his enemies), composes a hybrid ceremony using old and new traditions, ancient and modern ritual objects. The ceremony's spontaneity and openness to change ritualize hybridity itself, and so validate Tayo's mixed parentage and modernity's inevitable mixture of people and customs. For successfully completing the first half of his ceremony, Tayo is authorized to meet *Ts'eh*, the *katsina*, or embodied spirit of the mountain that marks the north of the pueblo. *Ts'eh* and Tayo complete the ceremony, restoring a delicate harmony to the landscape and evading the narrative traps that would ensnare Tayo in yet another story about a drunken Indian.

Installing Western history within an indigenous American epistemic framework certainly qualifies the novel as a "counterhistory," but upon closer inspection, "history" itself is not quite the right term. In an interview discussing her novels *Ceremony* and *Almanac of the Dead*, Silko explains that she understands time as like an "ocean, always moving," with all moments of time contiguous with all others, in constant circulation.[42] Because of an unbroken tradition of perhaps thousands of years of oral storytelling, Pueblo culture is constantly changing, yet always with different moments in time continuously merging. For Silko, then, the vast span of time under consideration not only precedes and exceeds European colonization, but also coheres rather than progresses linearly.

Tayo's ceremony involves reclaiming his family's stolen cattle, which amounts to a rebellion against the very idea of property, which is itself the basis of modernism and coloniality. Tayo is assaulted by the poachers, but "rescued" when they leave to hunt a mountain lion. The lion, we learn, has baited the men, and it returns to commune with Tayo: "Mountain lion, becoming what you are with each breath, your substance changing with the earth and the sky."[43] This oft-cited poetic line stands in for an ecology of becoming (over an ontology of being just one thing) within the novel at large, as all earthly elements are in deep relation with all others, and each corresponds to a flux of spiritual forces. The novel suggests that there is no difference between, say, the mountain's relationship to the plain and the spirit woman *Ts'eh*'s relation to her lion/hunter-partner who visits Tayo. When the lion reappears as a human hunter carrying a fresh-killed deer, Tayo is assured of the ubiquity of spiritual forces and of the productive mutability of the world. For a reader, there is no distinction between people and place, nor between the objects of a place and their ongoing interaction.

Ceremony is not postmodern in the way Castillo's or Everett's novels are. Where those authors pull threads of history and geography, unraveling the dense fabrics of the nation, Silko's novel is about repairing the weave of the world (her recurring motif is the spider, spinning a web, itself a metaphor of storytelling). She aims beyond nationalism and is not focused solely on the priority of Native Americans. Rather, her novel valorizes and reconstructs hybridity, the bedrock for a future better than the past. The title *Ceremony* is easily understood as a description: reading the novel *is* a ceremony, and the novel aims to heal the reader's world while narrating a story of healing between its covers. The novel begins with the evocative prelude, "Ts' its'tsi' nako Thought woman/ is sitting in her room/ and what ever she thinks about appears/ ... She is sitting in her room/ thinking of a story now/ I'm telling you the story/ she is thinking."[44] Taking Silko at her word, the novel is not only titled "Ceremony," but *is* a ceremonial story in which the teller and the told are the same, and through which a reader becomes subject to and subject of the ceremony. Reading makes the ceremony happen.

Though it is critically expedient to classify the literature as more or less historical, more or less geographical, much of the literature discussed here links history and geography, bringing forth the uncanny and irresolvable plurality of nations within the nation that constitute the United States, or even asserting a mode of belonging prior to the nation, as in the case of *Ceremony*. If Delgadillo is right about Castillo's challenge to Western epistemology, it is precisely because that epistemology projects historical progress and Western expansion in providential lockstep. Though terms like "Manifest Destiny" and the late-nineteenth-century endorsements of empire and colonialism are now treated as relics of another time, the epistemic frames of history and geography as modes of understanding the nation nonetheless persist. A hallmark of postmodern ethnic American literature, therefore, is a recasting of those frames, yielding dramatically new narratives of space and belonging that do not easily resolve into a national literature of ascent.

Further Reading

Fiction

Acosta, Oscar Zeta. *Autobiography of a Brown Buffalo*. New York: Vintage, 1989.
Díaz, Junot. *The Brief Wondrous Life of Oscar Wao*. New York: Riverhead Books, 2008.
Howe, LeAnne. *Shell Shaker*. San Francisco: Aunt Lute Books, 2001.
Roth, Philip. *The Counterlife*. New York: Vintage International, 1996.
Whitehead, Colson. *The Intuitionist: A Novel*. New York: Anchor Books, 2000.

Literary Criticism

Brogan, Kathleen. *Cultural Haunting: Ghosts and Ethnicity in Recent American Literature*. Charlottesville: University of Virginia Press, 1998.
Chuh, Kandice. *Imagine Otherwise: On Asian Americanist Critique*. Durham, NC: Duke University Press, 2003.
Palumbo-Liu, David, ed. *The Ethnic Canon: Histories, Institutions, and Interventions*. Minneapolis: University of Minnesota Press, 1995.
Rody, Caroline. *The Interethnic Imagination: Roots and Passages in Contemporary Asian American Fiction*. New York: Oxford University Press, 2009.
Saldívar, José David. *Border Matters: Remapping American Cultural Studies*. Durham, NC: Duke University Press, 1997.
Sollors, Werner. *Beyond Ethnicity: Consent and Descent in American Culture*. New York: Oxford University Press, 1986.
Vizenor, Gerald, and James Seaver. *Narrative Chance: Postmodern Discourse on Native American Literatures*. Albuquerque: University of New Mexico Press, 1989.

NOTES

1 Though much of this paragraph draws on the OED, the genealogy of "ethnic" is indebted to Werner Sollors's *Beyond Ethnicity: Consent and Descent in American Culture* (Oxford: Oxford University Press, 1986), chap. 1.
2 Ralph Ellison, *Invisible Man* (New York: Vintage Books, 1980), 217.
3 Homi Bhabha, *The Location of Culture* (New York: Routledge, 2004), 171–197.
4 Toni Morrison, *Song of Solomon* (New York: Vintage, 2004); and Michael Chabon, *The Yiddish Policemen's Union* (New York: Harper Perennial, 2008).
5 Bhabha, *Location of Culture*, 149.
6 Ibid.
7 Benedict Anderson, *Imagined Communities: Reflections on the Origins and Spread of Nationalism* (New York: Verso, 1998).
8 Toni Morrison, *Paradise* (New York: Vintage International, 2014).
9 Cynthia Ozick, *The Messiah of Stockholm* (New York: Vintage, 1988).
10 Idelber Avelar, *The Untimely Present: Postdictatorial Latin American Fiction and the Task of Mourning* (Durham, NC: Duke University Press, 1999), 232.

11 Ibid.
12 Scholar Kandice Chuh has gone so far as to advocate for a "subjectless" identity – one where there is no standing political or social subject, but an ethnic subject ceaselessly under construction. Kandice Chuh, *Imagine Otherwise: On Asian Americanist Critique* (Durham, NC: Duke University Press, 2003), 10.
13 Toni Morrison, *A Mercy* (New York: Vintage, 2009); and *Beloved* (New York: Vintage, 2004).
14 Philip Roth, *Portnoy's Complaint* (New York: Vintage International, 1994); and *The Human Stain* (New York: Vintage International, 2001).
15 Roth, *The Human Stain*, 209.
16 Werner Sollors, *Neither Black Nor White, Yet Both: Thematic Explorations of Interracial Literature* (Cambridge, MA: Harvard University Press, 2007).
17 Américo Paredes, *With His Pistol in His Hand: A Border Ballad and its Hero* (Austin: University of Texas Press, 1970).
18 Fredric Jameson, *The Political Unconscious: Narrative as a Socially Symbolic Act* (Ithaca, NY: Cornell University Press, 1982); and José Limón, *Mexican Ballads, Chicano Poems: History and Influence in Mexican American Social Poetry* (Los Angeles: University of California Press, 1996).
19 Sandra Cisneros, *Woman Hollering Creek and Other Stories* (New York: Vintage Contemporaries, 1991).
20 Charles Johnson, *Middle Passage* (New York: Scribner, 1998).
21 Ontology refers to the philosophy of being, though here I use it more generally to indicate what we know are the "ontic" facts of the world – capture, enslavement, torture. Epistemology is the philosophy of knowledge, though we may use the term to indicate the frameworks that allow us to know the world. By suggesting a "seam" between ontology and epistemology, I mean that we may know things to be true, but we may lack a framework of knowledge for really understanding the truth of, say, the traumatic past. Also, here I depart from Amy Hungerford's description of "postmodern belief" as a content-less belief in belief itself. Rather, Everett, Morrison, Cisneros, Viramontes, and others posit belief as the outside or beyond of reality, and with *Beloved* and Viramontes's *Their Dogs Came With Them* (discussed below), the object of belief along with the affective attachments that cathect between subject and object are transformative for a history of the present. Amy Hungerford, *Postmodern Belief: American Literature and Religion Since 1960* (Princeton, NJ: Princeton University Press, 2010).
22 Dominick LaCapra, *Writing History, Writing Trauma* (Baltimore, MD: Johns Hopkins University Press, 2000), 8.
23 "Toni Morrison on Love and Writing," interview by Bill Moyers, *billmoyers.com*, accessed March 17, 2016, www.billmoyers.com/content/toni-morrison-part-1/.
24 Morrison, *Beloved*, 324.
25 Jacques Derrida, *Specters of Marx: The State of the Debt, The Work of Mourning, and the New International*, trans. Peggy Kamuf (New York: Routledge, 1994), 51.
26 Gloria Anzaldúa, *Borderlands/La Frontera: The New Mestiza* (San Francisco: Aunt Lute Books, 1987).
27 Ibid., 194.
28 Cisneros, *Woman Hollering Creek*, 228.

29 Helena María Viramontes, *The Moths and Other Stories* (Houston: Arte Público Press, 1995).
30 Helena María Viramontes, conversation with the author, February 12, 2013.
31 Helena María Viramontes, *Their Dogs Came With Them* (New York: Atria Books, 2007), 325.
32 Octavia Butler, *Kindred* (New York: Beacon, 2003); Alejandro Morales, *The Rag Doll Plagues* (Houston: Arte Público, 1993); and Karen Tei Yamashita, *Tropic of Orange* (Minneapolis: Coffee House Press, 1997).
33 Percival Everett, *Erasure* (New York: Greywolf Press, 2011).
34 Richard Wright, *Native Son* (New York: Harper Perennial Modern Classics, 2005).
35 Percival Everett, *Watershed* (New York: Beacon Press, 2003).
36 Ana Castillo, *So Far from God* (New York: Norton, 2005).
37 Theresa Delgadillo, *Spiritual Mestizaje: Religion, Gender, Race and Nation in Contemporary Latina Narrative* (Durham, NC: Duke University Press, 2011), 55.
38 See B. J. Manriquez, "Ana Castillo's *So Far from God*: Intimations of the Absurd," *College Literature* 29, no. 2 (2002): 37–49.
39 Leslie Marmon Silko, *Ceremony* (New York: Penguin Books, 2006).
40 See, for instance, G. M. Mullett, *Spider Woman Stories: Legends of the Hopi Indians* (Tucson: University of Arizona Press, 1984).
41 Silko, *Ceremony*, 135.
42 Thomas Irmer, "Interview with Leslie Marmon Silko," *Altx.com*, accessed March 17, 2016, www.altx.com/interviews/silko.html.
43 Silko, *Ceremony*, 204.
44 Ibid., 1.

8

ELANA GOMEL

The Zombie in the Mirror

Postmodernism and Subjectivity in Science Fiction

One of the central features of postmodernism is its embrace of popular culture. The "vernacular" architecture celebrated in Robert Venturi's *Learning from Las Vegas* (1977), the gory sensationalism of the film *Pulp Fiction* (1994), and the convoluted mystery of the television series *Lost* (2004–2010) and *Twin Peaks* (1991) are all examples of the blurring of the boundary between "high" and "low" art forms. But the most obvious example of this blurring is the close connection between postmodernism and science fiction (SF). Previously relegated to the ghetto of pulp magazines, derided as the fodder for socially challenged nerds, SF suddenly became artistically and academically respectable in the 1990s. Brian McHale in *Constructing Postmodernism* singled out SF as perhaps *the* representative postmodern genre, pointing out that even "mainstream" postmodern literature had been "*'science-fictionized' to some greater or lesser degree*" (emphasis in the original).[1] Many other critics have also argued that there exists a "continuity... between the registers of the postmodern and the science-fictional."[2]

But how are we to understand this continuity? Is it merely a matter of postmodernism's fascination with fantasy worlds, impossible events, and mysterious coincidences? Or is there a deeper connection, related to the way postmodernism challenges the very definition of what it means to be human?

Seen as a cultural shift rather than just an artistic trend, postmodernism articulated new forms of subjectivity that did not fit into the conventional mold of realist representation. The cyborg, the alien, the AI, and the zombie are science-fictional icons of these new forms, corresponding to the theoretical debate within postmodernism around the definition of the human subject. This debate has given rise to postmodernism's philosophical heir: posthumanism, the ethical, philosophical, and political critique of humanism. At the center of postmodernism and posthumanism is the conviction that technological and scientific breakthroughs, such as the Internet, social media, synthetic biology, neuroscience, GMOs, and others, have profound implications not just for the way we live but for the way we are. Art and literature, whether of the "high" or "popular" variety, have to develop appropriate narrative tools to represent the new ways of being in the world.

Readers who do not like SF often complain that it has no "people." To put it into more academically respectable terms, SF characters are "flat": devoid of psychological complexity, predictable, and clichéd.[3] I would agree with this claim but argue that it is a feature, not a bug. Characterization is the narratological term for the suite of techniques that literature develops to represent human psychology, motivations, and actions. SF characterization, often underestimated and overlooked by critics, is precisely where genre fiction meets the postmodern critique of humanism.

Bits of Subjectivity

Nineteenth-century psychological realism created a particular view of what it means to be human. The traditional subject (often referred to as the liberal-humanist subject) was seen as complex but psychologically integrated; individualistic but socially engaged; and, above all, special and unique. Characterization in the realist novel corresponded to this view of the subject and included first-person narration, consistent point of view, and the protagonist-centered plot.

Postmodernism brought with it a complete reassessment of subjectivity. Fredric Jameson famously diagnosed the postmodern self as broken and fragmented, a cloud of emotional "affects" rather than a unified personality: "...the liberation, in contemporary society, from the older *anomie* of the centered subject may also mean a liberation from every other kind of feeling as well, since there is no longer a self present to do the feeling."[4] The fluidity of the categories that previously defined subjectivity, such as gender, social and familial role, and economic status (to say nothing of nationality and political ideology), has created a subject of bits and pieces, only loosely held together by individual choice.

While some scholars saw the demise of the humanist subject as a tragedy, others welcomed it as a liberation. Among the latter, perhaps the most influential was Donna Haraway in her 1985 "A Cyborg Manifesto."[5] The "cyborg" of the title is often misunderstood as referring to a technological augmentation of the body. We are used to the cyborg of movies and graphic novels – a miraculous superhero with high-tech implants and impenetrable armor like Batman or Judge Dredd. But Haraway used the cyborg as a metaphor for a particular psychological structure that rejected the old dichotomies that bound the liberal-humanist self. Haraway's cyborg was neither male nor female, neither straight nor gay, neither human nor animal: s/he was all of the above. The cyborg was a fluctuating, flexible, self-creating subject, gleefully transgressing the social conventions that defined its predecessors. S/he was a political icon of what Haraway called "socialist feminism": a utopian ideology that redefined Jameson's gloomy diagnosis of self-fragmentation as a genuine liberation of the self.

Today "A Cyborg Manifesto" seems naïve and outdated in its political predictions. Nevertheless, Haraway accurately described the processes, both technological and social, that the postmodern era unleashed upon the subject. There is a seamless continuity in her description between science, economy, politics, and representation: "the cyborg is our ontology; it gives us our politics. The cyborg is a condensed image of both imagination and material reality."[6]

There are two main types of literary strategies for representing the postmodern subject. On the one hand, there is the experimental prose of such avant-garde writers as Thomas Pynchon, Kathy Acker, Joseph McElroy, and others who deliberately undermine the realist conventions of psychological representation. Their work ranges from playful to obscure, from ironic to unreadable, but it is highly self-aware of its own status as a verbal artifact. In terms of characterization, it emphasizes what Mark Currie calls "the conquest of cultural schizophrenia over narrative identity."[7] In other words, it deliberately draws the reader's attention to its own subversive status. The focus is on language rather than plot; on style rather than narrative. Avant-garde postmodernism often employs sliding pronouns, unreliable or enigmatic narrators, and unaccountable shifts of perspective, and occasionally dispenses with character altogether. Currie describes it as "narrative shipwreck."[8]

But while avant-garde narratives sometimes wreck themselves on the shoals of linguistic innovation, other ships have boldly gone where no one had gone before, carrying their crews of genetically enhanced supermen and -women, aliens, mutants, and androids. Ostensibly these crews fit into the more traditional modality of characterization: they speak in coherent sentences, have proper names and more-or-less stable identities, and fulfill specific roles in the plot. But I will argue that the "flat" characters of SF and adjacent popular genres, such as fantasy and horror, are, in fact, as close to Jameson's "decentered subject" or Haraway's utopian cyborg as their esoteric avant-garde counterparts. Seemingly more conventional, they are, in fact, just as subversive.

AIs and Other Anti-Heroes

The term "cyberspace" was coined in the 1984 SF novel *Neuromancer* by William Gibson.[9] The novel depicts a dystopian future of global corporations, ubiquitous crime, godlike AIs, and "cyber cowboys" – whom we today would call hackers – who interact with the matrix of the proto-Internet via a neurochemical interface. Case, the novel's protagonist, lives most of his life online and grows desperate when cut off from cyberspace and confined to what he contemptuously calls "the meat" of his physical body. Engaged in a complex heist, he is aided by Molly, a female assassin with implanted mirrorshades and stainless-steel claws; a dead man whose personality has been uploaded into a computer; and some clones. This motley crew inadvertently brings about the emergence of a godlike AI who does not even bother to try to exterminate humanity, unlike its later brethren in movies such as *Lawnmower Man* (1992) and *Ex Machina* (2015).

Case is literally a cyborg: a hybrid of organics and electronic technology. But perhaps more interestingly, he is also a narrative hybrid. Much of his description in the novel is old-fashioned psychological realism, focusing on his brooding over an unhappy love affair. But at the same time, in his interaction with cyberspace and with the AIs, he is represented through narrative devices impossible in a realist novel. These include a neural fusion with the matrix, in which he effortlessly shifts between physical reality and the "consensual hallucination" of cyberspace.

Gibson and other writers of the 1980s, such as Bruce Sterling, Pat Cadigan, and Rudy Rucker, developed the modality of SF known as "cyberpunk," which combines noir plots with the emerging subculture of nerds and hackers. Bruce Sterling writes that cyberpunk is an ideal vehicle for representing the "theme of mind invasion: brain-computer interfaces, artificial intelligence, neurochemistry – techniques radically redefining the nature of humanity, the nature of the self."[10] He means "techniques" in the sense of technologies. But it is equally possible to argue that cyberpunk, and SF in general, have developed *narrative* techniques for "redefining ... the nature of the self."

The classification of postmodern/posthuman subjects in SF is often thematic. Critics have identified popular culture "icons" that incarnate specific aspects of posthumanism: the alien, the mutant, the superhero, and, of course, the cyborg.

The "iconic" approach has many merits, enabling an overview of a large number of SF texts, both literary and visual, and finding common threads in what otherwise appears to be an insanely proliferating mass of cultural productions. I have employed this approach in my own research.[11] But here I want to take a different tack. Instead of comparing character types, I want to focus on the narrative strategies whereby such types are created.

I identify three such strategies here. They are *character eversion* (which I elsewhere called "character degree zero" and which is to be explained below); *zombification*, which is a decoupling of action and intentionality; and *un-self-creation*, which is the use of first-person narration to indicate the infestation of the human subject by the un/non-human.

Being (in) Place

In "Narratology beyond the Human," David Herman asks how narrative can represent the interaction between humans and their environment in less anthropocentric terms.[12] He analyzes Lauren Groff's 2011 story "Above and Below," whose female protagonist becomes homeless and wanders through a wilderness populated by animals and outcasts. Herman's point is that while traditional narrative privileges temporal progression (overcoming obstacles, achieving goals), postmodernism focuses on the spatial aspects of the plot (known in narratology as the setting). Groff's protagonist's aimless wanderings through strange places can be read as "her growing recognition of her place within a more-than-human world."[13] She loses time but gains space.

But SF offers far more radical examples of the same narrative modality; indeed, the strong emphasis on, and the textual elaboration of, the setting is the genre's standard *modus operandi*. In SF, space ceases to be the passive medium for the protagonist's actions in time. Instead, the subject is embedded in, and integrated with, the setting. Such subjects are the opposite of the "round," psychologically complex characters of the realist novel. SF characters are flat because their inner space is outside them. They have no interiority of their own but inhabit a landscape that is complex, active, and psychologically charged. The process that generates such subjects might be called *character eversion* (in the dictionary meaning of eversion as the state of being turned inside out). As opposed to the *pathetic fallacy*, in which the landscape echoes the character's inner state, in the eversion of subjectivity the character's inner state becomes an echo of the landscape. Space and subject exchange places.

Character eversion was pioneered by cyberpunk. Case's inner odyssey is inseparable from the multidimensional topology of cyberspace. His communion with his lost lover, his moments of sublimity, and his ultimate defeat all occur in cyberspace rather than in the "meat space" of physical reality. In the postmodern SF novel *Snow Crash* (1992) by Neal Stephenson, the protagonist (named, tongue-in-cheek, Hiro Protagonist) operates in the virtual Metaverse that contains simulacra of physical locales, such as Hong Kong, Shanghai, and Paris, all strung together in cyberspace without any regard for distances or boundaries.[14] Protagonist's actions are mapped onto the impossible space of the Metaverse in such a way that his actions and decisions become mere extensions of its vertiginous topology. Indeed, cyberspace contains the very text that describes it, since the premise of the novel is that language itself is a computer virus that infects the "real" world.

The way in which a character's search for identity becomes embedded in the configurations of the setting is illustrated in the late cyberpunk novel *Solitaire* by Kelley Eskridge (2002), in which the heroine Jackal is locked up in a virtual cell for a crime she has not committed.[15] The three spaces of the novel – the virtual, the physical, and the psychological – are all mirror reflections of each other, avatars of the city of Hong Kong. To achieve redemption, Jackal has to integrate all three. Her liberation from her virtual jail becomes simultaneously a return to the city and a return to sanity.

But cyberpunk is not the only kind of SF to use character eversion; indeed, the most striking examples of this narrative technique are in the texts that, like Groff's story, describe the relationship between a human character and the (often alien) wilderness. Two examples will suffice: Kim Stanley Robinson's novella *A Short, Sharp Shock* (1990) and Jeff Vandermeer's *Southern Reach* trilogy (2014).

Robinson's novella follows the amnesiac protagonist who wakes up in the otherworldly ocean alongside a woman known only as "the swimmer." Together they hike the only land on this ocean world – the endless girding spine, a peninsula without a mainland. The identity of the protagonist (who calls himself Thel) is unknown. He never recovers his memory, nor are we told whether his exile on the spine is an accident, a punishment, or perhaps a reward. Lost in a flow of strange encounters and striking impressions, Thel becomes merely a roving eye, a moving point of view through which the reader is experiencing the landscape.

The spine is vividly evoked in poetic and yet precise descriptions. It is topologically impossible, "a landscape in reverse," the "earth river."[16] It is also double, harboring its own reflection, which Thel periodically accesses by diving through a magic mirror. There is no explanation for any of the events surrounding the mirror, or for the peculiar creatures inhabiting the spine – fractal-faced women, tree people, and humanoid mollusks – who behave toward Thel and the swimmer with the capriciousness of a fever dream, intermittently helping and harming them. The novella deliberately undermines our expectations of causality, narrative coherence, and explanatory closure. The spine becomes the plot: Thel and the swimmer are literally driven on by the topography of the land. They have no desires and no goals independent of the place that contains them. The narrow strip of rock and sand, with its mesmerizing beauty and elusive mystery, is the true protagonist of the novella, while Thel's transparent consciousness is the narrative space it inhabits.

The inversion of space and character is emphasized by the very beginning of the novella, in which the drowning man is brought into consciousness by "a shattered image of a crescent moon," at which "a whole cosmology bloomed in him."[17] Thel is given reality by his impossible world, cosmology filling the void of his hollowed self.

Jeff Vandermeer's *Southern Reach* trilogy, consisting of three books – *Annihilation, Authority,* and *Acceptance* – has a plot similar to Arkady and Boris Strugatsky's *Roadside Picnic* (1972). A mysterious alien incursion has created a topologically distorted space – Area X – located somewhere in the south of the United States. The area is only accessible through a single portal, but those who venture inside either do not come back or come back psychologically and physically changed, mutated in unpredictable and often horrifying ways. The organization known as the Southern Reach Authority sends successive expeditions to Area X, but the information they collect does not elucidate either the nature of the incursion or the ways of combatting it. Instead, the Authority becomes a bureaucratic labyrinth, infected by the same strangeness as the area itself.

Annihilation is narrated in the first person by a member of one of the expeditions, a nameless female biologist. *Authority* is exclusively focalized through a male agent named John, who interrogates the biologist (or, rather, her copy) when she comes out of Area X and eventually follows her back there. *Acceptance* is intermittently focalized through this copy and the lighthouse keeper who becomes the beachhead for the alien incursion. It also contains chapters narrated in the second person and addressed to the director of the Authority, who dies in Area X.[18]

The most striking feature of the biologist's narrative voice in *Annihilation* is its flatness.[19] Even when referring to her own emotional reactions, she sounds remote, an observer rather than a participant. Referring to her life before she was recruited to the expedition, she says, "my existence back in the world had become at least as empty as Area X. With nothing left to anchor me, I *needed* to be here."[20] This need is what drives her on, even as the other expedition members perish or disappear. She is following in the footsteps of her husband, who had been in another expedition and came back as an empty shell filled with the strangeness of Area X. Her quest is not to find what happened to him but to become like him: a human-shaped alien site. As she says at the beginning of her quest, "Desolation tries to colonize you."[21] The very notion of colonization is inverted: instead of space being taken over by humans, space takes them over.

Like Robinson's novella, Vandermeer's books are filled with elaborate descriptions of a magical terrain where time is subsumed into space. Area X is pristine wilderness, cleansed of the signs of human habitation and inhabited by alien entities, such as the monstrous Crawler, composed of human brain cells, who "writes" incomprehensible lines on the walls of its lair in living moss. Language, along with subjectivity, is absorbed into the landscape. As the biologist in *Annihilation* puts it: "Slowly the history of exploring Area X could be said to be turning into Area X."[22] This process of absorption continues in *Authority*, where Area X literally takes over the human institution meant to study and contain it.

Going back to Herman's call for "narratology beyond the human," character eversion is a perfect strategy for representing subjects that straddle the borderline between human and animal. Animals are incapable of temporally organized narrative. But neurological research suggests that many animals do organize their experience in terms of visual or olfactory "maps" of their environment. Character eversion brings us closer to the animal vision of the world. In Vandermeer's trilogy, the biologist eventually metamorphoses into a many-eyed, multidimensional "leviathan" who passes beyond the limits of human language and human understanding.

The fusion between place and character in SF can also be seen politically, as an expression of the emerging eco-consciousness in the age of Anthropocene. Character eversion generates subjects who give up the temporal coherence of the liberal-humanist self in favor of a more capacious and inclusive sense of belonging. They lose themselves but gain the world.

Zombification

The popularity of the zombie in contemporary genre fiction and visual media is a source of bewilderment to many critics. The zombie – as opposed to the sexy vampire, the mysterious alien, or the seductive cyborg – is not just ugly but also boring. The undead rise, eat the living, and rise again – rinse and repeat. And yet, this simplistic formula has conquered the world: "the zombie is more popular now than ever before; it has even seemed to have crashed the boundaries of narrative and stepped into real life."[23]

If the zombie has indeed "stepped into real life," we must consider what it indicates about life in the twenty-first century. While postmodernism precedes the current wave of the walking dead, its articulation of subjectivity resonates with the poetics of zombification. Indeed, beyond Jameson's subject-in-pieces looms an even more extreme form of the postmodern self – its absence.

The zombie has no interiority whatsoever. It is a subject with no subjectivity, a corporeal entity with no mental life. Zombies act but do not reflect on their actions; they bite but do not taste; kill but do not murder. For all their destructiveness, they are as innocent as houseplants because they have as little sentience. This is the point of David Chalmers's famous thought experiment of the philosophical zombie: a creature that acts *as if* it had conscious experiences (or qualia) but in fact has none whatsoever.[24]

Jean-François Lyotard in "What Is Postmodernism?" and later in *The Inhuman* describes the human subject as a precarious and brittle construct that depends for its very existence on what is rejected and repressed as "the inhuman." This "inhuman" may be the subconscious, the body, or even the invisible social forces that mold and determine the subject. But in any case, according to Lyotard, the human self is always "hostage" to the inhuman.[25] The inhuman signifies the "death of Man" as a philosophical concept.[26]

Zombies may be seen as popular-culture icons of the inhuman within humanity. They dramatize the "death of Man" in the figure of the shambling animated corpse. They are subjects without subjectivity. In narratological terms, zombies are actants but not agents, which means that they fulfill specific plot functions but have no choice in how they act.

In traditional narratology, agents are characters who have the capacity to choose among several courses of action. Traditional plots, whether of Hamlet's revenge or Elizabeth Bennet's marriage (in Jane Austen's *Pride and Prejudice*), hinge on the protagonist's choice. Hesitation, deliberation, uncertainty, and the ultimate decision provide the character with psychological richness and complexity. But zombies cannot choose. Nor can their victims: once bitten by a zombie, any human automatically becomes one of them. The trajectory of the zombie novel is exactly the opposite of the psychological novel's: it is about the absence of choice, the withering of alternatives, and the demise of free will. Zombies have no other needs or desires than to consume the living. The physical terror they unleash is a displacement of the deeper terror of a subject without subjectivity, of action without agency, of violence without intentionality. The zombie is Lyotard's inhuman made (rotting) flesh.

Zombie narratives create suspense by the juxtaposition between agents and actants. The protagonist is the one who has choices; his or her enemies are soulless, mindless automata. But zombie texts never let us forget that an agent is only a bite away from becoming an actant. We are all potential zombies. Often zombie narratives underscore this point by depriving their protagonist of some salient aspect of identity, thus reminding us that the inhuman is always lurking within humanity. Language is frequently the first victim of zombification. In Mira Grant's *Newsflesh* trilogy (2010–2011), for example, the blogging heroine enacts her transformation into a zombie by posting online increasingly disjointed posts that end in a splatter of gore. In Manel Loureiro's *Apocalypse Z* (2007–2008), the resourceful protagonist that battles zombies across the entire continent of Europe has no name: it is only in the last sentence that we find out that he has the same name as the author, thus collapsing the distinction between body and text, fantasy and reality, agency and action.

Lyotard distinguishes between two kinds of the inhuman: that of the individual psyche, the unconscious or preconscious machinery of the brain; and that of the system, the supra-individual structure of society the individual has no control over. Zombies represent both those aspects. Insofar as it is an entity with a brain but no consciousness, the zombie is the inhuman within (it is no accident that it can only be stopped with a bullet to the head). Insofar as it is part of a larger but equally unconscious collective (zombies are always rampaging in hordes), it is the inhuman without.

Probably the most famous zombie text, Max Brooks's *World War Z: An Oral History of the Zombie War* (2006), made into a blockbuster movie of the same title in 2012, illustrates these two aspects of the zombie void of subjectivity.[27] The most striking aspect of Brooks's novel is its narrative form. It is modeled on Studs Terkel's *The Good War: An Oral History of World War Two* (1984), evoking the feel-good patriotic spirit of the 1940s. Like Terkel's collection of witness accounts, Brooks's novel is composed of first-person narratives of people fighting the zombie hordes created by a viral epidemic originating in China. The scope of the novel ranges from the United States to Israel, China, Russia, and other countries. Global in scale and yet woven of multiple individual voices, *World War Z* seems to offer a revivalist view of subjectivity, based on such old-fashioned virtues as agency, loyalty, and dedication to a common cause.

But the nature of the enemy undermines Brooks's simulacrum of the Greatest Generation. In the Good War, two ideological narratives opposed each other: democracy versus totalitarianism or, seen from the opposite side, racial pollution versus racial purity. In each narrative, the division between "us" and "them" was sharply drawn and delineated in moral terms: our side stood for light, theirs for darkness. But in *World War Z*, there is only one side, perpetually fighting itself. Making war on the dead is a self-defeating enterprise. Once involuntarily infected by the zombie virus, anyone can become one's own enemy.

The trope of reanimation mocks the heroics of the characters, as the text itself becomes a zombie, feeding on the historical memory for its existence. In one of the mini-narratives, a Ukrainian soldier appeals to the memorials of the Great Patriotic War, seeing himself as part of "a seething wave of strength and courage that crashed upon the Germans and drove them from our homeland."[28] But this battle had been fought and won long ago. By reanimating the past, Brooks's characters reveal themselves as merely zombies-in-waiting, and history is resurrected as an empty simulacrum. Even the use of multiple first-person narrators becomes a subtle parody of Terkel's poetics of witnessing. If in Terkel's book the first-person pronoun is attached to unique and specific individuals, in Brooks's imitation it is merely a linguistic virus that briefly animates the speaker, creating an illusion of subjectivity, before moving on to somebody else.

On the collective level, the novel exposes "the inhuman of the system" despite its ostensible ideological dedication to personal responsibility and self-reliance. It critiques the passivity, self-absorption, and lack of patriotism of Brooks's generation. One of the concluding narrators, Mrs. Miller from Montana, declares: "My grandparents suffered through the Depression, World War II, then came home to build the greatest middle class in human history ... Then my parents' generation came along and fucked it all up – the baby boomers, the 'me' generation. And then you got us. Yeah, we stopped the zombie menace but we're the ones who let it become the menace in the first place. At least we're cleaning up our own mess, and maybe that's the best epitaph to hope for. 'Generation Z, they cleaned up their own mess.'"[29]

But generations, viruses, and zombies are collective and impersonal forces that care little for individual pluck and virtue. The wave of zombification that engulfs America is not very different from the wave of anomie that is supposedly responsible for America's fall from greatness. Zombies represent the loss of agency, but they are not responsible for what happened to them. They are the blankness and passivity of the "me generation" taken to its logical extreme of non-being. And since the zombie virus cannot be totally eradicated, the fight against them is never-ending, repetitious, and ultimately futile. The "mess" that "Generation Z" is fated to clean up forever is Generation Z itself.

Despite its attempts to extol individual heroism, Brooks's novel derives its moments of genuine power from the images of the shambling zombies, rotting but moving, dead but alive:

"The trickle was now turning into a stream ... Most were either in hospital gowns, or pajamas and nightshirts. Some were in sweats or their undies ... or just naked, a lot of them completely buck bare. You could see their wounds, the dried marks on their bodies, the gouges that made you shiver even inside that sweltering gear."[30]

These images are instantly familiar, endlessly recyclable, circulating across media in a closed loop of thrills. This circulation collapses the distinction between sign and its meaning. As Julia Round points out in her discussion of *The Walking Dead*, zombies are pure negation, "emptied of metaphorical or symbolic significance," denying the very thing that brings them into being: language and narrative.[31]

Zombification as a narrative technique precedes the current popularity of the rampaging undead. In less obvious ways, it can be found in Philip K. Dick's SF novels and stories where characters who appear to be agents are ultimately revealed as actants, unconscious puppets of forces they are unaware of. In "Impostor" (1953), for example, an android believes himself to be a human being acting under his own volition, even though all of his acts are the result of programming to bring about a powerful explosion. In "The Golden Man" (1953), the incredibly charismatic and attractive mutant turns out to have "the intelligence of a dog," acting solely on instinct. From Dick's mutants and androids to today's zombies, postmodern SF undercuts humanism's insistence on choice and free will, revealing the powerful forces of which "the soul is a mute hostage."[32]

Un-Self-Creation

One of the most important postmodernist insights into the nature of subjectivity was the rejection of the humanist idea of individual autonomy: "Postmodernism not only views the subject as contradictory and multilayered, it rejects the notion that individual consciousness and reason are the most important determinants in shaping human history. It posits instead a faith in forms of social transformation that are attentive to the historical, structural, and ideological limits which shape the possibility for self-reflection and action."[33]

In his 1980 book *Renaissance Self-Fashioning*, Stephen Greenblatt described how Renaissance humanism developed narrative strategies for "the generation of identities."[34] Postmodern SF, to the contrary, produces narrative techniques of *un-self-fashioning*: the dissolution of stable identities and the unraveling of the subject.

Greenblatt points out that the humanist self is always constructed through a contrast with the rejected or threatening Other: "Self-fashioning is achieved in relation to something perceived as alien, strange, or hostile. This alien Other – heretic, savage, witch, adulteress, traitor, Antichrist – must be discovered or invented in order to be attacked and destroyed."[35] This "alien Other" may be related to Lyotard's inhuman. But while the inhuman is an elusive concept that resides beyond language and discourse, the Other is far more concrete. The inhuman is a philosophical category; the Other – a political one. In SF, the inhuman is represented through zombification: the reduction of the subject to the mute horror of the mindless flesh. But the

Other is a far more varied category that embraces aliens, mutants, cyborgs, and other intelligent but non-human entities.

Many books have been written analyzing images of the alien Other in SF. My focus here is on one particular narrative technique whereby such images are constructed. I will call it, by analogy with Greenblatt, *un-self-fashioning*: the invasion or corruption of the human self by the alien Other. Often, though not always, this technique involves the first-person narration by the subject being so invaded.

There is a long SF tradition of alien infestation. Robert Heinlein in *Puppet Masters* (1953), for example, employed a first-person narration to demonstrate the insidious power of alien "slugs."[36] His protagonist, a patriotic secret agent named Sam, is infested by the slugs but continues his narration uninterrupted, even when under the control of the alien Other whom he is otherwise trying to exterminate. This strange situation puts such a strain on the narrative fabric that it results in what Currie calls "narrative shipwreck," as Sam unaccountably shifts pronouns from "I" to "we" to "they," describes his own actions as if they belonged to somebody else, and eventually erupts in an insane orgy of violence.

More narratively and conceptually sophisticated SF employs un-self-fashioning to tease out the implications of postmodernism's insight into the "contradictory and multilayered" nature of subjectivity. But it also interrogates the political aspects of the alien Other, especially in relation to the problematic of gender and race.

Gene Wolfe's *The Fifth Head of Cerberus* (1972) deploys un-self-fashioning to probe the complexities of postcolonialism.[37] The colonial situation generates what Homi Bhabha called "hybrid" selves, as the colonized both mimic and subvert the culture of the colonizer. In Wolfe's novel, the hybrid selves speak in complex and contradictory voices, leaving the reader with the unanswered questions of who is, and is not, human.

The novel is composed of three interdependent tales set on the twin planets of St. Croix and St. Anne, populated by the descendants of human settlers. Before their advent, there had been aboriginal inhabitants on St. Anne (called "abos") who possessed the gift of mimicry. The so-called Veil's hypothesis, articulated by one of the characters, suggests that the "abos" had imitated the humans so successfully that they had forgotten their own origin. In other words, all the human characters may, or may not, be aliens. This house-of-mirrors situation results in a proliferation of simulacra, copies without an original, speaking in borrowed voices.

The first novella is narrated by the clone Number Five, whose story culminates in his killing his "father" (actually his genetic original) and resuming the latter's profitable slave trade, in which the slaves bought and sold are in fact genetically identical to himself. The second novella, a hallucinatory exploration of the "abo" culture, is supposedly written by an anthropologist from Earth, John Marsh, who tries to prove Veil's hypothesis. In the third novella, composed of Marsh's diary, we realize that Marsh himself may have been imitated and supplanted by his native guide who, of course, has no memory of what he had been.

The three tales have unreliable narrators whose search for a stable identity results in self-disintegration.[38] Number Five's chilling bildungsroman is the most narratively stable of the three, but his final self is so morally and psychologically repulsive that the process of self-narration becomes a parody of social and psychological integration. He is a copy of a copy, a flesh-and-blood simulacrum who, if Veil's hypothesis is correct, may be an amnesiac alien who can never recover his lost memory. In the hall of mirrors that is the world of Wolfe's novel, one does not destroy the Other to become a self; one destroys oneself to create another self, which then replicates the whole meaningless cycle. Marsh is an even more unreliable narrator, as his inexplicable shifts of style, constant second-guessing, and fascination with the "abo" culture he does not understand make it more than plausible that he is either mad or an imitation himself. Neither the psychological nor the cultural identity can be recovered or established: the chaos in which self and Other interpenetrate and commingle leads only to violence.

There is, however, a positive, almost utopian aspect to un-self-fashioning, which is exemplified by Octavia Butler's *Lilith's Brood* trilogy (originally published as *Xenogenesis;* 1984–1989).[39] In these novels, the fusion between human self and alien Other is celebrated as an escape from patriarchy and racism. The alien Oankali, coming to the war-devastated Earth and imposing genetic and reproductive exchange upon the survivors, are seen as friends rather than enemies. Their non-dichotomous gender structure and nonviolent culture are embraced by the trilogy's heroine Lilith, a black woman who has firsthand experience of being the Other in a white-dominant culture. The Oankali have three reproductive sexes, and their genetic "trade" with the humans results in hybrid families and individuals possessing both human and alien characteristics. Narratively speaking, Butler's novels attempt to utilize un-self-fashioning in a less disorienting way than *The Fifth Head of Cerberus.* The first novel of the trilogy is focalized through Lilith; the second and third are narrated/focalized by her hybrid progeny. Their voices are relatively consistent throughout the text despite the corporeal modifications they undergo. Nowhere do we encounter the extreme version of the "narrative shipwreck" in which the narrative voice falls into incoherence.

However, the more traditional form of Butler's text militates against its subversive content. One wonders just how different the human–alien hybrids are if they speak like Jane Austen characters. It seems that by toning down the experimental technique of un-self-fashioning, Butler inadvertently blunts its subversive edge. If Wolfe's characters are incomprehensible, hers are too familiar.

SF and postmodernism in general have been trying to find the balance between self and Other without quite succeeding. But perhaps it is this failure that best exemplifies the dynamic, unstable, interconnected nature of the postmodern self.

Postscript: SF Bodies, Postmodern Minds

In developing its own unique techniques of narrative characterization, SF vividly brings to the general audience the artistic and philosophical critique of the liberal-humanist subject that is the core insight of postmodernism. Not all SF texts are either politically subversive or narratively innovative. But the genre itself is particularly attuned to the sense that the contemporary era produces not only new gadgets but new people as well. As Michel Foucault says in *The Order of Things*, "Man is a recent invention."[40] The time to reinvent is now.

Further Reading

Bould, Mark, Andrew M. Butler, Adam Roberts, et al., eds. *The Routledge Companion to Science Fiction*. New York: Routledge, 2009.
Broderick, Damien. *Reading by Starlight: Postmodern Science Fiction*. London: Routledge, 1995.
Foucault, Michel. *The Order of Things: An Archaeology of the Human Sciences*. New York: Random House, 1974.
Hayles, N. Katherine. *How We Became Posthuman: Virtual Bodies in Cybernetics, Literature and Informatics*. Chicago: University of Chicago Press, 1999.
Lyotard, Jean-François. *The Inhuman*. Stanford, CA: Stanford University Press, 1991.
McHale, Brian. *Constructing Postmodernism*. London: Routledge, 1992.

NOTES

1 Brian McHale, *Constructing Postmodernism* (London: Routledge, 1992), 229.
2 Damien Broderick, *Reading by Starlight: Postmodern Science Fiction* (New York: Routledge, 1995), 111.
3 The distinction between "flat" and "round" (psychologically complex and multi-faceted) characters goes back to E. M. Forster's classic study *Aspects of the Novel* (1927).
4 Fredric Jameson, *Postmodernism, or, The Cultural Logic of Late Capitalism* (Durham, NC: Duke University Press, 1991), 319.

5 Donna J. Haraway, "A Cyborg Manifesto: Science, Technology, and Socialist-Feminism in the Late Twentieth Century," in *Simians, Cyborgs, and Women: The Reinvention of Nature* (New York: Routledge, 1991), 149–181.

6 Ibid., 150.

7 Mark Currie, *Postmodern Narrative Theory*, rev. ed. (New York: Palgrave Macmillan, 2011), 116.

8 Ibid., 125.

9 William Gibson, *Neuromancer* (London: Grafton Books, 1990).

10 Bruce Sterling, ed., "Introduction," in *Mirrorshades: The Cyberpunk Anthology* (New York: Arbor House, 1986), xiii.

11 See Elana Gomel, *Science Fiction, Alien Encounters, and the Ethics of Posthumanism: Beyond the Golden Rule* (London: Palgrave/Macmillan, 2014).

12 David Herman, "Narratology beyond the Human," *DIEGESIS. Interdisziplinares E-Journal fur Erzahlforschung / Interdisciplinary E-Journal for Narrative Research* 3, no. 2 (2014): 131–143, accessed March 17, 2016, https://www.diegesis.uniwuppertal.de/index.php/diegesis/article/download/165/229.

13 Ibid., 136.

14 Neal Stephenson, *Snow Crash* (New York: Bantam Dell, 1992).

15 Kelley Eskridge, *Solitaire* (Easthampton, MA: Small Beer Press, 2010).

16 Kim Stanley Robinson, *A Short, Sharp Shock* (Grand Rapids, MI: Anti-Oedipus Press, 1990), 24.

17 Ibid., 2.

18 Focalization is the narratological term for representing the events from the perspective of one of the characters but in the third person.

19 Jeff Vandermeer, *Annihilation* (Book 1 of the *Southern Reach* Trilogy) (New York: Farrar, Straus and Giroux, 2014).

20 Ibid.

21 Ibid.

22 Ibid.

23 Sarah Juliet Lauro and Deborah Christie, eds., "Introduction," in *Better off Dead: The Evolution of the Zombie as Post-human* (New York: Fordham University Press, 2011), 1.

24 See www.consc.net/zombies.html. Chalmers's idea has been the subject of a heated debate, with some critics claiming it is incoherent. I am not entering this debate but only refer to the philosophical zombie as an emblem of postmodernism's fascination with the void of subjectivity.

25 Jean-François Lyotard, *The Inhuman* (Stanford, CA: Stanford University Press, 1991), 2.

26 Jean-François Lyotard, "What is Postmodernism?" in *The Post-Modern Reader*, ed. Charles Jencks (New York: Academy Editions, 1992), 147.

27 Max Brooks, *World War Z: An Oral History of the Zombie War* (New York: Three Rivers Press, 2006).

28 Ibid., 121.

29 Ibid., 334.

30 Ibid., 97.

31 Julia Round, "The Horror of Humanity," in *The Walking Dead and Philosophy*, ed. Wayne Yuen (Chicago: Open Court, 2012), 155–167, 166.

32 Lyotard, *The Inhuman*, 2.

33 Henry Giroux, "Postmodernism as Border Pedagogy: Redefining the Boundaries of Race and Ethnicity," in *A Postmodern Reader*, ed. Joseph Natoli and Linda Hutcheon (Albany: State University of New York Press, 1993), 452–497, 467.
34 Stephen Greenblatt, *Renaissance Self-Fashioning: From More to Shakespeare* (Chicago: University of Chicago Press, 1980), 1.
35 Ibid., 9.
36 Robert A. Heinlein, *The Puppet Masters* (New York: Doubleday, 1951; reprint, New York: Ballantine Books, 1990).
37 Gene Wolfe, *The Fifth Head of Cerberus* (New York: Tom Doherty Associates, 2000).
38 Unreliability in narratology is a technical term meaning that the narrator is presented by the author as being in some way untrustworthy or problematic.
39 Octavia Butler, *Lilith's Brood* (New York: Warner Books, 2000).
40 Michel Foucault, *The Order of Things: An Archaeology of the Human Sciences* (New York: Random House, 1974), xxiii.

9

PATRICK O'DONNELL

Postmodern Styles

Language, Reflexivity, and Pastiche

At one end of the arc that extends from the postmodernist experiments of the American 1960s and 1970s to the "post-postmodernism" of the twenty-first century, there is a heterogeneous array of writers who play fast and loose with style, form, and language, and who are invested in challenging inherited assumptions attendant upon readership and readability.[1] Following in the wake of the Beat era, at the height of the Cold War, and with a country in the throes of youth culture rebellion and deep civic unrest, these writers, who engaged with stylistic and formal innovations that contend against the literary realism of the 1940s and 1950s, represent the onset of postmodernism in American letters. Since then, many of the energies of "early postmodernism" have been refined, attenuated, and contained, while many others have been transformed or released in new forms of contemporary experimentation. As Bob Dylan remarks in "Things Have Changed," "a lot of water under the bridge / a lot of other stuff too" in the nearly fifty years that separate the examples of metafictional experimentation to be found in Thomas Pynchon's *The Crying of Lot 49* (1966), Toni Morrison's *Song of Solomon* (1977), Ishmael Reed's *Mumbo Jumbo* (1972), Kathy Acker's *The Childlike Life of the Black Tarantula by the Black Tarantula* (1973), William H. Gass's *Omensetter's Luck* (1966), and John Barth's *Lost in the Funhouse* (1968) from a post-millennial group of novelists whose formal and stylistic experimentation rivals that of their contemporary forebears, including Ben Marcus, Marisha Pessl, Mark Z. Danielewski, Colson Whitehead, Shelley Jackson, Junot Díaz, Carole Maso, and Monique Truong.[2] In this chapter, I will survey a broad array of formal and stylistic experiments ranging across these five decades that have been essential to the formation of literary postmodernism leading to its contemporary aftermath.

Among the highlights in the story of postmodern American fiction are the Gardner–Gass debates of the 1970s, recently recollected and recalibrated by Nick Ripatrazone in *The Quarterly Conversation*, currently one of the best online journals critiquing and reviewing cutting-edge contemporary writing and translation. The novelists John Gardner and William H. Gass engaged in a vigorous series of conversations in letters, public forums, and print about the social relevance and meaning of art. Two writers more at opposite ends of the spectrum on questions of art and morality, or the power of representation versus the potential of fabulation, could not have been found. Gardner was known for works such as *Grendel* (1971) and *The Sunlight Dialogues* (1972) that combine realism and myth for allegorical purposes. Gass, the premiere "high postmodernist" of the era, was the author of a series of "difficult" experimental fictions, including *Omensetter's Luck* (1966), the stories of *In the Heart of the Heart of the Country* (1968), the illustrated novella *Willie Masters' Lonesome Wife* (1968), and a monumental work in progress that would not emerge until 1995 as *The Tunnel*. It has always been the case with avant-garde and experimental literature that questions of aesthetics, politics, and the social order often arise in terms of a binary opposition between the referential aspects of literary language and its nonrealistic, metalinguistic, or mannerist capacities. In the Gardner–Gass contestations, the direction and importance of contemporary writing were at issue as Gardner, during the decade of the 1970s in Ripatrazone's account, became increasingly critical of Gass and others who represented what he considered to be the stylistic excesses of emergent literary postmodernism – views formalized in the essays of *On Moral Fiction* (1978). For his part, Gass had consistently argued in his essays collected in *Fiction and the Figures of Life* (1970) onward that art existed primarily for its own sake, that the construction of form was the highest goal of the artist, and that, in the case of the novel, when it comes to the crucial element of character, as Ripatrazone summarizes, "it is not the primary function of a novelist to create dramatized, lifelike characters" but, rather, to construct character as "pure internal discourse."[3]

The writing that Gardner criticizes is that of experimental postmodernism, which was gaining increasing visibility during a time of intense domestic and international turmoil as the Vietnam War and the Cold War pursued their intertwined courses over the 1960s and 1970s. A symptomatic example occurs with the novels of John Hawkes, who had said in a 1964 interview that "the true enemies of the novel [are] plot, character, setting, and theme," which left "totality of vision or structure" as "all that remained."[4] In tandem, there are the novels of John Barth, who becomes something of a spokesman for American literary postmodernism with his twinned essays, "The Literature of Exhaustion" (1967) and "The Literature of Replenishment" (1980), which addressed the novel as a resource that reflexively exhausts and recycles its elements in the work of its serious play. Now largely forgotten, Richard Brautigan's lyrical experiments, *Trout Fishing in America* (1967) and *In Watermelon Sugar* (1968), had become the iconic embodiments of reality as hallucinated and communally experienced in the late-1960s drug culture. In his stories and novels of the 1960s and 1970s, Robert Coover shattered the very opposition between politics, the social order, and aesthetics that Gardner and Gass were discussing in such works as *The Universal Baseball Association* (1968), *Pricksongs & Descants* (1969), and *The Public Burning* (1977); to this day, Coover remains one of the primary avatars of American literary postmodernism as it progresses into the digital age. To be sure, these examples come exclusively from a limited group of writers – all white, all male, and all (with the exception of Brautigan) working in the academy. Thus, the debate over the value or excesses of postmodern experimentalism might be seen as one preserving a kind of mandarin exclusivity, but this would be a misconception that artificially limits the terms of a contestation between forms of social realism and forms of experimentation – not always easily divisible into categories – that was implicitly occurring amongst a diverse group of writers of the era, including Reed (*Yellow Back Radio Broke-Down* [1969] and *Mumbo Jumbo*), Susan Sontag (*Death Kit* [1967]), Maxine Hong Kingston (*The Woman Warrior* [1976]), Morrison (*The Bluest Eye* [1970], *Sula* [1973], and *Song of Solomon* [1977]), and Leslie Marmon Silko (*Ceremony* [1977]). It is important to note as well that amidst the ongoing Gardner–Gass conversations and the proliferation of novels that were engaging in various forms of stylistic and formal experimentation that challenged traditional notions of representation, realism, and narrative aesthetics, other forms of a dominant social realism were visible in novels by writers such as John Updike, Saul Bellow, Joyce Carol Oates, and William Styron. This is the backdrop against which something definable as a postmodern style emerges. The Gardner–Gass debates illuminate this emergence in placing at the forefront questions about the conflicts or alignments that occur in locating language and its effects at the center of the narrative enterprise.

Whether engaged in the writing of "historiographic metafiction" – a term, now canonical, initially developed by Linda Hutcheon to describe the conflation of facticity, realism, and fantasy in contemporary writers such as Pynchon, Coover, Morrison, and E. L. Doctorow[5] – or in postmodern experiments such as Gilbert Sorrentino's *Mulligan Stew* (1979), where fictional characters in the novel debate their status *as* fictional characters, one of the most visible elements of a definable postmodern style is reflexivity. Indeed, as Robert Alter argues in his study of the novel from Cervantes to Nabokov, the novel has always been a "self-conscious" genre that reflects on its own form and status as an artifice, and thus on its relation to the material conditions of existence.[6] While, in Alter's view, the novel may have gone through periods in which the degree of reflexivity or self-consciousness was on the wane, as was the case in the early to mid-nineteenth century with the ascendency of Stend-halian realism, modernist experiments such as James Joyce's *Ulysses* (1922), Virginia Woolf's *The Waves* (1931), and Samuel Beckett's *Watt* (1953) evidence vigorous "returns" of the novel's generic self-consciousness to levels matching those of *Don Quixote* (1605; 1615) and *Tristram Shandy* (1767). All of these are well-exceeded by Joyce's *Finnegans Wake* (1939), which still stands as the limit-case for what the novel can achieve as a reflection on its capacities for imitating the complexities of a planetary reality. For the postmodern writer who, as John Barth once stated, "neither merely repudiates nor merely imitates either his twentieth-century modernist parents or his nineteenth-century premodernist grandparents," and who "has the first half of our century under his belt, but not on his back," reflexivity is an integral part of the narrative work of the novel, equally visible in plot, style, and thematic array.[7]

An integral part of that work – occurring alongside the novel's traditional project of representing the construction of identity within the imaginative mapping of a social order – is reflecting upon the novel's contribution to a larger discursive reality that at its furthest, Borgesian reach contains all texts ever written in an infinite library. Here, perhaps, is one possible resolution to the Gardner–Gass contestation, in that, reflexively, any novel can be considered as integral to itself as an artifice and, at the same time, as contributing to the larger context of a "reality" in process, always unfolding in its social, historical, and linguistic dimensions. The examples of postmodern style that inculcate this understanding of reflexivity are many and operate in myriad ways, but for many writers who can be characterized as operating under the aegis of postmodernism, it is a critical part of faithfully pursuing, in words, an understanding of the world and worlding. Barth's *LETTERS* (1979) offers a prime example. It is an epistolary novel comprising seven correspondents, five of whom appear in or descend from protagonists in Barth's six fictions preceding it. Here, reflexivity, far from being a sign of authorial solipsism, is a matter of intertextuality, as texts proliferate, circulate, repeat, and refer to themselves in generating a set of cultural rules that "expose how America, as narrative and object, is called into being by competing discourses, and how these, in turn, regulate the institutions, behaviors, and social and political practices of those who articulate and are articulated by these discourses."[8] At the other end of the arc that extends from postmodernism to post-postmodernism, reflexivity becomes a form of intertextuality in Mark Z. Danielewski's *House of Leaves* (2000), ostensibly a horror novel complete with a Poesque haunted house, which is composed of multiple texts, narrators, and myriad footnotes distinguished by changes in font size and color. The novel materially and parodically foregrounds its own bookishness in delivering an amalgamation of networked narratives that, N. Katherine Hayles has argued, reflect the "neural connectionism" of contemporary culture and a reality that comes to us "intermedially," composed of multiple, "hyperlinked" sources and discourses that we constantly scan, cognitively and affectively.[9] In both LETTERS and House of Leaves, the internal reflection on the capacity of multiple texts and discourses to connect across time and space in the shaping of contemporary reality occurs through the work of authors and readers interacting to piece things together into the narrative patchwork termed "novel."[10]

The notion of the novel as patchwork leads to that of pastiche, or the assemblage of traditional forms and imitated styles recombined into innovative narrative patterns; but before focusing on this key element of postmodern narrative, let us consider how reflexivity is manifested in an equally thematic concern of many contemporary novels: the reach of language. In 1965, Donald Barthelme published in the New Yorker an enigmatic story entitled "The Indian Uprising," which would later appear in Unspeakable Practices, Unnatural Acts (1968), a collection sandwiched between Come Back, Dr. Caligari (1964) and City Life (1970). Together, these volumes established Barthelme as one of the premier experimental authors of the times. Often anthologized as a "representative" Barthelme story (a misconception, as Barthelme was always experimenting with story forms and narrative language – no Barthelme story is really typical), "The Indian Uprising" begins with these sentences:

> We defended the city as best we could. The arrows of the Commanches came in clouds. The war clubs of the Commanches clattered on the soft, yellow pavements. There were earthworks along the Boulevard Mark Clark and the hedges had been laced with sparkling wire. People were trying to understand. I spoke to Sylvia. "Do you think this is a good life?" The table held apples, books, long-playing records. She looked up. "No."[11]

From its outset, "The Indian Uprising" continuously shifts contextual grounds and compels a reflection, sentence by sentence, of the relationship between language and the construction of narratable worlds. The reader, "trying to understand" the narrative's circumstances, is thrust into a space that appears to be both modern-day Paris and nineteenth-century America, and into a war that appears to be both indigenous and domestic. But we may also be in Oz, with its "soft, yellow pavements," or inspecting a contemporary still life in the described objects of an ordinary living room. The story goes on to expound connections between love and war, contemporary culture and media, barbarity and civilization, and while it certainly encourages us to comprehend these linkages on the thematic level, it is primarily concerned with exploring how, in a reality saturated with signs, messages, and narratives, we construct stories and relations that allow us to navigate the absurd conjunctions and antinomies of contemporary existence. For the close reader of "The Indian Uprising" (and, in fact, there could be no other kind – this is fiction that requires the reader to fill in the contextual gaps and forge the links of semiotic chains), the story serves to mirror simultaneously the constructedness of narrative and the work/pleasure of reading in such a way as to participate in the composition of a narrative landscape.

This is to focus on language and linguistic experiments as the primary elements of narrative reflexivity, and the range of such experiments across the postmodern era – often indebted to surrealism and the modernist literary and cinematic avant-garde – can be seen in the writing of William S. Burroughs, Kathy Acker, David Markson, and Carole Maso, to name a few among many. We can observe a significant, elaborate example of linguistic narrative reflexivity – one "updated" for the digital age – in Ben Marcus's *The Flame Alphabet* (2010). The premise of Marcus's dystopic novel is that the speech of children has become toxic to adults, resulting in a world in which parents must go into hiding, children are quarantined off into unruly collectives, and communication can only occur through Rube Goldberg–like devices that can only produce nonsense and noise. The novel contains a quest for a lost child and an attempt to preserve the family in an environment of total social and linguistic dysfunction, but above all it serves as an alternatingly comic and sad meditation on the corrosive capacity of language when it is regarded merely as instrumental in the era of the soundbite and text messaging, its meaning reducible to the scanned phrase or tagline. In *The Flame Alphabet*, adults must either be mute or attempt to communicate in a language that is rapidly devolving into sheer noise, composed of "hisses and blips, a language ripped apart, turned into flesh and then shredded," a self-poisoning discourse of signals communicating "the vestiges of a message that might once have mattered, but by now had been hacked into nonsense."[12] The solution proposed by the novel's protagonist, an inventor who has lost his wife and daughter due to the plague of language, is to invent a new alphabet composed of a hodgepodge of materials that will result in an iconic new language of nonsense. The impossibility of this enterprise, however, only serves to underscore the novel's reflection on the paradoxical relation between language and the social order: language as the connective tissue that binds identities and societies; language, with its power to distort reality, as a destructive force that prophesies, in its own production, the world's end.

The postmodernist attention to the divergent potential of language to both construct worlds and deconstruct its own capacities, observable across the period that runs from Barthelme to Marcus, is reflected in narrative form, particularly those novels that can be described as encyclopedic or instances of pastiche, and that, in Tom LeClair's characterization, often constitute a literature of excess. By "excess," LeClair does not necessarily mean fictions that appear to be open-ended and formless, full of plots and subplots that sometimes connect, but often do not, and containing a cast of hundreds – the "loose, baggy monsters" of Henry James's famous description.[13] Rather, LeClair is referring to a category of postmodern novels by such writers as Coover, DeLillo, Gaddis, Le Guin, McElroy, Heller, and Pynchon that are paradoxically "excessive" in size, scope, and discursive range and variety, often made up of dozens of intersecting stories, motifs, riffs, plots, and characters, but at the same time narratives about mastery, about excesses of power, force, and authority in arenas small and large: the self's mastery of itself, economic and political hegemony, force in history and culture, the transforming power of science and technology, the control of information and art. These novels too are about the size and scale of contemporary existence: how multiplicity and magnitude create new relations and new proportions among persons and entities, how quantity affects quality, how massiveness is related to mastery ... [they] are themselves long, large, and dense.[14]

Made up of many parts intimating an expanding universe and systems – discursive, aesthetic, and technological – that intersect with varying degrees of order and randomness in that universe, excessive narratives continue to be prominent well beyond the heyday of the "high postmodernist" fiction that LeClair discusses. In the work of such writers as David Foster Wallace, Junot Díaz, Colson Whitehead, and Shelley Jackson, the art of excess continues to evolve, though in different terms at a moment when the concept of authorial or discursive mastery has given way to one of collectivity.

The novels LeClair considers, most of them published in the 1970s, reflexively foreground two traits that have been evident in the history of the novel from its beginning: pastiche (in the general sense of an entity constructed of many imitative parts of varying provenance) and encyclopedism (that is, comprising or referring to several different disciplines and forms of knowledge woven into the narrative patchwork).[15] These constant elements of the history of the novel have been manifested in countless ways in literary modernism as it moves across the twentieth century into the postmodern era, as in the encylopedic divagations of Joyce's *Ulysses* (1922) and Gaddis's *The Recognitions* (1955), the historical collages of John Dos Passos's *U. S. A. Trilogy* (*The 42nd Parallel* [1930], *1919* [1932], and *The Big Money* [1936]), or postwar fictions where the encyclopedic impulse conjoins with narrative reflexivity in the linguistic "cut-ups" of William S. Burroughs's *Nova* trilogy (*The Soft Machine* [1961], *The Ticket that Exploded* [1962], and *Nova Express* [1964]). The line can be traced as well between avant-garde experiments from surrealism (André Breton's *Nadja* [1928] and Louis Aragon's *Le Paysan de Paris* [1928]) to those of the Oulipo movement (Raymond Queneau, Georges Perec, Italo Calvino) and of the French *nouveau roman* (Nathalie Sarraute, Alain Robbe-Grillet, Marguerite Duras).

All of these influences inform what is, for many, the single-most important novel of the post–World War II era in America, Thomas Pynchon's *Gravity's Rainbow* (1973). Ostensibly a hallucinatory journey through the war and postwar "zones" of Europe with a titular protagonist, Tyrone Slothrop, who has become a textual fragment by the novel's end, Pynchon's novel is a compendium of Western culture and the cultural imaginary in the twentieth century. Composed of songs, shaggy dog stories, hallucinatory drug trips, road narratives, lists of everything from the myriad dishes of the world's most elaborate single-ingredient breakfast (bananas) to the outlandish variety of sweets available in a baroque English candy sampler, and plots of all kinds, ranging from the divine and the imperialistic to the telemetric and the paranoiac, *Gravity's Rainbow* combines pastiche and the impulses of encyclopedic narrative – to create a fictional analogue to the "world" in its multilayered complexity – in a labyrinth of discourse. The encyclopedic dimensions of this "interdisciplinary" novel that references Eastern and Western mythologies, the history of comics, jazz, ballistics, quantum physics, rocket science in Germany during World War II, drug culture, military science, and a host of other disciplines and knowledge result in what Ursula Heise has termed a "data bank, or a cosmic web … a textual space or cognitive field whose tightly woven symmetries and correspondences promise coherence, but ultimately defy attempts at ordering them into a meaningful pattern."[16] As a "data bank," the novel compels seemingly random or disparate forms of knowledge to come into contact: thus, in one set of sequences in the novel, the diaspora of the Herero people of Southern Africa is made contiguous to the development of the V-2 rocket in Nordhausen, Germany, as tragic nomadic and fascistic histories collide. Heise views *Gravity's Rainbow* "primarily as a temporal construct that makes information only gradually available and molds it according to genre conventions that prompt the reader to ask certain questions at the expense of others, and to select specific types of information to answer these questions."[17] This suggests the extent to which encyclopedism and pastiche conspire in a novel where multiple genres, the imitation of manifold styles, and the parodic representation of disparate cultural stereotypes generate a patchwork narrative that illuminates both the structures and seams of an unfolding, incomplete, and heterogeneous contemporary reality. If we place the novel's encyclopedic forays alongside its mashups of genres and styles, then it can be seen that *Gravity's Rainbow* is not "blank parody, a statue with blind eyeballs," as Fredric Jameson has famously characterized the work of postmodern pastiche, but a work that compels the reader to see the relation between scattered and dissimilar objects, microhistories, and cultural orders in the fallout of Western twentieth-century history.[18]

No other novel in the annals of contemporary American fiction, with the notable exception of Don DeLillo's *Underworld* (1997), offers such a panoptic display of the "novel as world" compared to *Gravity's Rainbow* when it comes to aligning the history of objects, technologies, and nations. But the encyclopedism and pastiche of Pynchon's masterwork can be perceived in a broad range of "big" novels in the last quarter of the twentieth century, from Coover's *The Public Burning* (1977) and Gaddis's *JR* (1975) to somewhat less familiar examples such as Alexander Theroux's unfortunately neglected *D'Arconville's Cat* (1981); Samuel R. Delany's *Dhalgren* (1975), often pigeonholed as "sci fi"; and Leslie Marmon Silko's *Almanac of the Dead* (1991). In the twenty-first century, a number of significant novelists, including Shelley Jackson, Junot Díaz, Colson Whitehead, and David Foster Wallace, have been using pastiche and the centrifugal referentiality of encyclopedic narrative to portray the complexities of contemporary reality as simulated and experienced.

Half Life (2006) is Shelley Jackson's first novel in print. Prior to its publication, she had authored a number of hypertext novels in electronic format such as *Patchwork Girl* (1995) and digital experiments such as *Skin* (2003–present), an online project that archives images tattooed on the bodies of thousands of volunteers. A Frankensteinian mashup of stories, images, songs, and poems, *Half Life* traces the episodic adventures of Nora and Blanche Oakley, twins conjoined at birth who are fated to lives that are always partial and disconnected, their "other halves," joined in body but separate in mind, both intimate and alienated, their identities a contradictory mix of physical singularity and psychological doubling. Jackson draws upon multiple genres, including science fiction, gothic romance, fantasy, and the political thriller, in relating the twins' bizarre and improbable journey toward becoming one, "neither singular nor plural,"[19] in an integrated "book" (the one we are reading) that contains the twins as conflated physical and textual identities. Jackson thus materializes pastiche and encyclopedic digressiveness both as formal elements of the novel and as figurative means of graphing identity in a contemporary world where identities of all kinds are threatened with atomization. The novel's title bears reference not just to the halved and doubled lives of the twins, but also to atomic half-life, and to the nuclear test range near the twins' childhood home in Nevada, a symbol of Cold War binarism and mutually assured destruction policies existing between twinned/doubled superpowers.²⁰

The politics of identity is explored as well in Colson Whitehead's remarkable first novel, *The Intuitionist* (1999).²¹ Set in a near-future Manhattan, *The Intuitionist* takes place amidst a welter of encyclopedic discourses, from the theological to the technical, as it relates the narrative of Ida Mae Watson, the first African American female elevator investigator in the metropolis – a position of great importance in a striated, "vertical" world where rising up and going down are movements at once physical and metaphysical. In the novel, an elevator is not just a mechanical conveyance: like the automobile in horizontal time and space, in the novel's organization of vertical hierarchies, the elevator is a vehicle that enables connection, progress, and the speedy navigation of multiple microworlds. In Whitehead's allegory of a binary reality where everything from religion to the transportation system is ideologized, those who investigate the causes behind technical breakdowns, which can range from mechanical failure to political conspiracy, are divided between the Intuitionists, who can experientially "feel" the trouble at hand by simply standing in a disabled elevator, and the Empiricists, who must tear it apart in order to effect a repair. *The Intuitionist* is both a detective novel and a *bildungsroman* that traces Ida Mae's journey from innocence to experience as she attempts to discover the invisible parties responsible for a series of catastrophic elevator failures. In investigating the lines of force and power of a world premised upon a singular notion of perfection in the form of a theoretical "black box," or perfect elevator, she is compelled to come to terms with discursive and material fragmentations of a diasporic reality in which all identities are partial and scattered. For Whitehead, pastiche and a traversal of paralleled and disparate religious, scientific, and technical discourses are the apt formal mechanisms for navigating contemporaneity.

In turning to Junot Díaz's capacious *The Brief Wondrous Life of Oscar Wao* (2007), we can observe the classic form of the *bildungsroman* rendered as a patchwork of genres and styles that reflect the voracious reading and consumer habits of its protagonist, Oscar De León, an overweight adolescent moving into adulthood who bears the burden of a tragic family history.²² Initially, the novel appears to be told through an assemblage of narrative perspectives, but as it progresses it becomes apparent that the primary narrator of the novel is Yunior, who relates the story progressively in the first, second, and third person, and who is Oscar's college roommate and the boyfriend of his runaway sister, Lola. Yunior's account of Oscar's life and that of his sister and his parents, who are natives of the Dominican Republic and victims of the brutal thirty-year dictatorship of Rafael Trujillo, is thus, like the identities of the Oakley twins, both singular and plural.²³ Formally, the intertwined familial stories that Yunior tells are generic, imitative assemblages of science fiction, comic books, fantasy, metahistorical documentary, and folklore. In its recurrent use of slang, dialect, and numerous footnotes that range in tone and style from the scholarly to the anecdotal, the novel literally becomes a patchwork of voices, texts, and languages, even as it operates under the rubric of a single narrator within the framework of the classic *bildungsroman*. Both exuberant and tragic, Díaz's novel takes up themes of masculinity, cultural identity, the relation between "high" and popular cultures, and the omnipresence of the past and collective history in the individual life; its multiple registers allow Díaz to convey within the vestigial form of the family novel the sense that everyone on the planet is both fatally connected to and inexorably alienated from all the others.

Even before his death in 2008, David Foster Wallace had become widely regarded as the most important novelist and essayist of his generation, and, for many, something of an heir to Thomas Pynchon in the "post-postmodern era." Wallace's three novels – *The Broom of the System* (1987), *Infinite Jest* (1996), and the unfinished *The Pale King* (2011; published posthumously) – are all large, encyclopedic collages that appear to be the loose, baggy monsters of James's description, perhaps infinite in their variety, yet they potentially also exist as responses to the integrity and systematicity of the novel, as Wallace's first title might suggest. Certainly the most widely read and critiqued of Wallace's novels is *Infinite Jest*, but interestingly, *The Broom of the System* predicates Wallace's career-long interest in writing that registers the inheritance of the "high postmodernism" of the 1970s and 1980s, while suggesting the degree to which, for him, the novel is a collective enterprise that depends more on the capacities of the author as a channeling entity rather than one who, however invisible, instills systematicity.[24] The encyclopedism of *The Broom of the System* is evident in the variety of its settings: a college campus, Cleveland office buildings, various apartment dwellings, the city sewer system, a nursing home, and the huge, manmade "Great Ohio Desert" (acronym = GOD), a simulacrum created in an unlikely location for the purposes of jump-starting the state's tourist industry. The novel's titular protagonist, Lenore Stonecipher Beadsman, a telephone switchboard operator at "Frequent & Vigorous" in Cleveland, undertakes a bizarre odyssey to locate her great-grandmother, who has run away with a group of fellow advanced-age rebels from the Shaker Heights Rest Home, but this is only one of the novel's many intersecting stories and projects that exist collectively as an assemblage of loose ends and red herrings.[25] Indeed, *The Broom of the System* can be viewed as an anthology of genres and discourses: jokes, mathematical puzzles, rhetorical figures, philosophical conundrums, transcripts of psychotherapy sessions and town-meeting minutes, religious sermons, the vocalizations of a talking bird with an extensive vocabulary, office dictation, dream book entries – all make their way into a novel whose story-arcs are both extensive and incomplete. Wallace's novel can be seen on multiple levels as a parodic response to systems of all kinds – political, historical, and literary – in their tendency to project a *telos* or end in the fulfillment of time. He evolves this response throughout his work, which might be seen as a redress to both modernism and postmodernism in its encyclopedic aspects – one that questions, and ultimately rejects, the system-producing "isms" or critical back-formations of his twentieth-century forebears.

In considering the experiments in language, reflexivity, and form of postmodern American fiction, it becomes clear that, in retrospect, the conversations between William H. Gass and John Gardner that I discussed in the beginning may have not foreseen the ways in which contemporary American writers (including Gass and Gardner themselves) inculcate what the poet John Shade refers to as "combinatorial delight" in Nabokov's *Pale Fire* (1962), resulting in new fictional constructions that merge traditional and innovative elements.[26] Nor does Gardner's concern that what he considered to be the stylistic excesses of an emergent postmodernism would lead to a body of work without ethical dimension or social relevance seem well-founded in the long run. From Pynchon's portrayals of the cruelties of war and oppressive bureaucratic systems to Wallace's suspicion of bureaucracies, governments, and writing systems of all kinds, from Barthelme's resurrections of linguistic relevance through the fragmentation of discourse to Marcus's sobering dirge on the commodification of language, and from the effects of a simulated social order on the formation of identity that one can observe in novels from Coover and Silko to Whitehead, Jackson, and Díaz, contemporary writing across postmodernism that experiments with language and form continues to be fully engaged with the "world," or worlds, as both projected and experienced. Especially in its reflexive dimension, this is writing that will continue to question – as did the Gardner–Gass conversations – the lineaments and reach of its own making.

Further Reading

Harvey, David. *The Condition of Postmodernity: An Inquiry into the Origins of Cultural Change*. Oxford: Blackwell, 1989.

Hassan, Ihab. *The Postmodern Turn: Essays in Postmodern Theory and Culture*. Columbus: Ohio State University Press, 1987.

Hutcheon, Linda. *A Poetics of Postmodernism: History, Theory, Fiction*. New York: Routledge, 1988.

Jameson, Fredric. *A Singular Modernity: Essays on the Ontology of the Present*. London: Verso, 2002.

Jameson, Fredric. *Postmodernism, or, The Cultural Logic of Late Capitalism.*
Durham, NC: Duke University Press, 1991.
Lyotard, Jean-François. *The Postmodern Condition: A Report on Knowledge.* Trans.
Geoff Bennington and Brian Massumi. Minneapolis: University of Minnesota
Press, 1984.
McHale, Brian. *Postmodernist Fiction.* New York: Methuen, 1987.
Nealon, Jeffrey T. *Post-postmodernism, or, The Cultural Logic of Just-in-Time Capitalism.* Stanford, CA: Stanford University Press, 2012.

NOTES

1 The conceptualizations of postmodernism are prolific, and in this essay I do not
take on the task of defining it or indicating a preferred version; rather, in focusing on the specificities of style that writers often categorized as postmodernist
exhibit, my intention is to work from the inside out, from symptom to rubric.
But, of course, and ironically, one of the grand narratives of postmodernism is
to be found in Fredric Jameson's *Postmodernism, or, The Cultural Logic of Late
Capitalism* (Durham, NC: Duke University Press, 1991), and the response to
Jameson, in one of the leading accounts of "post-postmodernism," can be found
in Jeffrey T. Nealon's *Post-Postmodernism, or, The Cultural Logic of Just-in-Time
Capitalism* (Stanford, CA: Stanford University Press, 2012).
2 The lists at both ends of the arc are merely indicative, and in no way suggest the
degree to which American postmodern writers are influenced by and have contributed to a broader international postmodernism. As I will suggest, the French
nouveaux romans of Alain Robbe-Grillet, Nathalie Sarraute, and Michel Butor
(as well as the successor Oulipo movement embraced in the work of Georges
Perec, Raymond Queneau, Italo Calvino, and Harry Mathews), as well as the
Latin American "Boom" inspired by the Vanguardia movement and the work
of Jorge Luis Borges that includes such figures as Gabriel García Márquez, Carlos Fuentes, Julio Cortázar, and Mario Vargas Llosa, discernibly influenced the
literary experimentalism of a host of American postmodern writers. Equally, the
"late" modernism of Joyce and Beckett; the literary productions of the Beat movement; the surrealist art and film of such figures as Jean Cocteau, Max Ernst, and
André Breton; and the Theater of the Absurd as represented in the plays of Luigi
Pirandello, Eugène Ionesco, and Jean Genet can be seen as a few among the many
sources of and influences upon American postmodern fiction from the 1960s to
the present.
3 Nick Ripatrazone, "Let Me Make a Snowman: John Gardner, William Gass, and
'The Pedersen Kid,'" *Quarterly Conversation*, accessed March 17, 2016, www.
quarterlyconversation.com/let-me-make-a-snowman-john-gardner-william-gass-and-the-pedersen-kid.
4 John J. Enck, "John Hawkes: An Interview," *Wisconsin Studies in Contemporary
Literature* 6, no. 2 (1965): 149.
5 Linda Hutcheon, *A Poetics of Postmodernism: History, Theory, Fiction* (New
York: Routledge, 1988), 108–123.
6 Robert Alter, *Partial Magic: The Novel as Self-Conscious Genre* (Berkeley: University of California Press, 1975), 1–30.

7 John Barth, *The Friday Book: Essays and Other Nonfiction* (New York: G. P. Putnam's, 1984), 203.

8 Kim McMullen, "The Fiction of Correspondence: LETTERS and History," *MFS: Modern Fiction Studies* 36, no. 3 (1990): 406.

9 N. Katherine Hayles, "Intermediation: The Pursuit of a Vision," *New Literary History* 38, no. 1 (2007): 100.

10 For an incisive comparison of the forms of reflexivity to be found in Barth and a postmodern counterpart, David Foster Wallace, see Charles B. Harris, "The Anxiety of Influence: The John Barth/David Foster Wallace Connection," *Critique: Studies in Contemporary Fiction* 55, no. 2 (2014): 103–126.

11 Donald Barthelme, "The Indian Uprising," in *Sixty Stories* (New York: Penguin, 2003), 102.

12 Ben Marcus, *The Flame Alphabet* (New York: Knopf, 2010), 78.

13 The comment comes in James's Preface to *The Tragic Muse* (1890) in the project of self-canonization that constitutes The New York Edition of his novels. There, James is comparing his own narrative aesthetic to that of Thackeray, Tolstoi, and Dumas: "A picture without composition slights its most precious chance for beauty ... There may in its absence be life, incontestably, as *The Newcomes* has life, as *Les Trois Mousquetaires*, as Tolstoi's *Peace and War*, have it; but what do such large, loose, baggy monsters, with their queer elements of the accidental and the arbitrary, artistically *mean*? We have heard it maintained, we well remember, that such things are 'superior to art'; but we understand least of all what that may mean, and we look in vain for the artist, the divine explanatory genius, who will come to our aid and tell us. There is life and life, and as waste is only life sacrificed and thereby prevented from 'counting,' I delight in a deep-breathing economy and an organic form. My business was accordingly to 'go in' for complete pictorial fusion, some such common interest between my two first notions as would, in spite of their birth under quite different stars, do them no violence at all" (Henry James, *The Art of the Novel: Critical Prefaces by Henry James*, intro. R. P. Blackmur [New York: Scribner's, 1934], 84). Clearly, James would regard many of the works LeClair names as examples of excess and the paradoxical discourse of postmodern mastery as such "monsters."

14 Tom LeClair, *The Art of Excess: Mastery in Contemporary American Fiction* (Urbana: University of Illinois Press, 1989), 6.

15 The foundational discussion of these traits as constitutive of the novel as such in history is that of M. M. Bakhtin, where he focuses as well on the heterogeneity of speech in the novel as a key element of its making. See M. M. Bakhtin, *The Dialogic Imagination: Four Essays*, ed. and trans. Michael Holquist (Austin: University of Texas Press, 1982).

16 Ursula Heise, *Chronoschisms: Time, Narrative and Postmodernism* (Cambridge: Cambridge University Press, 1997), 179.

17 Ibid., 179.

18 Jameson, *Postmodernism*, 17.

19 Shelley Jackson, *Half Life* (New York: Harper Perennial, 2007), 136.

20 This discussion of *Half Life* derives in part from an earlier discussion of the novel in my *The American Novel Now: Reading Contemporary American Fiction Since 1980* (New York: Wiley-Blackwell, 2010), 77–79.

21 Colson Whitehead, *The Intuitionist* (New York: Random House, 1999).

22 Junot Díaz, *The Brief Wondrous Life of Oscar Wao* (New York: Riverhead, 2007).
23 Trujillo's regime ran from 1930 until he was assassinated on May 30, 1961.
24 David Foster Wallace, *The Broom of the System* (New York: Viking Press, 1987).
25 For a fuller account of the novel's encyclopedic and anti-systematic dimensions, see my "Almost a Novel: *The Broom of the System*," in *A Companion to David Foster Wallace Studies*, ed. Marshall Boswell and Stephen J. Burn (New York: Palgrave Macmillan, 2013), 1–22.
26 Vladimir Nabokov, *Pale Fire* (New York: Vintage, 1989), 69.

10

PAULA GEYH

Between Word and Image

The Textual and the Visual in Postmodern
American Fiction

Introduction

This chapter explores the relationships between word and image in post-modern American fiction, from literary works that experiment with typography or other visual or material aspects of the book, to those that include images (drawings, photographs, and so on), to the graphic novel, a form that came of age in the late twentieth and early twenty-first centuries and developed into an important genre of postmodern fiction. These works reflect, and reflect upon, the postmodern world, and they share the conceptual issues and thematic preoccupations of other postmodern narratives. They also exhibit many of the same formal devices, including self-reflexivity and pastiche, but they add the use of images and other visual elements, which offer powerful means for the expression of postmodern thought and experience. Rather than simply illustrating or embellishing the text, the images and other visual elements found in these works are integral to the narrative, and they produce remarkable effects within it and on its readers. They require new approaches to reading and literary interpretation, and foreground the readers' active role in the construction of the text and its meanings as they read.

There are several types (sometimes shared by the works considered here) of relationships between word and image, three of which will be discussed in this chapter. First, I discuss works that aim to counteract the historically prevailing (albeit occasionally tested) assumption that a work's meaning is not significantly, if at all, affected by such "surface" features as the typeface in which it is printed, how the book is bound, what's on its cover, and so on. These works actively engage with the materiality of the text and consider the physical features of books as essential parts of their meaning-producing machinery. Their creative uses of different fonts and sizes of type, of the space of the page, and of the book's format and covers merge form and content and make it difficult, if not impossible, to separate them from each other. Such works as William H. Gass's *Willie Masters' Lonesome Wife*

(1968), Theresa Hak Kyung Cha's *Dictee* (1982), and Jonathan Safran Foer's *Extremely Loud and Incredibly Close* (2005), for example, use varying typefaces and the distribution or absence of words on the page to embody the characters' voices, their hesitations, and their silences – to make us *see*, and thus synesthetically *hear*, them.

Second, I consider the use of images in concert and sometimes in conflict with the written narrative, as exemplified by Gass's and Cha's works. This use is also essential to several of the novels' explorations of postmodern historicity, with their emphasis on the constructedness of history and their skepticism toward narratives of American history that have claimed to be objective and complete, but that omit the histories of many ethnic and racial "others." The irreverent drawings in Kurt Vonnegut's *Breakfast of Champions* (1973), for instance, are indispensable to the novel's iconoclastic demystification of America's founding myths and symbols. The critique of American history and historiography in Ishmael Reed's *Mumbo Jumbo* (1972) is partly accomplished through its uncaptioned photographs and unidentified images, which compel its readers to struggle with the ambiguous nature of historical evidence and question the reliability of the historical narratives based on it. Cha's and Foer's uses of uncaptioned photographs and film stills, by contrast, are less demonstrations of historical indeterminacy than of the difficulty of constructing a coherent narrative of traumatic historical events, a difficulty shared by readers as they endeavor to decipher the images, connect them to the written text, and assemble them into constellations of meaning.

The third type of works I shall discuss are postmodern graphic novels. They also exploit the expressive potential of typefaces and sizes, of the space of the page, and, obviously, of images, but they are substantially different from other works just mentioned, which remain predominantly written texts. In graphic novels, the relationships between the words and images can be quite complex, but it is usually the images, rather than the words, that carry most of the narrative. Moreover, graphic narratives have their own, primarily visual, narrative forms (or "vocabulary") and conventions. Like Gass, Cha, and Foer, graphic novelists make expressive use of different typefaces for speech and other sounds, but they also have their specific visual techniques for depicting them, beginning with expressively shaped speech balloons. The traditional narrative vocabulary of the graphic novel, which builds on those developed throughout the history of comics, includes panels and sequences or tiers of panels, gutters (the empty space between and around panels), and the page itself. These formal elements offer ways of representing time and space that are especially suited to narratives, like those to be discussed here, exploring history and spatiality. Art Spiegelman's *In the Shadow of No Towers* (2004), Alison Bechdel's *Fun Home* (2006), and Chris

Ware's *Building Stories* (2012) not only make use of this graphic vocabulary, but also extend it beyond the pages of the text proper to the book's paratext (covers, endpapers, and so on) to create additional dimensions of spatiality.

As with many other formal or stylistic markers of postmodernist fiction, there are precursors for these combinations of words and images, and for the transformation of words *into* images. In the "pattern poems" of the third or second century BCE, forerunners of what's now called "concrete poetry" or "concrete prose," words morphed into images as the poem's lines were arranged to create shapes that represented or complemented its subject. Early twentieth-century avant-garde movements such as Futurism and Dadaism revived the pattern poem and experimented with other arrangements of text and with typefaces to produce synesthetic effects that make the reader *hear* or *feel*. The concrete poems of Guillaume Apollinaire's *Calligrammes* (1918) not only *look* like their subjects, but also, through a kind of typographic onomatopoeia, *sound* like them: words explode in large, dark type or fade out as the type dwindles in size and thickness. In Stéphane Mallarmé's "A Throw of the Dice Will Never Abolish Chance" (1914), words and lines move in a rhythm consonant with the poem's images, so that, for example, readers *feel* the foundering ship list and sink. This remarkable capacity of words and, or *as*, images to physically affect or kinetically involve the reader will subsequently be used to great effect in several of the postmodern novels discussed in this chapter.

Early experiments with typefaces and other visual aspects of the text were not limited to poetry. The preeminent predecessor of these postmodernist novels is arguably Laurence Sterne's *The Life and Opinions of Tristram Shandy, Gentleman* (1759–1767). Since it is a self-reflexive (or metafictional) work that is much concerned with the materiality of the text and issues of signification and meaning, *Tristram Shandy* might easily be seen as a postmodern novel avant-la-lettre. In this comic novel, diagrams map the narrative's tangled progress; rows of asterisks and dashes stand in for what cannot be expressed, at least in polite company; and different typefaces create a variety of comic and onomatopoetic effects. Sex and the body and the mishaps to which they may fall prey are major preoccupations of the novel's eponymous narrator, Tristram, and they are mirrored in the obsession with the fragility of the material "body" of the text and the hazards of the (re)productive processes of printing, which are dramatized by the book's misplaced and missing chapters. Even the page itself is used to dramatic effect: there is an entirely black mourning page for "poor Yorick" and a blank page on which the reader is invited to paint the "concupiscible" widow Wadman "to your own mind."[1]

Words and (actual) painted images combined in the illuminated manuscripts of the Middle Ages and merged in the illuminated works of the late nineteenth-century poet and artist William Blake, creating "the marriage of painting and poetry."[2] In 1913, at the height of early-modernist experimentation, the poet Blaise Cendrars and the painter Sonia Delaunay-Terk created "The Prose of the Trans-Siberian and of Little Jehanne of France," an illuminated story poem that bridges all these histories of combining words and images, and anticipates aspects of postmodern fiction's incorporations of images into texts and of the graphic novel. Bound accordion-style, the poem unfolds in space and time, like the trans-Siberian train trip it chronicles and the childhood memories it evokes. The nearly 6½-foot-long page is divided lengthwise, like a train track, with Delaunay-Terk's brilliantly colored abstract painting dominating the left, and the lines of Cendrars's poem rocking back and forth across the right side. The images' and text's movement across and down the page evokes the train's rocking motion and makes readers *feel* it while they simultaneously experience the visual sensation of a swiftly passing landscape. The poem's words and images are intended not just to be read sequentially or alternately, however, but rather, as much as possible, simultaneously. Thus, the poem's two sides are connected by the text's multicolored type and by the fields of color surrounding and permeating it, just as, in its speaker's mind, experience and memory merge into a continuous present.

While its history overlaps at points with the one just sketched out, the graphic novel (or "long-form comics" or "sequential art" or "comix") has its own precursors and historical trajectory, beginning with medieval illuminated manuscripts, William Hogarth's eighteenth-century narrative serial engravings, and Blake's illuminated poetry. Rodolph Töpffer's satirical *The Adventures of Obadiah Oldbuck* (1842), which uses panels, was the first American comic book. Richard F. Outcault's *The Yellow Kid* (1897), the first collection of comic strips published as a book, popularized the use of the speech balloon. This and subsequent books of collected strips represent a significant step in the development of long-form comics, but their stories were inherently episodic and didn't cohere into novelistic narratives. The Expressionistic woodcut novels of Frans Masereel and Lynd Ward in the 1920s and 1930s had unified narratives but no words. Charlotte Salomon's *Life? or Art?* (1941–1943) combined gouache paintings and transparent overlays with texts and captions into what is arguably the first "graphic novel." Like many of the graphic narratives of the past forty years, Salomon's work was mostly autobiographical, but its fantastic elements make determining its genre complicated. By the 1940s, superhero comic books had extended narratives, and from that point on, the distinction between "long-form comics" and "graphic novels" may be less a matter of form than of the perceived "seriousness" and literary quality of the work.[3] As the authors of graphic novels have created increasingly sophisticated narratives, the genre has become the focus of much critical and scholarly attention. The emergence of the graphic novel as an important genre of postmodern fiction is, in fact, an excellent instance of the collapse of the distinctions between "high" and "low" culture forms that is one of the hallmarks of postmodern culture and cultural production.

Text as Image and Image into Text

Even as they extend or surpass them, postmodernist novelists who incorporate visual elements into their texts and graphic novelists alike draw upon the inspired devices and experiments of their precursors. William H. Gass's metafictional novella *Willie Masters' Lonesome Wife* builds on the creative uses of typefaces, arrangements of words and lines, and methods of combining or merging text and image discussed above, and goes beyond these experiments in its innovative uses of the book's covers and title pages.[4]

As in *Tristram Shandy*, obfuscatory asterisks proliferate in *Willie Masters' Lonesome Wife*, filling entire pages, but there's a self-consciousness about them, as the author observes in a direct address to the reader, "*********************** It's easy enough to think of them as star*s. It's a little ostentatious, perhaps, like having God's name up in lights, but they run on overlong now, in my opinion, don't you think? Yes, I feel these star*s about to droop ... " Words careen across and even *off* the page, and different discourses interpenetrate one another, forcing readers to abandon their habitual, linear reading practices. Gass employs a plethora of typefaces (nineteen in all) to indicate different speakers' voices and lines of thought, while others, like the swooping, pulsing, multi-sized letters of a moan, "oo-ooo-oo," produce onomatopoetic effects.

Willie Masters' Lonesome Wife also shares *Tristram Shandy*'s thematic preoccupations with the human body and the material body of the text. Here, the book *is* a body: the body of the "lonesome wife," Babs. The novella's punning title and the author's name are inscribed across a black-and-white photograph of Babs's naked, headless torso on the front cover; the back cover features her buttocks. Scattered throughout the book, Babs's naked, fragmented body mirrors the fragmented text. She is not only the book's narrator and narrative subject, she is also "its physical manifestation ... literally and figuratively, the 'flesh and bones' of this book."[5] To "read" the book, is, in effect, to make love to it (and her). Thus, the book's engagement with the body extends beyond the bodies of the text, its subject, and its author, to the body of the reader. The desire of the reader (apparently assumed to be male) is solicited throughout the text, from the front cover to the back.

Babs is (the book is) endlessly, and sometimes outrageously, accommodating to this desire: "I'll be a little mouse of a woman, blond and skinny, and there'll be rings on my belly where men have set down drinks," she says. But the author, who intrudes and obsesses and pontificates inside the text, is, he suggests, something else entirely (despite his hilariously Tristram-like phallic anxieties and fixations): "You are your body," he informs Babs, "you do not choose the feet you walk in – and the poet is his language."

Yet, if "the poet is his language," he's in trouble, as the text's fretful, again, *Tristram Shandy* – like (*and* characteristically postmodern) meditations on signification, the uncontrollable plurality of meaning, and interpretation reveal. "What's in a name but letters, eh?" the text demands, "And everyone owns *them* ... So use any names you like." The author's intention may well be beside the point, and he cannot, he resentfully acknowledges, control the reader's interpretation of even the most mundane, material traces of his own "text": "The muddy circle you see just before you and below you represents the ring left on a leaf of the manuscript by my coffee cup. Represents, I say, because, as you must surely realize, this book is many removes from anything I've set pen, hand, or cup to ... But why put a ring in the book? Kiss mine – why not? It can be a map of Dante's seventh circle if you like. Why not?" As Babs predicted, the last page features a photo of her naked torso with a ring around her navel – perhaps it is the author's, but it might as easily be the reader's. It is the final mark of Babs's, and the text's, submission to the reader's interpretation.

Kurt Vonnegut's transgressive drawings in *Breakfast of Champions* are essential components of his metafictional satire. As in *Willie Masters' Lonesome Wife* and many other early works of postmodern metafiction, the author appears as a figure within his own narrative and directly addresses the reader. "I am programmed at fifty to perform childishly – to insult 'The Star-Spangled Banner,' to scrawl pictures of a Nazi flag and an asshole and a lot of other things with a felt-tipped pen," Vonnegut informs his readers. "I think I'm trying to clear my head of all the junk in there – the assholes, the flags ... "[6] Vonnegut uses two principal techniques for his satirical "clearing" of the "junk": *defamiliarization*, a presentation of a familiar thing in a way that makes it appear strange, so that we see it anew, and *demystification*, a "drawing back of the curtain" to reveal the reality behind an illusion. The objects of his satire are defamiliarized by the author-narrator's matter-of-fact explanations of their manifestations, much as one would explain them to a very young child or an alien from another planet, accompanied by their equally matter-of-fact and demystifying display ("It looked like this:") in his artlessly childlike drawings.

Vonnegut's send-up of pornography ("Wide-Open Beavers Inside!"), prudery, and censorship features a sketch of a vagina, followed by the observation, "This was where babies came from." With deadpan gravity, the author-narrator reports, "It was the duty of the police and the courts to keep representations of such ordinary apertures from being examined and discussed by persons not engaged in the practice of medicine. It was somehow decided that wide-open beavers, which were ten thousand times as common as real beavers, should be the most massively defended secret under law."[7] Vonnegut's acerbic commentary renders porn and prudery equally absurd. The drawing of the vagina, like the preceding one of the asshole, defiantly *enacts* the transgression of the law, propriety, and "good taste," as it simultaneously drains the forbidden image of its allure.

In his demystifying discussion of American history, Vonnegut rejects the blinkered "traditional" narrative and instead offers a corrective "history from below," which adopts the perspective of those routinely omitted from the historical record, an example of the postmodern genre known as historiographic metafiction. He points out that 1492 – here inscribed in large, handwritten numbers – was not, as generations of schoolchildren were routinely taught, "when their continent was discovered by human beings. Actually, millions of human beings were already living full and imaginative lives on the continent in 1492. That was simply the year in which sea pirates began to cheat and rob and kill them."[8] The conceit that "the sea pirates eventually created a government which became a beacon of freedom to human beings everywhere else" is accompanied by a description of "this supposed imaginary beacon" as "sort of an ice-cream cone on fire," followed by a drawing that looks like an ice-cream cone on fire.[9] Referring to the "discoverers" and founding fathers of America as "sea pirates" casts them in a harsh but revealing light; the faux naïve explanations sharply illuminate the hypocrisy and obfuscations of America's founding narratives; and the drawings of the beacon and the flag, for all their technical accuracy, irreverently rob them of their patriotic aura.

Ishmael Reed's *Mumbo Jumbo* (1972) was one of the first postmodern historiographic metafictions, this time rewriting American history from an African American point of view. Reed's counterhistory of 1920s America reimagines this history as an epic struggle between the repressive forces of Atonism, defenders of monotheism, the "white-washed" history of the United States and its white-dominated power structures, and the polytheistic, African and African American creative spirit of "Jes Grew" and the Harlem Renaissance it inspires.

To create this counterhistory, Reed mixes reproductions of authentic documents, news clippings, and photographs, all of which might function in the text as historical "evidence," with apparently invented ones. It is not always easy to tell them apart or determine their connection to the narrative. A few, like the Cotton Club program, are easily identifiable or, like the photograph of Duke Ellington's orchestra, glossed in the text, and their contribution to the story's verisimilitude is clear. In other cases, like the photograph of a 1960s Black Panthers march that is embedded in a discussion of a 1920s plot against Jes Grew, readers must deduce the connection. The identity of many other images, however, remains obscure, as does their relation to the narrative. This uncertainty or ambiguity is exacerbated by the lack of captions or other identifications. In effect, Reed puts his readers in the position of a historian who must identify artifacts from the past, determine their authenticity or validity, decide upon an interpretation of them, and use them to create a coherent and cohesive history.

Many of these images inevitably test the reader's willingness to accept a persistent uncertainty and a multiplicity of possible meanings. The exciting, jazz-like visual polyphony of the text's images is a powerful contrast to – and rejection of – the "thin flat turgid dull grey bland like a yawn" Atonist aesthetic.[10] This polyphony expresses and enacts the lively, inventive Jes Grew aesthetic, in which meanings are plural and multivalent. *Mumbo Jumbo* is both a critique of received history and a counterhistory, and amid these contending histories, it makes sense that its images would share the written text's indeterminate historical "truth."

Theresa Hak Kyung Cha's *Dictee* (1982), the author's experimental memoir of her Korean mother's and her own experiences of exile, is, like *Mumbo Jumbo*, a work that seeks to recover lost histories and voices through an array of discourses and images. Cha was a filmmaker as well as a writer, and her use of images that are not always explicitly connected to the narrative seems inspired by the dialectical montage of early twentieth-century Soviet film, which required viewers to look for implicit comparisons, convergences, contrasts, and other relations among the shots. The intertwining of national and personal history – the Japanese occupation of Korea that sent Cha's mother into exile, and, later, the Korean Civil War, during which Cha and her parents emigrated to the United States – is dramatized by uncaptioned images of historical events that punctuate, but are not referenced in, the women's stories. A photograph of bound, blindfolded Korean prisoners about to be executed by Japanese soldiers, for example, attests to the brutality of the Japanese occupation.[11] Later, there is a post–Civil War map of Korea divided into North and South that is not only the marker of a historical event, but also a "map" of Cha's imminent exile.[12]

The issues of identity, voice, and language suggested by the book's title, *Dictee* (in French: "dictation" or "dictated"), are developed through the fragmented and multilingual text and, visually, through typography, the space of the page, and images. In addition to English, the text is in mostly untranslated French, Latin, Korean, Japanese, and Chinese. Absent translation, these texts easily become lacunae or, in the case of the ideographs, indecipherable images. The array of untranslated texts puts most readers in a linguistic exile that mirrors that of Cha's mother, who was compelled to forsake her native Korean for Japanese and Chinese, and of Cha herself, who, after emigrating from Korea was sent to a school where only English and French were spoken. A French–English parallel-text poem is arranged on the page to emphasize the brokenness of Cha's speech and her growing withdrawal into silence. Just as her sense of herself has been "cut," separated from her Korean home and language, the poem's text is cut, fragmented: "Cracked tongue. Broken tongue."[13] Opposite this text are diagrams of the mouth, throat, larynx, and lungs.[14] At stake, however, is not simply anatomy, but rather the extent to which the postmodern subject is constructed (and deconstructed) in and through language.

Cha's and her mother's experiences of exile echo one another, and their identities are in turn reflected or refracted through the images of historical figures of heroines and saints, which appear, icon-like, in the text (much as in *Orlando*, Virginia Woolf used photographs to represent Orlando's many subject positions). A photograph of the Korean heroine Yu Guan Soon complements photos of Cha's mother.[15] Photographs of Cha's girlhood idols, Saint Thérèse of Lisieux and Joan of Arc, as portrayed by Maria Falconetti in Dreyer's film *The Passion of Joan of Arc*, reveal her youthful idealism and, not incidentally, indicate how her subjectivity is mediated by filmic images.[16] The overexposed black-and-white class photograph of young Korean women on the back cover of the book could be read as a coda: an image of Cha's and her mother's fragmented subjectivities.

Cha graphically represents absence and forgetting through blank spaces or pages. There are moments that ironically call to mind the blank page Tristram Shandy leaves for the reader to draw his own portrait of the widow Wadman. Here, a blank half page is followed by the mordant observation, "One expects her to be beautiful," but rather than opening up a space in which the female subject could materialize (albeit in whatever form the reader might imagine), this blank marks her erasure.[17] Four chapters conclude with blank pages, as if to mark the absence of all the things that cannot be remembered or said by the exiled subject. The silence is eloquent.

Trauma, silence, and absence are also central themes of Jonathan Safran Foer's *Extremely Loud and Incredibly Close*, and, like Cha, Foer develops them through his creative use of the visual elements of the text itself and of images. The novel contains two interlocking narratives: the story of 9-year-old Oscar's quest to find the lock to fit the mysterious key left behind by his father, who died on 9/11; and his grandparents' stories of the trauma of World War II and its aftermath, told through their letters.

Most of the book's experimentation with typography and the space of the page is found in these letters. In them, blank or nearly empty pages make silence tangible. Oscar's grandfather's first letter to his unborn son explains that he carries a blank book in which to write all the things he cannot say, and the brief inscriptions ("I want two rolls," for example, or "Do you know what time it is?") are surrounded on the page by the empty space of silence.[18] The silence infects Oscar's grandmother's attempts at writing, too. Her memoir, we see, consists only of blank pages.[19] Communication also breaks down, ironically, when there is too much to be said. In Oscar's grandfather's last letter to his already-dead son, he is thwarted by trying to say too much. "I want an infinitely blank book and the rest of time," he thinks, but the book isn't infinite.[20] The type in the letter grows increasingly tightly spaced until it overwrites itself and becomes illegible; and still, page after page, it grows denser, until it is finally a nearly solid black field through which only tiny fragments of the white page glimmer.[21]

Oscar's world and his quest are copiously documented by photographs throughout the text, but here I'll focus on two key recurrent images: a doorknob (sometimes with a keyhole) and "the falling man." Both of these images function not just visually, as images: they also involve the reader physically or, again, kinetically. Some of the doorknobs, which appear as full-page black-and-white photographs, belong to Oscar's grandparents' story and seem to embody the barriers between the unhappy couple and his grandfather's inability to find a way past his grief and trauma after the war. Most of them, however, belong to the doors Oscar knocks on in his citywide search for the owner of the lock that will fit the key left by his father. The search is an act of mourning, and the doorknobs represent the obstacles to Oscar's acceptance of his father's death and, perhaps, his progress toward it. These doorknob images, however, do more than symbolize Oscar's search: nearly all of them appear on the recto (right-hand) page, so that, turning the page, the reader is, in effect, turning, or trying to turn, the knob and open the door. Thus, the reader shares – and physically enacts – the search *with* Oscar.

"The falling man," full-page stills from a video of a man plummeting from one of the World Trade Towers on 9/11, is the most repeated image in the novel.[22] It appears twice (once as a blow-up of the figure) among the photographs Oscar keeps in his scrapbook entitled "Stuff That Happened to

Me," and, like the other television images in the scrapbook, it raises questions of how media images construct and *mediate* our senses of ourselves and the world. Later, the falling man image is inserted, like a flashback, amid the fragments of a conversation Oscar overhears between his mother and his psychiatrist. The novel ends with Oscar narrating the events of 9/11 in reverse, followed by a 16-page flipbook, in which the series of video stills is reversed so that the falling man floats upward to safety. Flipping the pages, the reader enacts Oscar's fantasy, physically joining him in those last moments of wish fulfillment. This dynamic use of the physical space between the novel's pages to produce action over time brings it to the threshold of the distinctive uses of space and time in the graphic novel.

The Space and Time of Graphic Narratives

As a spatial medium, the comics' or graphic novel's page has, as Hillary Chute observes, "a kind of serialized architecture, either gridded conventionally ... or deviating meaningfully from the grid. ... The fundamental form of comics, then, is like a building, composed of rows of windows, or frames."[23] Within that architecture of the page, time is spatialized, captured in moments depicted in panels, and elapsing in the gutters between them. Past, present, and future can be juxtaposed on one page or traversed from panel to panel and page to page. Art Spiegelman, Alison Bechdel, and Chris Ware, the three authors I shall discuss here, use these formal elements in their graphic novels to explore history and the passage of time, and issues of spatiality, including how the spaces we inhabit shape us and our experience of the postmodern world. Moreover, they expand the graphic novel's architectural form to encompass the format, covers, endpapers, and "front matter" (the frontispiece and title and copyright pages), which they use to transform their books into architectural embodiments of towers, a house, and an apartment building.

Art Spiegelman's *In the Shadow of No Towers* defies attempts to situate it within one genre: it is at once a graphic memoir of 9/11 and its aftermath, a political polemic, and an homage to early twentieth-century comics.[24] The book narratively – and structurally – reenacts the trauma of World Trade Towers' collapse and the work of mourning and memory. The nature of this memorial is not solely rhetorical: as a physical object, the book *becomes* the towers.

Literally and figuratively, the towers are the book's organizing structural principle, its architecture. They materialize throughout the book's text and, strikingly, through its covers and endpapers. Printed on heavy cardboard like children's "board books," *In the Shadow of No Towers* is a large

(20 × 14.5"), heavy, rectangular black block. The front cover depicts the towers in solid glossy black on a matte black background, a reproduction of Spiegelman's acclaimed post-9/11 *New Yorker* magazine cover. Coupled with the book's title, this image makes present, in the form of two black shadows, the towers' absence. The shadow towers are bridged by the title and the author's name, and by a color inset panel containing images of some of the early twentieth century's most iconic comics characters, tumbling through space and, apparently, time. The panel bridge evokes and, obviously, contrasts with the unforgettable image of Philippe Petit's famous 1974 "Man on Wire" walk between the towers. The tumbling comics characters also evoke the haunting video image of "the falling man." The back cover continues the black-on-black motif, but it features the glossy shadows of the comics characters, falling through the matte black void. This motif continues inside both covers to the first third or so of the front and back endpapers, where, in black, tower-like rectangles, they are the background for the title page information and the author's bio (and a drawing of Spiegelman himself, tumbling with them).

The book's double structure is both spatial and, in its division into two parts (the 9/11 narrative and "The Comic Supplement"), temporal. With September 11, 2001, as its "Year Zero" and fulcrum, the book's text and images reach back to the first decades of the twentieth century and forward to the first few years after 9/11. Next to the black tower of falling figures, the front endpapers feature a reproduction of the front page of the September 11, 1901, New York newspaper *The World*, which is devoted to news of President William McKinley's deteriorating physical state following the attempt on his life. Setting up a parallel between the two imminently fatal "wounds," a circular, pixilated image of one of the World Trade Towers, glowing and about to fall, is superimposed on the center of the newspaper page. On the back endpapers, the space not taken up by the black tower of falling characters is devoted to newspaper headlines – some from the run-up to 9/11, some from 9/11, and others afterwards. Ricocheting back and forth between these front and back endpapers and the text's two parts are a series of thematic resonances across time – of shock and horror, of suspicions of dark conspiracies and hasty arrests, of ongoing trauma and irreparable loss.

Inside the book, the towers are omnipresent: they bracket the length of many of the pages, march in multiple iterations across them, and cast shadows that diagonally traverse them. If one regards the panels as windows, every tier is a floor and every page a tower. Spiegelman violates the panel grid on nearly all the pages: these are toppling buildings. The panels move across, down, and even zigzag, and they can be read in many orders. The effect is spatially vertiginous and temporally disorienting; they seem, as Martha Kuhlman suggests, "intended to convey 'that all-at-onceness' that was the 'overwhelming feeling of September 11th.'"[25]

This sense of synchronicity is amplified by the second part of the book, "The Comic Supplement." "The blast that disintegrated those Lower Manhattan towers also disinterred the ghosts of some Sunday supplement stars born on nearby Park Row about a century earlier," Spiegelman explains.[26] Like prophetic dreams, these comics proleptically resonate with 9/11. In his dream, Little Nemo (from Winsor McCay's "Little Nemo in Slumberland") and his African friend struggle to climb down a building and find their way through crowded city streets, while in the distance, Flip the clown topples buildings in his rush to catch up with them. In the book's final comic, Jiggs (from George McManus's "Bringing Up Father") encounters the Leaning Tower of Pisa, which he dreams collapses onto him; the next day, he props it up with wooden beams, and that night, sleeps secure. Yet as we close the book, we see Little Nemo's and Jiggs's shadow figures among all the others, forever falling through the dark.

In Alison Bechdel's graphic memoir *Fun Home: A Family Tragicomic*, the traumatic space she inhabits is the family's house (the title is short for "funeral home," the family business, and also an ironic comment on what it was like to grow up there). The narrative depicts Bechdel's ambivalent childhood relationship with her closeted gay father, Bruce, and her discovery and experience of her own lesbian identity. Postmodern subjectivity is frequently understood to be "positional" – constructed through one's position within social structures such as the family. In *Fun Home*, Bechdel explores both her own and her father's sexual identities as they were worked out within the family (here, a traditionally patriarchal one). She also spatializes this positionality through her depiction of how the family's house shaped and was shaped by their identities. Throughout her childhood, her father spent his time endlessly renovating their house – a Victorian Gothic Revival, fittingly enough, since it is "haunted by the uncanny ghosts of repressed desires."[27] The constant renovations may be understood as a displacement of her father's continual attempts to construct a normative, heterosexual identity for himself, and his failure to do so. His historical restoration of the house was, Bechdel recalls, "his passion, and I mean passion in every sense of the word. Libidinal. Manic. Martyred."[28] On this page, she depicts her father in a Christ-like, "on the road to Calvary" posture, weighed down by the carved column he's carrying. His stooped figure barely fits beneath the roof of the entirely black house that looms behind him like a shadow, emphasizing the constriction of the space – a parallel to the constriction of the role of heterosexual, patriarchal father to which he consigned himself.

This constriction is apparent in many of the book's representations of Bechdel and her father in and around the house. The first chapter's title page, for example, depicts her father from the waist up, his face turned defiantly outward but half in shadow, framed by the front door and its doorjamb, shutters, and porch supports – an excessive framing that strongly suggests confinement. The chapter's title, printed beneath, is "Old Father, Old Artificer," a quotation from the conclusion of James Joyce's *Portrait of the Artist as a Young Man*. Joyce's works become reference points for Bechdel's thinking through not only of her father's identity, but also of her own: *Fun Home* is a self-portrait of the artist as a young woman. Bechdel's father was, she recalls, "an alchemist of appearance, a savant of surface, a Daedalus of décor," who "used his skillful artifice not to make things, but to make things appear to be what they were not."[29] The Bechdel family was a part of his artifice: the children "lent an air of authenticity" to his normative façade, behind which he struggled with his conflicted sexuality.[30] "It's tempting to suggest, in retrospect," Bechdel remarks, "that our family was a sham, that our house was not a real home at all but a simulacrum of one. Yet we really were a family, and we really did live in those period rooms."[31]

The Bechdels' family life is figuratively and literally enclosed within the house, which materializes around the narrative through the book's covers, endpapers, and frontispieces. On the cover, there's a snapshot of Bechdel as a child, sitting with her father on the front porch, multiply framed, as in the "Old Father, Old Artificer" image. Behind the photograph, the cover is decorated with a reproduction of flowered wallpaper from the house. The wallpaper also covers the front and back endpapers, encompassing the narrative as it surrounded Bechdel inside the house. The wallpaper resembles, but is not the same as, the girly pink flowered wallpaper Bechdel's father, over her vehement protests, puts up in her bedroom, confining her, as he confined himself, in an ill-fitting gender identity.

The frontispiece depicts the exterior of half the house with three members of the family revealed in circular cutaways that emphasize their confinement and their isolation from one another. This isolation is repeated in several other places in the text, where each family member appears enclosed in a different window. On one of these scenes, Bechdel observes, "Our selves were all we had."[32] The back frontispiece provides the other half of the house with the two remaining members of the family. Although the two parts of the image of the family appear united inside the book,[33] on the two frontispieces, the front and back halves are reversed (the right side is in front, the left in back), as though the divided halves of the house and the members of the family were headed in opposite directions. These images foreshadow the future, in which Bechdel, deciding to live openly as a lesbian, takes a different path from her father. On the title page, the peaked roof of the house frames "Fun Home," but there are no sides or border, as though leaving the space open for Bechdel's eventual escape, both echoing and refiguring that of Stephen Dedalus from Ireland at the end of Joyce's *Portrait of the Artist*.

The effects of physical spaces on those who inhabit them are also explored in Chris Ware's "graphic novel-in-a box," *Building Stories*, a fragmented narrative of the lives of an apartment building and its four tenants. Ware is fascinated by "how houses and buildings affect the shapes and structures of our memories, and how these shapes can continue to live on in our minds years or decades once the buildings are gone."[34] The novel's fragmented form reflects its city dwellers' experience of space and time, and the interpenetration of thought and memory.

Comprising "14 distinctively discrete Books, Booklets, Magazines, Newspapers, and Pamphlets," as described on the box that contains it, *Building Stories* is an experiment in disjunctive form, perhaps the most radical one yet in "hard" copy, as opposed to electronic texts and hypertexts.[35] Like Julio Cortázar's borderline postmodernist novel *Hopscotch*, the parts of *Building Stories* can be read in any order, and the narrative – the characters' intertwined stories and their symmetries and counterpoints – must be pieced together, "built," by the reader.

Building Stories can be seen as a three-dimensional exploration of how form and content interact and merge. The nature of the narrative in each part determines its format, which, in turn, determines how the reader physically handles – and reads – it. The story of a young woman's solitary evening walk in the snow, for example, takes the form of a 3½″ high by 7″ wide pamphlet that unfolds lengthwise into four segments that trace her path, segment by segment and panel by panel. Halfway through her walk, the reader turns the pamphlet over and continues until she arrives back at the apartment building. The text thus unfolds (in a movement reminiscent of *The Prose of the Trans-Siberian*) in space and time, like the walk itself, and formally reproduces its circularity, from home and back. In turn, the reader's physical experience of the text, its unfolding and reversing, reproduces the walk's motion and temporality.

Ware is acutely aware of the reader's physical and cognitive (which are no more separable than form and content) experience of his work. "In comics you make the strip come alive by reading it, by experiencing it beat by beat as you would playing music," he says.[36] This rhythm is produced through the sizes and arrangement of the panels and gutters: tightly packing many narrow panels into a single tier can speed up the rhythm, for example, but fewer, longer panels with bigger gutters in between can slow it down. A splash page can freeze a moment for as long as the reader wishes to contemplate it. The graphic novel's page also, as we've seen, has an architectural gestalt (panels as windows and tiers as stories): "Another way is to pull back and consider the composition all at once," Ware continues, "as you would the façade of a building."[37] This spatiality of the page can be extended beyond two dimensions, thus defining the general structure of the graphic novel: "You can look at a comic as you would look at a structure that you could turn around in your mind and see all sides of at once."[38]

"The crossings or hybridizations of the media release great new force and energy as by fission or fusion," Marshall McLuhan observed in his 1964 essay, "Hybrid Energy: Les Liaisons Dangereuses."[39] The crossings of literature and art in postmodernist novels that incorporate images into the text and the hybridization of image and text in graphic novels have created new forms of fiction with which to explore the time and space of human experience. It is ironic that, as texts increasingly "dematerialize" into digital forms that become displays on screens, electronic images of themselves, these combinations of words and images make readers engage with and sometimes become aware of the importance of the materiality of the text as never before. They offer new ways of conceiving of the book as a physical object and reading as a physical interaction, not just a mental one. They create complex relations between form and content, and, in many cases, demonstrate their inseparability. They challenge readers to develop different modes of interpretation for understanding the powerful synergies of word and image. One cannot predict how far these combinations, hybrids, and syntheses of word and image will reach, but one could hardly doubt that they will continue to expand, redefine, and reinvent the future of the book and the literature of the future.

Further Reading

Baetens, Jan, and Hugo Frey. *The Graphic Novel: An Introduction.* Cambridge: Cambridge University Press, 2015.
Chute, Hillary. "Graphic Narrative," in Joe Bray, Alison Gibbons, and Brian McHale, eds., *The Routledge Companion to Experimental Literature.* New York: Routledge, 2012. 407–419.
Chute, Hillary, and Patrick Jagoda, eds. *Comics & Media.* A special issue of *Critical Inquiry* 40, no. 3 (Spring 2014): 1–284.
Drucker, Johanna. *The Visible Word: Experimental Typography and Modern Art, 1909–1923.* Chicago: University of Chicago Press, 1994.
Eisner, Will. *Graphic Storytelling and Visual Narrative.* New York: Norton, 2008.
Gardner, Jared. *Projections: Comics and the History of Twenty-First Century Storytelling.* Stanford, CA: Stanford University Press, 2012.

Gardner, Jared, and David Herman, eds. *Graphic Narratives and Narrative Theory.* A special issue of *SubStance: A Review of Theory and Literary Criticism* 40, no. 1, issue 124 (2011): 3–202.

McCloud, Scott. *Understanding Comics: The Invisible Art.* New York: HarperPerennial, 1994.

NOTES

1 Laurence Sterne, *The Life and Opinions of Tristram Shandy, Gentleman* (New York: Modern Library, 1941), 28, 426–427.

2 David V. Erdman, *The Illuminated Blake* (New York: Dover, 1974), 10.

3 The term "graphic novel" was popularized by Will Eisner in reference to *A Contract with God* (1978), his collection of four thematically related graphic short stories.

4 "Metafictions" call attention to their own fictionality and narrative conventions. In many metafictions, the author appears in the narrative and directly addresses the reader. William H. Gass, *Willie Masters' Lonesome Wife* (1968; reprint, Normal, IL: Dalkey Archive Press, 1992), n.p. (There are no page numbers in the book.)

5 Karen L. Schiff, "Reading Body-Books: *Willie Masters' Lonesome Wife* reconsiders *Tristram Shandy*" (Normal, IL: Dalkey Archive Press), accessed March 12, 2016, www.dalkeyarchive.com/reading-body-books-willie-masters-lonesome-wife-reconsiders-tristram-shandy/.

6 Kurt Vonnegut, *Breakfast of Champions* (New York: Delacorte Press, 1973), 5.

7 Ibid., 23–24.

8 Ibid., 10.

9 Ibid., 11.

10 Ishmael Reed, *Mumbo Jumbo* (1972; New York: Scribner, 1996), 62.

11 Theresa Hak Kyung Cha, *Dictee* (1982; Berkeley, CA: Third Woman Press, 1995), 39, 34–36.

12 Ibid., 79.

13 Ibid., 75.

14 Ibid., 74.

15 Ibid., 24; 44, and 59.

16 Ibid., 119, 93.

17 Ibid., 98.

18 Jonathan Safran Foer, *Extremely Loud & Incredibly Close* (2005; New York: Houghton Mifflin, 2006), 19, 125.

19 Ibid., 120–123.

20 Ibid., 281.

21 Ibid., 280–284.

22 Ibid., 59, 62, 205, and 327–end.

23 Hillary Chute, "Temporality and Seriality in Spiegelman's *In the Shadow of No Towers*," *American Periodicals: A Journal of History, Criticism, and Bibliography*, 17, no. 2 (2007): 228–244, 235.

24 Art Spiegelman, *In the Shadow of No Towers* (New York: Viking, 2004). As with Spiegelman's earlier works, *Maus I* and *II*, categorizing this work as fiction is problematic, although one could argue that its fictionality lies in the comics that

compose the second half of the book. Yet, like several other graphic works discussed in this chapter, such as Salomon's *Life? or Art?* and Bechdel's *Fun Home*, it is a hybrid of historical fact (including parts of Spiegelman's own life) and fiction. In order to deal with such hybrid works, Hillary Chute refers to them as "graphic narratives" in *Graphic Women: Life Narrative and Contemporary Comics*; Lynda Barry has suggested the portmanteau term "autobifictionalography." One might see these works in more simple terms as "fictionalized graphic autobiographies."

25 Martha Kuhlman, "The Traumatic Temporality of Art Spiegelman's *In the Shadow of No Towers*," *The Journal of Popular Culture* 40, no. 5 (2007): 849–866. 850.

26 Spiegelman, *In the Shadow of No Towers*, 8.

27 Robin Lydenberg, "Under Construction: Alison Bechdel's *Fun Home: A Family Tragicomic*," *European Journal of English Studies* 16, no. 1 (April 2012): 57–68, 58.

28 Alison Bechdel, *Fun Home: A Family Tragicomic* (Boston and New York: Houghton Mifflin, 2006), 7.

29 Ibid., 6, 16.

30 Ibid., 13.

31 Ibid., 17.

32 Ibid., 139.

33 Ibid., 134.

34 Quoted in Chris Mautner, "'I Hoped That the Book Would Just Be Fun': A Brief Interview with Chris Ware," *The Comics Journal*, October 10, 2012, accessed 12 March 2016, www.tcj.com/i-hoped-that-the-book-would-just-be-fun-a-brief-interview-with-chris-ware/.

35 Chris Ware, *Building Stories* (New York: Pantheon, 2012).

36 Quoted in Daniel Raeburn, *Chris Ware* (New Haven, CT: Yale University Press, 2004), 25.

37 Ibid.

38 Ibid.

39 Marshall McLuhan, *Understanding Media: The Extensions of Man* (1964; Cambridge, MA: MIT Press, 1994), 48, 53.

II

ASTRID ENSSLIN

Electronic Fictions

Television, the Internet, and the Future of Digital Fiction

Introduction

This chapter focuses on a contemporary literary art form that emerged in the 1970s and 1980s in the wake of postmodernism and particularly poststructuralism, and has been developing alongside evolving electronic and digital media up to the present day. Digital fiction, as I will refer to it, is a form of literary, narrative expression that embeds the medium-specific elements afforded by the technologies used to create and consume it. It is digital-born, which means that it depends for its interaction and understanding on the distinct characteristics of the digital technologies (the hardware and software) chosen by their writer-programmers, who often work in teams rather than as individuals. Therefore, with digital fictions we cannot pin down one specific material manifestation, such as a printed text, because this would cause them to lose their characteristic dynamic, fluid quality as well as a strong sense of medium-specificity for their analysis.[1] Key genres of digital-born fiction include Interactive Fiction (IF), hypertext fiction, hypermedia fiction (produced using, for example, Flash, QuickTime, and JavaScript), app fiction for tablets and smartphones, as well as some videogames.[2]

To begin with, I shall outline some important theoretical, literary, and media developments that preceded and heralded digital fiction in its manifold forms. This discussion will involve the role of television vis-à-vis specific developments in postmodern fiction writing, as well as predigital forms of nonlinear writing such as protohypertext novels. I will then zoom in on diverse movements and forms of digital fiction over time, starting from interactive and hypertext fiction in the 1980s and the ways in which hypertext was theorized as the "embodiment" of poststructuralist critical theory. I will then look at the arrival of digital multimedia (hypermedia) in the 1990s, which gave rise to new forms of digital literary multimodality. Similarly, the growth of the games industry around the same time inspired various forms of literary-creative experimentation with the power of the program code vis-à-vis the reader as player or indeed the object of textual play. Finally, I shall examine how the rise of (micro)blogging and social media in the early twenty-first century has generated new forms of participatory fiction writing online. The last section will follow with a discussion of new platforms for creative literary expression, such as tabloids and smartphones, and how they have given rise to augmented, or medially enhanced, ebooks.

Digital fiction is one of the most recent and fastest developing phenomena in postmodern literature; it is generating new, experimental forms with almost every new artifact produced and incorporating newly evolving technologies as they emerge. Therefore, it is worth dedicating part of this essay to some speculations about where the future of digital fiction and literary "reading" more generally may lie. This discussion will form the final section of this essay and involve some deliberations about multimodal embodiment and ludoliterary artifacts, as well as the creative implications of digital and metamodernism.

Analog Precursors: Television and Proto-Hypertext

There are two key analog precursors of digital fiction: television and protohypertext (that is, predigital forms of nonlinear, networked, and cross-referenced writing). The former inspired forms of postmodern fiction writing that reflected the impact of the screen and viewer-driven channel zapping, whereas the latter foreshadowed the importance of electronic hyperlinking, nonlinear sequencing of pages that are characteristic of digital hypertext writing, as well as other forms of electronic narrative.

The rise of postmodernism in the 1960s coincided roughly with the popularization of television, "the postmodern medium *par excellence*."[3] The ease with which a range of postmodernist theories and concepts, such as hyperreality, simulation, fragmentation, decentering, pastiche, and intertextuality, offer themselves to television analysis is therefore hardly surprising.[4] Television epitomizes Guy Debord's idea of a postmodern "society of the spectacle," where "[t]he spectacle is not a collection of images; it is a social relation between people that is mediated by images."[5] The blurring boundaries between reality and simulation, where "there is no difference between the image and other orders of experience," were reflected artistically in postmodern literary fiction such as Robert Coover's short story "The Babysitter" (1969) and Thomas Pynchon's 1990 novel *Vineland*.[6] "The Babysitter" portrays the idea of the hyperreal both intra- and extradiegetically (within and outside the fictional world of the text), leaving readers wondering what actually did happen in the story, or whether the fragmented plot segments should indeed be understood as one of the characters' own experience of watching randomly sequenced, or "zapped," television episodes. *Vineland* in turn displays the "ontological plurality" of an entire "television world," suggesting a continuity between the worlds inhabited by audiences and TV characters.[7]

Clearly, the connectivity of Web 1.0 and the participatory nature of Web 2.0 weren't yet in sight in the 1960s and 1970s (despite visionary concepts such as Theodor Nelson's "docuverse" [1974] and Marshall McLuhan's "global village" [1962]).[8] Nevertheless, at the time, print precursors of nonlinear writing commonly associated with hypertextual media began to herald postmodern tenets of decentering (deconstructing logocentric thought), the rhizome, and the idea of the writerly text propagated by Barthes.[9] Important examples of such protohypertextual writing include a range of postmodernist novels such as Julio Cortázar's *Hopscotch* (1966) (*Rayuela* [1963]) and Vladimir Nabokov's *Pale Fire* (1962).[10] *Hopscotch* offers readers two different methods of reading: a sequential one, from chapters 1 to 56, or an alternative, crisscrossing path suggested by a character map in the text, starting with chapter 73 and proceeding in an apparently arbitrary fashion. Readers of *Pale Fire* are made to navigate between the individual sections of a 999-line poem and an extensive body of footnoted comments in a quasi-hypertextual, multilinear manner.[11]

Whilst canonical postmodernist novels such as those mentioned earlier in this section were not intended to appeal to mass consumerist, and specifically younger, audiences, other forms of proto-hypertextual, nonlinear writing did (and still do): early popular game culture (between 1970 and 1990) generated a host of so-called Choose Your Own Adventure books, in which readers select highly individualized reading paths according to their personal answers to questions posed by the narrator, or decisions they are asked to make in the storyworld. Works such as Edward Packard's *The Cave of Time* (1979) and R. A. Montgomery's *Space and Beyond* (1980) resemble the experience of playing an adventure game, which is corroborated by the fact that reader-players are addressed by the narrative in the second person, thus drawing them into the storyworld as the protagonist, player-character, or proto-first-person avatar. It is this particular stylistic feature that they have in common with Interactive Fiction, another form of experimental, ludic (playful and/or game-like) fiction writing that developed roughly at the same time using newly evolving digital technologies, which I will turn to in the following section.

Embodying Poststructuralist Theory? Interactive Fiction and "Serious" Hypertext

The 1980s and 1990s saw a historical shift from a society dominated by television, or "sit-back" media, to so-called "lean-forward,"[12] networked, and user-focused media, such as the home computer, the Internet, and the World Wide Web. The focus on a single screen through which masses of viewers would watch highly centralized media content shifted to multiscreen media, which epitomized like never before the plurality and fragmentation of mediated and mediatized reality. Yet even years before the actual advent and popularization of the World Wide Web, digital technologies were introduced to mass audiences that gave rise to radically new forms of postmodern literary creativity. The two main pre-WWW genres of digital fiction were Interactive Fiction and so-called "serious" hypertext fiction.

Interactive fictions (IFs) such as Steve Meretzky's *Planetfall* (1983) and Adam Cadre's *Photopia* (1988) are prime examples of ludic, or playful, digital postmodernism.[13] Readers assume the double role of extradiegetic "interactor" and diegetic "player character"[14] – a combination of reader-narratee and character-protagonist. They type natural language commands, such as "go north" or "open gate," into an interpreter that displays narrative content in verbal form. These commands are subsequently analyzed by a parser, which in turn triggers new narrative output from the system to the extratextual reader. However, the narrative output, which addresses readers in the second person, draws them into the storyworld by making "you" the crucial and driving element of the diegesis. This playful coexistence of various diegetic roles leads to myriad highly subjective plotlines and readings, which are often based on trial-and-error navigation loops and readers' attempts to apply their linguistic and conceptual creativity to "writerly"[15] narrative progress.

Many examples of IF exist, however, that do not afford narrative progression as we might expect it from a work of fiction. Nick Montfort's *Ad Verbum* (2000),[16] for instance, satirizes its own generic characteristics metafictionally and metamedially. Inspired by Oulipian linguistic and literary self-reflexivity, its aesthetic is based largely on language games, such as verbal puns, synonymy, and alliterations, and rather than projecting a complex storyworld in the vein of text adventures and other interactive fictions, "its creative focus lies in the micro- rather than macrostructures of narrative language."[17] Similarly, Emily Short's *Galatea* (2000)[18] revolves primarily around a dialogue between a statue-come-to-life and the reader-interlocutor, the latter of whom has the challenging task of finding out anything and everything about Galatea and her problematic relationship with her creator, Pygmalion. Hence, much like the novel has done since its emergence in the eighteenth century, and particularly in modernism and postmodernism, interactive fiction has used its own formal constraints to mock its own traditions and meanings.

Situated less on the ludic and more on the deconstructivist side of digital postmodernism, the first hypertext fictions were published by Eastgate Systems in the years immediately preceding the arrival of the World Wide Web. Hypertext writers took advantage of new software systems like Hypercard (a hypermedia editing and programming system using stacks and cards as desktop metaphors; first released in 1987) that were shipped free with contemporaneous Macintosh computers (for example, the Apple IIGS), as well as the tailor-made Storyspace program, a hypertext writing, editing, and reading application designed in the early 1980s specifically for Eastgate System's "serious" hypertext fictions, such as Michael Joyce's *afternoon: a story* (1987), Stuart Moulthrop's *Victory Garden* (1991), and Shelley Jackson's *Patchwork Girl* (1995).[19] *Afternoon*, for example, is a psychological hypertext novel featuring a homodiegetic narrator, Peter, who – so the narrative suggests – has lost his son in an accident. His overall confusion as well as feelings of personal bereavement, guilt, and failed responsibility are portrayed formally by the various layers of hypertextuality, yet due to the fiction's high levels of multilinearity and nonclosure, and the resultant overall feeling of disorientation, the ultimate answer to the question of what actually did happen in the story is left to the reader to answer and very much depends on his or her narrative and navigational choices.

Of particular importance for the debates surrounding digital postmodernism was the so-called first wave of hypertext theory,[20] which assumed that literary hypertext was an almost direct embodiment, or material manifestation, of numerous poststructuralist theoretical concepts. In his controversial and much debated convergence thesis, George Landow put forward the idea that "critical theory promises to theorize hypertext and hypertext promises to embody and thereby test aspects of theory, particularly those concerning textuality, narrative and the roles or functions of reader and writer."[21] Meanwhile, second-wave digital fiction scholars have moved away from these somewhat reductionist assumptions and have been focusing instead on close narratological, semiotic, and ludostylistic analyses of individual works.[22] Similarly, what we might call a third and more fledgling wave of digital fiction scholarship has been emerging around empirical approaches to studying actual reader responses to digital fiction and its specific interactive, narrative, and multimodal elements.[23]

New Generations: Hypermedia, Cybertext, and Beyond

Hypertext fiction has, since its inception, undergone major creative shifts and transformations. These "generational"[24] shifts have been afforded by the experimental possibilities offered by newly evolving digital technologies. The first generational shift, from hypertext to hypermedia, happened around the mid-1990s, which saw the launch of Mosaic, the world's first graphic browser (1993), as well as the popularization of the World Wide Web with HTML as its main mark-up language. HTML enabled the encoding and digital representation of diverse semiotic systems comprising text, graphics, audio (speech, sound, and music), animation, and film. Using, for instance, HTML, JavaScript, Flash, and Shockwave technologies, hypermedia enable a variety of pastiche and collage techniques, and thus a distinctly multimodal approach to literary creativity: "As opposed to first generation hypertexts, which use images sparsely and mainly as illustrative or decorative means, hypermedia writings form a coherent intertextual, intermedial, and multimodal whole, which is more than the sum of its constituent parts."[25] Amongst the most frequently discussed hypermedia fictions are geniwate and Deena Larsen's Flash-based *The Princess Murderer* (2003) and Lance Olsen and Tim Guthrie's hypermedia avant-pop novel, *10:01* (2005).

In *Canonizing Hypertext*, I describe a second general shift, from hypermedia to cybertext, manifested in digital literature programmed in such a way as to empower the software code and cause readers to "play against" the textual machine.[26] Inspired by the growth in the games industry and gamer culture from the 1990s onward, cybertext writers embed interactive, playful elements in the text that make readers part of a cybernetic feedback loop and diminish the agency (interactive freedom) they have vis-à-vis the reading process. In some extreme experimental forms, this has given rise to what I have termed physio-cybertexts,[27] which physically embody the reader in the software and hardware underlying the digital fiction. *The Breathing Wall* (2004) by Kate Pullinger, Stefan Schemat, and babel,[28] for instance, runs an especially developed software that measures the reader's breathing rate and intensity, and releases or withholds key textual information (clues for resolving the murder mystery, in this case) in line with "breathed" input.

Rustad proposes a further, fourth generation of digital fiction, which he refers to as a genre of "social media literature."[29] Since the first decade of the twenty-first century, social networking and microblogging sites, such as Facebook and Twitter, have given rise to highly participatory forms of digital literary engagement, or "co-construction," leading to radically new genres of digital fiction writing, such as Twitterfiction and "small stories" told through Facebook updates.[30] Participatory storytelling through social media can be seen as "a kind of performance, allowing for all kinds of creative interplay between [users'] offline and online selves."[31] Authors of Twitterfiction pitch their tweets (posts of no more than 140 characters each) specifically at their followers' expectation of being served minimalist snippets of information in a piecemeal and often abbreviated fashion. Matt Richtel's 2008 *Twiller* ("Twitter thriller"), for example, grounds its method of creating suspense in the real-time nature of the constantly evolving Twitter stream, "providing followers with short bursts of information and the tension that arises from knowing that the protagonist has no more clue as to how events will turn out than they do."[32]

Participatory electronic fiction through social media can take a myriad of forms, depending on the technologies and platforms chosen by users and writers. In a nonfictional approach to narrative tweeting, Nigerian-American writer Teju Cole describes his information-laden, sensationalist, documentary-style tweets as a new form of *fait divers*, "a compressed report of an unusual happening."[33] Much as in flash fiction, readers are made to construct the entire, mostly shocking news story from posts such as "In Ikotun, Mrs Ojo, who was terrified of armed robbers, died in her barricaded home, of smoke inhalation."[34] A new way of publishing short stories through social networking sites was explored by Alex Epstein, who published an electronic version of his microstory collection, "For My Next Illusion I Will Use Wings" (2012) on the Facebook page "Electric Literature."[35] The stories, some of which only span a few lines, are displayed in individual windows, accompanied by the "likes" and comments of other Facebook users.

Another recent form of participatory literary engagement is dedicated collaborative online fiction-writing platforms (for example, *Protagonize*, *One Million Monkeys*, and *StoryPassers*). They have sprung up in the past decade, offering "the perfect opportunity for nonprofessionals to write literary texts and gain recognition."[36] In line with the Web 2.0 concepts of user-generated content (UGC) and prosumption (a blend of "production" and "consumption" denoting the merging of producer and consumer, and writer and reader in networked media),[37] digital platforms and their interactive constraints shape both aesthetic expression and the meaning potential of collaborative digital writing. By the same token, the concept of the "wreader" (a blend between "writer" and "reader"), first coined by Landow to describe in a somewhat misleading way the alleged empowerment of hypertext readers to quasi-coauthors,[38] has come into its own. As Klaiber puts it, "the participant of a collaborative online writing project may truly be considered a 'reader-author' or a 'wreader.' It is, on the one hand, the interplay between multiple wreaders and emerging narrative, and on the other hand, the interaction of multiple wreaders that evoke the double plot in collaborative fiction."[39] Thus, by "double plot," Klaiber means the coexistence of two narrative levels in digital collaborative fiction: the paratextual interaction between users, documented in their metacommentary, and the actual coauthored plot as it evolves through their fictional turn-taking.

Arguably the most prolific type of participatory writing on the web is fan fiction, which is fiction written by fans of popular media texts, such as TV series, novels, films, and videogames. Particular theoretical and critical interest has been raised by fans constructing alternative and highly complex sexualities in their writings, thus creating what Halberstam refers to as counterpublics.[40] Similarly, the lack of rules and the rise of the fan-author as quasi-equivalent to the likes of J. K. Rowling and Stephenie Meyer have been attributed to "fandom's postmodern moment,"[41] and the rise of widely accessible fan communities via multifandom archives such as FanFiction.net has given global dimensions to what used to be a largely localized set of social and creative practices.

New Platforms, New Narratives

The previous looked at the medium-specificity of digital fiction mostly from a software perspective, taking for granted that the core hardware components used are desktop and laptop computers. That said, the past five to ten years have seen a sea change from static to mobile devices – most importantly, smartphones and tablets – and this technological paradigm shift has given rise to a multitude of new narrative forms. Indeed, the alternatives to keyboard and mouse interaction offered by mobile media have inspired digital writers to experiment with radically new forms of literary creativity. Published under the label "app fiction," fictional artifacts are now read using touchpad technologies that enable readers to simply swipe and tab on the interface. In Inkle's interactive adaptation of *Frankenstein*,[42] for example, readers turn book pages by swiping across the screen, as well as choosing – much as in a choose-your-own-adventure book or point-and-click adventure game – where to take the narrative. Readers are addressed by "you" and are thereby drawn into the storyworld, where they take the role of Victor's friend and confidant, talking to him directly and triggering different responses and narrative paths depending on the choices they make. This direct, kinetic, and communicative involvement of the reader leads to a strong sense of embodiment and presence as readers are made to invest in and reflect about the narrative (and often moral) decisions they make.

The concepts of embodiment, presence, and immersion have been all-pervasive in discourses of cyberculture and digital postmodernism.[43] As users become part of the cybernetic feedback loop and have themselves impersonated by the likes of avatars and other forms of online representation, they develop a strong sense of reality and immediacy. This is partly due to the direct, kinetic interaction with hardware and software, and partly to the multisensory experience of reading and playing. In "New Generations:

Electronic Fictions

Hypermedia, Cybertext and Beyond" section, I mentioned the multimodal nature of hypermedia, which has been continued and further developed to the present day. The recent games industry focus on next-generation 3D technologies, such as the Oculus Rift (a virtual reality headset for stereoscopic 3D gaming, allowing 360° head tracking and hyperperipheral vision), is a response to the growing audience need for hyperrealistic and hyperembodied gaming experiences (note the emphasis on "hyper," meaning "beyond natural," thus enabling superhuman experiences of embodiment).

In a similar move to enabling enhanced multisensory, embodied experiences without changing between hardware platforms, ebook publishers have started moving away from this historical legacy and experimenting with new forms of multimodality, interactivity, and connectivity. Whilst ebooks, in their most traditional formats, are strongly anchored in print culture, thereby refashioning the book in its material form, vooks (video books), also called "advanced ebooks," "V-books," or "digi-books," are app-based, multimedia artifacts for tablet computers and smartphones, combining written text with video, maps, illustrations, ephemera like authors' research materials, and deleted manuscript sections, as well as links to social networking sites and the Internet more widely. In an attempt to modify and amplify Gerard Genette's concept of paratextuality and particularly epitextuality[44] for recent ebook developments, Ellen McCracken uses the terms "centrifugality" and "centripetality" to refer to the kind of outward and inward movements afforded by epitextual material that either draws the reader away from the text per se (by tapping links to other readers' comments, author information, or interviews, for instance) or into it (by moving from a browse through Amazon's website and the reader comments posted there to the actual vook itself, for instance).[45] The digi-book amplification of Jack Kerouac's *On the Road*, for example, provides a host of centripetal elements, such as "photos, audio of Kerouac reading, his essays on the Beat Generation and other writing, maps and sketches of his late 1940s trips across the United States and Mexico, textual comparisons between the scroll and the first edition, commentary, memos and letters, and photos and brief biographies of the members of the Beat Generation. Throughout the digital text of the novel are links in the margins to the corresponding biographies of the people that various characters represent."[46] Thus, electronic fictions, whether digital-born or ebook-derived, are increasingly turning into convergent media that, for their analysis and theorization, require a comprehensive, cross-disciplinary range of skills, thought processes, and methodological frameworks, not only transcending established disciplinary boundaries but indeed creating their own fields of investigation within the overarching paradigm of digital humanities.

New Convergences: The Future of Digital Fiction and Literary Reading

The present and future of electronic fiction, or, if you will, its post-postmodern existence, is and will remain strongly shaped by multiple convergences, involving all three classical components of media research: producers, texts, and audiences. Participatory fiction writing as covered in the "New Generations: Hypermedia, Cybertext and Beyond" section exemplifies the convergence between producers and consumers. The convergence between platforms and modes of representation mentioned in the preceding section pertains primarily to the textual aspect of the triad yet simultaneously affects both production and consumption practices. This section attempts to convey further, new convergences by examining some current trends and emergent formations in digital fiction that can be expected to grow in the future and transform our understanding and practices of literary reading.

Twenty-first-century media convergence transgresses our conventional understanding of multisensory perception and multimodal representation. It involves location-based, site-specific experiences exemplified by participatory and immersive theater (Punchdrunk, for example), vertical dance (Kate Lawrence, for example), and GPS-based mobile narratives (Blast Theory, for example). Hence, fictional experiences are becoming increasingly embodied in the sense that our actual rather than virtual bodies are part of a physical, three-dimensional setting that merges intra- and extradiegesis and makes narrative progress contingent on readers' mobility and interaction with the spaces in which fictional worlds are situated or "installed." By the same token, site-specific digital fictions are no longer intended for private, individual consumption. The 2015 digital fiction installation, Dreaming Methods' *WALLPAPER*, by Judi Alston and Andy Campbell, was set up in an art gallery (Sheffield, United Kingdom) and accessed by numerous, co-situated users at the same time. Readers/players experience *WALLPAPER* through the eyes of the protagonist, a middle-aged man who, after the death of his mother, returns to the isolated, derelict family mansion in the North Yorkshire Moors to discover the secret behind the mysterious room he was never allowed to enter during his childhood. An employee of a futuristic corporation, the player-character needs to unlock the room to be able to test a new technology with a view to reconstructing and "playing back" the past. WALLPAPER is conceptualized as a travelling installation, which will exploit the characteristics of the sites where it will be located, and the specific physical and atmospheric aspects of each site will shape readers' experiences and understandings of the text.

The concept of embodiment is likely to attain even further reaching significance in the wake of the popularization of virtual reality technologies and wearable technologies. The MIT Media Lab's recently prototyped "wearable" book, or "sensory fiction," *The Girl Who Was Plugged in* (James Tiptree Jr., originally published in 1973), connects an augmented book with a wearable vest through which readers' emotions activate changes in temperature and ambient lighting. Thus, "[b]y using a combination of networked sensors and actuators, the sensory fiction author is provided with new means of conveying plot, mood, and emotion while still allowing space for the reader's imagination. These tools can be wielded to create an immersive storytelling experience tailored to the reader."[47]

Another trend in electronic fiction that has emerged in the past decade and promises to grow in the future is the phenomenon of literary gaming.[48] Fictional works that fall within this category combine literary reading and gaming, and can roughly be described as hybrids between ludic digital fictions (digital-born fictions that exhibit specific game-like and playful mechanisms) and literary games (videogames that contain a strong element of literary language). Hence, literary gaming constitutes another form of convergence, albeit in terms of cognitive states rather than platforms and modes.

Literary gaming happens along a spectrum of playful activities, and these activities give rise to a spectrum of cognitive engagement. On the left hand of the spectrum is deep attention,[49] which is a cognitive condition that allows us to focus on an artifact like a print novel for an extended period of time without, however, losing a sense of the actual world surrounding us. Hyperattention is a state where the activity in which players are immersed becomes a basic human priority or need (like food or drink). Hyperattention occurs frequently with people immersed in game worlds, who find it difficult to tear themselves away from gameplay. As far as literary gaming is concerned, there is a literary and a ludic end of the spectrum, where the literary end correlates with deep attention and the ludic end with hyperattention.

Two striking, albeit radically different, examples of ludic digital fiction are episodes 3 and 5 of Kate Pullinger et al.'s *Inanimate Alice* (2005–2016), and Tale of Tales' *The Path* (2009).[50] *Inanimate Alice* sits near the literary end of the spectrum: it is a digital story that needs to be read, first and foremost, yet it contains mini-games, such as a Russian Doll catching game in Episode 3 ("Russia") and a dexterity-type skateboard game ending in a cliffhanger situation to implicitly announce the next episode (Episode 5, "Hometown 2"). *The Path* is first and foremost a 3D horror game (and therefore nearer the ludic end of the spectrum), yet it contains literary devices, such as interior monologues, superimposed onto the 3D storyworld, providing psychological and contextual information about the backstory, the storyworld, and its dramatis personae.

A third important contemporary trend in fiction writing follows the paradigm of digital modernism. Adding another semantic component to the concept of convergence, digital modernism "seeks to build bridges between modernism and digital literature, print textuality and computational technologies, literary criticism and media studies."[51] Works that lend themselves to this critical framework offer new, avant-garde ways of "making it new" and rebel against the dictates of networked mass media and popular culture by following an aesthetic of difficulty. At the same time, however, they make use of the very technologies underlying mass culture, albeit to subvert their "culinary" uses (to use a Brechtian term). Judd Morrissey's *The Jew's Daughter* (2000), for example, can be read as a database narrative in the Manovichian sense that "database is potential and narrative is its resulting output."[52] Subverting the mass cultural expectations of hypertextual navigation, *The Jew's Daughter* operates via links that replace and thereby delete sections of the same page rather than opening new windows. Reader interaction therefore changes the text in subtle ways, thereby diminishing reader agency and navigational transparency. Since most digital fiction writers operate under an experimentalist, neo-avant-garde paradigm, it can be expected that they will continue to explore the subversive potential of newly evolving technologies to critique and question the conventions and expectations of mass media consumption.

Finally, an increasing number of digital fictions are and will engage with metamodernist concerns. Generally speaking, metamodernism is understood to converge in a compromise or reconciliation of modernist engagement and postmodern ironic distance.[53] Of particular importance here is Vermeulen and van den Akker's core metamodernist concept, the "aesth-ethical": "[a]esth-ethical commitment pervades ... metamodernist writing: it is opposed to the injustices of global capitalism, concerned by the increased digitalization and hyper-reality of society, conscious of the shifting social relationships in a globalizing world, and it hopes for a shared sustainable future, however untenable that may be. In other words, metamodernism is concerned with global ethics."[54] Importantly, this adds a keen sense of socio-political engagement to an artistic and critical tradition that for over a century concerned itself mostly with nonreferential, structuralist, and formal concerns – a tendency for which digital fiction has frequently been criticized. Thus, what we may call engaged digital fictions, such as Sachiko Hayashi's semi-documentary hypermedia remix of historical human-rights abuses, *Last Meal Requested* (2003), and Zoe Quinn's 2013 Twine fiction-game, *Depression Quest*, which stages the loss of agency perceived by sufferers of depression, are important examples of how electronic writing can

and will increasingly succeed in blending an aesthetic concern with technological innovation and aesthetic subversion with a strong commitment to
providing new avenues of coming to terms with global human issues.

Further Reading

Baldwin, Sandy. *The Internet Unconscious: On the Subject of Electronic Literature.*
London: Bloomsbury, 2015.
Bell, Alice, Astrid Ensslin, and Hans K. Rustad. *Analyzing Digital Fiction.* New York:
Routledge, 2013.
Brillenburg Wurth, Kiene. *Between Page and Screen: Remaking Literature through
Cinema and Cyberspace.* Bronx, NY: Fordham University Press, 2012.
Cornis-Pope, Marcel. *New Literary Hybrids in the Age of Multimedia Expression:
Crossing Borders, Crossing Genres.* Amsterdam: John Benjamins, 2014.
Ensslin, Astrid. *Literary Gaming.* Cambridge, MA: MIT Press, 2014.
Schäfer, Jörgen and Peter Gendolla. *Beyond the Screen: Transformations of Lit-
erary Structures, Interfaces and Genres.* Bielefeld: transcript, 2010. Accessed
March 17, 2016, http://www.transcript-verlag.de/978-3-8376-1258-5/
beyond-the-screen.

NOTES

1 N. Katherine Hayles, "Print Is Flat, Code Is Deep: The Importance of medium-
specific Analysis," *Poetics Today* 25, no. 1 (2004): 67–90. See also Alice Bell
and others, "A [S]creed for Digital Fiction," *electronic book review,* last modified on March 7, 2010, www.electronicbookreview.com/thread/electropoetics/
DFINative.
2 Alice Bell, Astrid Ensslin, and Hans K. Rustad, *Analyzing Digital Fiction* (New
York: Routledge, 2013).
3 Marc O'Day, "Postmodernism and Television," in *The Routledge Companion to
Postmodernism,* ed. Stuart Sim (New York: Routledge, 2013), 112.
4 For more on simulation, see Jean Baudrillard, *Simulations* (New York: Semio-
text(e), 1983). For more on decentering, see Jacques Derrida, *Of Grammatology*
(Baltimore, MD: Johns Hopkins University Press, 1976); and Jacques Derrida,
"Structure, Sign and Play in the Discourse of the Human Sciences," in *Writing
and Difference* (Chicago: The University of Chicago Press, 1978), 278–293. For
more on pastiche, see Fredric Jameson, *Postmodernism, or, The Cultural Logic
of Late Capitalism* (Durham, NC: Duke University Press, 1991); and for more
on intertextuality, see Julia Kristeva, *Desire in Language: A Semiotic Approach
to Literature and Art* (New York: Columbia University Press, 1980).
5 Guy Debord, *Society of the Spectacle* (Detroit: Black & Red, 1983), 1:4.
6 Robert Coover, "The Babysitter," in *Pricksongs and Descants* (New York: Dut-
ton, 1969), 206–239; and Thomas Pynchon, *Vineland* (Boston: Little, Brown,
1990). The quote is from John Fiske, "Postmodernism and Television," in *Mass
Media and Society,* ed. James Curran and Michael Gurevitch (London: Edward
Arnold, 1991), 58.

7 Brian McHale, *Constructing Postmodernism* (New York: Routledge, 2012), 136, 118.

8 Theodor Nelson, *Computer Lib/Dream Machines* (Chicago: Hugo's Book Service, 1974); and Marshall McLuhan, *The Gutenberg Galaxy: The Making of Typographic Man* (Toronto: University of Toronto Press, 1962).

9 For more on deconstruction of logocentric thought (the structuralist assumption of fixed meanings inherent in language), see Derrida, *Of Grammatology* and "Structure, Sign and Play." The poststructuralist rhizome metaphor is generally used as a subversion of or alternative to logocentrism. It is characterized by ramifying, nonhierarchically organized root structures, which are decentralized, that is, there is no core or visible hierarchy or sequence for readers to follow. For more on rhizomatic thought, see Gilles Deleuze and Félix Guattari, *A Thousand Plateaus: Capitalism and Schizophrenia*, trans. Brian Massumi (Minneapolis: University of Minnesota Press, 1987). For more on the writerly text (texts that require active readers, who metaphorically co-write the text as they read it), see Roland Barthes, *S/Z* (New York: Farrar, Straus and Giroux, 1975).

10 Julio Cortázar, *Hopscotch*, trans. Gregory Rabassa (New York: Random House, 1966), originally published as *Rayuela* (Buenos Aires: Editorial Sudamericana, 1963); and Vladimir Nabokov, *Pale Fire* (New York: G. P. Putnam's Sons, 1962). Nonlinear writing and its accompanying phenomena of multilinear reading, annotating, and cross-referencing via nonelectronic hyperlinks (such as footnotes and verbal references) date back over 1000 years. Proto-hypertexts go as far back as medieval glosses in the Bible, the Talmud, medical texts, and Canon law.

11 Astrid Ensslin, "Nonlinear Writing," in *The Johns Hopkins Guide to Digital Media*, ed. Marie-Laure Ryan, Lori Emerson, and Benjamin J. Robertson (Baltimore, MD: Johns Hopkins University Press, 2014), 360–362.

12 Steve Jobs quoted in Steven Johnson, *Everything Bad Is Good for You* (London: Penguin, 2005), 118.

13 Steve Meretzky, *Planetfall* (Cambridge, MA: Infocom, 1983); and Adam Cadre, *Photopia*, last modified 1998, www.adamcadre.ac/if.html. Playfulness is mentioned as a prime stylistic and attitudinal component of postmodern writing by Linda Hutcheon in *A Poetics of Postmodernism: History, Theory, Fiction* (New York: Routledge, 1988).

14 Nick Montfort, *Twisty Little Passages: An Approach to Interactive Fiction* (Cambridge, MA: MIT Press, 2003), 26–28.

15 Barthes, *S/Z*.

16 Nick Montfort, *Ad Verbum*, last modified 2000, www.nickm.com/if/adverbum .html.

17 Astrid Ensslin, *Literary Gaming* (Cambridge, MA: MIT Press, 2014), 118.

18 Emily Short, *Galatea*, in *Electronic Literature Collection*, vol. 1, ed. N. Katherine Hayles and others, 2000, www.collection.eliterature.org/1/works/short__galatea .html.

19 Michael Joyce, *afternoon: a story* (Cambridge, MA: Eastgate, 1987); Stuart Moulthrop, *Victory Garden* (Cambridge, MA: Eastgate, 1991); and Shelley Jackson, *Patchwork Girl, Or a Modern Monster* (Cambridge, MA: Eastgate, 1995).

20 Key examples include J. David Bolter, *Topographic Writing: Hypertext and the Electronic Writing Space* (Cambridge, MA: MIT Press, 1991); Paul Delany and George P. Landow, *Hypermedia and Literary Studies* (Cambridge, MA: MIT

Press, 1991); and George P. Landow, *Hypertext 2.0: The Convergence of Contemporary Critical Theory and Technology* (Baltimore, MD: Johns Hopkins University Press, 1997).

21 Landow, *Hypertext 2.0*, 2.

22 Bell, Ensslin, and Rustad, *Analyzing Digital Fiction*; Ensslin, *Literary Gaming*; Alice Bell, *The Possible Worlds of Hypertext* (Basingstoke: Palgrave Macmillan, 2010); and David Ciccoricco, *Reading Network Fiction* (Tuscaloosa: University of Alabama Press, 2007). The term "ludostylistic" refers to a type of literary-linguistic analysis that embeds ludological and medium-specific concepts; see Ensslin, *Literary Gaming*.

23 See, for example, David S. Miall and Teresa Dobson, "Reading Hypertext and the Experience of Literature," *Journal of Digital Information* 2, no. 1 (2001), accessed March 17, 2016, www.journals.tdl.org/jodi/index.php/jodi/article/view/35/37; Colin Gardner, "Meta-Interpretation and Hypertext Fiction: A Critical Response," *Computers and Humanities* 37 (2003): 33–59; and James Pope, "A Future for Hypertext Fiction," *Convergence: The International Journal of Research into New Media Technologies* 12, no. 4 (2006): 447–465.

24 N. Katherine Hayles, *Writing Machines* (Cambridge, MA: MIT Press, 2002).

25 Astrid Ensslin, "'Hypertextuality,'" in *The Johns Hopkins Guide to Digital Media*, 262.

26 Astrid Ensslin, *Canonizing Hypertext: Explorations and Constructions* (London: Continuum, 2007). The idea of the text/machine was put forward by Espen J. Aarseth in *Cybertext: Perspectives on Ergodic Literature* (Baltimore, MD: Johns Hopkins University Press, 1997).

27 Astrid Ensslin, "Respiratory Narrative: Multimodality and Cybernetic Corporeality in 'physio-cybertext'" in *New Perspectives on Narrative and Multimodality*, ed. Ruth Page (London: Routledge, 2009), 155–165.

28 Kate Pullinger, Stefan Schemat, and babel, *The Breathing Wall* (London: The Sayle Literary Agency, 2004). I'd like to add here that the choice of some non-American authors and developer teams in this essay has been made deliberately to show an important trend within digital creative practice of bringing together international teams of artists and writers, who produce electronic literature as a new form of world literature that transgresses territorial boundaries and in many cases uses English as an international medium of native and non-native creative expression. Pullinger, for example, is Canadian-born yet works primarily in the United Kingdom, with various international collaborators, and a lot of her digital work is available multilingually.

29 Hans K. Rustad, "A Short History of Electronic Literature and Communities in the Nordic Countries," *dichtung digital* 41, last modified 2012, www.dichtung-digital.org/2012/41/rustad.htm.

30 Ruth Page, *Stories and Social Media: Identities and Interaction* (New York: Routledge, 2012), 91.

31 Bronwen Thomas, "140 Characters in Search of a Story: Twitterfiction as an Emerging Narrative Form," in Bell, Ensslin, and Rustad, *Analyzing Digital Fiction*, 95.

32 Matt Richtel, *Twiller*, 2008, accessed March 17, 2016, www.twitter.com/mrichtel. The quote is from Thomas, "140 Characters," 95.

33 Teju Cole, "Small Fates," 2011, www.tejucole.com/small-fates/.

34 Ibid.

35 Alex Epstein, "The Facebook Book," 2012, www.facebook.com/media/set//set=a
.10150607010303011.404919.90126328010&type=1&l=60835bb6f1.

36 Isabell Klaiber, "Wreading Together: The Double Plot of Collaborative Digital
Fiction," in *Analyzing Digital Fiction*, ed. Bell, Ensslin, and Rustad, 124.

37 Don Tapscott and Anthony D. Williams, *Wikinomics: How Mass Collaboration
Changes Everything* (New York: Portolio, 2006).

38 George P. Landow, "What Is a Critic to Do? Critical Theory in the Age of Hypertext," in *Hyper/Text/Theory*, ed. George P. Landow (Baltimore, MD: Johns Hopkins University Press), 1–47.

39 Klaiber, "Wreading Together," 29–130.

40 Judith Halberstam, *In a Queer Time and Space: Transgender Bodies, Subcultural
Lives* (New York: New York University Press, 2005).

41 Francesca Coppa, "A Brief History of Media Fandom," in *Fan Fiction and Fan
Communities in the Age of the Internet: New Essays*, ed. Karin Hellekson and
Kristina Busse (Jefferson, NC: McFarland, 2006), 41–60.

42 Dave Morris, *Frankenstein, for iPad and iPhone* (Cambridge: Inkle Studios,
2012).

43 See, for example, Pierre Lévy, *Cyberculture* (Minneapolis: University of Minnesota Press, 2001); Bonnie Mak, *How the Page Matters* (Toronto: University of
Toronto Press, 2011); and Jessica Pressman, *Digital Modernism: Making It New
in New Media* (New York: Oxford University Press, 2014).

44 Gerard Genette, *Paratexts: Thresholds of Interpretation* (Cambridge: Cambridge
University Press, 1997). According to Genette, paratext is the text, or rather the
textual ecology, surrounding an artifact like a novel, film, or game, such as a title,
blurb, reviews, interviews, and product websites. It subdivides into peritext (the
texts immediately surrounding a text, such as title, blurb, and contents page) and
epitext (the texts relating to but not physically accompanying another text, such
as reviews, interviews, and diaries).

45 Ellen McCracken, "Expanding Genette's Epitext/Peritext Model for Transitional
Electronic Literature: Centrifugal and Centripetal Vectors on Kindles and iPads,"
Narrative 21, no. 1 (2013): 104–123.

46 Jack Kerouac, *On the Road* (New York: Penguin, 2011), accessed March
17, 2016, www.penguin.com/static/pages/features/amplified_editions/on_the_
road.php. The quote is from McCracken, "Expanding," 117–118.

47 Felix Heibeck, Alexis Hope, and Julie Legault in Alison Flood, "Sense and Sen-
sorbility: The Book That Lets You Feel Your Protagonist's Pain," *The Guardian
online*, last modified January 28, 2014, www.theguardian.com/books/2014/jan/
28/sensory-fiction-mit-technology-wearable-fiction-books.

48 Ensslin, *Literary Gaming*.

49 N. Katherine Hayles, "Hyper and Deep Attention: The Generational Divide in
Cognitive Modes," *Profession* 13 (2007): 187–199.

50 Kate Pullinger, Chris Joseph, and Andy Campbell, *Inanimate Alice*, 2009–2014,
accessed March 17, 2016, www.inanimatealice.com; and Tale of Tales, *The Path*,
2009, accessed March 17, 2016, www.tale-of-tales.com/ThePath.

51 Pressman, *Digital Modernism*, 22.

52 Judd Morrissey, *The Jew's Daughter*, last modified 2000, www.thejewsdaughter
.com; the quote is taken from Pressman, *Digital Modernism*, 101–102, drawing

on Lev Manovich, *The Language of New Media* (Cambridge, MA: MIT Press, 2002).

53 James MacDowell, "Wes Anderson, Tone and the Quirky Sensibility," *New Review of Film and Television Studies* 10, no. 1 (2012), accessed December 22, 2016, http://www.tandfonline.com/doi/abs/10.1080/17400309.2012.628227.

54 Timotheus Vermeulen and Robin van den Akker, "Notes on Metamodernism," *Journal of Aesthetics and Culture*, 2 (2010), accessed March 17, 2016, www.aestheticsandculture.net/index.php/jac/article/view/5677/6304; the quote is taken from Alison Gibbons, "'Take that you intellectuals!' and 'kaPOW!': Adam Thirlwell and the Metamodernist Future of Style," *Studia Neophilologica*, 3, accessed March 17, 2016, www.tandfonline.com/doi/abs/10.1080/00393274 .2014.981959#.VOdXX_msVoY.

INDEX

magical realism, 59
Robber Bride, The, 62
Auden, W. H., 15
Austen, Jane, 145
Pride and Prejudice, 139
Auster, Paul, 34, 37, 38
author
as character, 1, 38, 87–8, 94, 98, 103–4,
140, 168
quasi-coauthors, 187
Authority (Vandermeer), 137, 138
Autobiography, An (Rodriguez), 46
autobiographical narratives, 52–3, 57,
180
autogenealogies, 53, 54–6
avant-garde, 58, 133, 149, 153, 155, 165
Avelar, Idelbar, 116
Untimely Present, The, 128
Aztlán, 121

babel
Breathing Wall, The, 186, 195
"Babysitter, The" (Coover), 182–3, 193
Badiou, Alain, 69
Being and Event, 79
Baker, Nicholson
Human Smoke, 91–3, 94, 96
U and I, 91
Vox, 91
Bakhtin, M. M.
Dialogic Imagination, The, 161
Baldwin, James, 33
Go Tell It on the Mountain, 33
Bambara, Toni Cade, 21, 83
Salt Eaters, The, 89
Barnes, Djuna, 15
Barry, Lynda, 180
Barth, John
End of the Road, The, 33
Floating Opera, The, 33
Friday Book, The, 161
history and fiction, 82
LETTERS, 151, 152
"Literature of Exhaustion, The", 13, 16,
26, 33, 149
"Literature of Replenishment, The", 149
Lost in the Funhouse, 148
modern–postmodern split, 38, 39
from modern to postmodern, 31, 32, 33,
34
postmodern styles, 149, 151, 161
postmodern theory, 14, 17, 22, 28, 68
Sot-Weed Factor, The, 31, 33, 84

Barthelme, Donald
City Life, 152
Come Back, Dr. Caligari, 152
global literature, 59
history and fiction, 82
"Indian Uprising, The", 152–3, 161
periodization, 31, 33, 38
postmodern styles, 28, 152, 159
Snow White, 62
Unspeakable Practices, Unnatural Acts,
152
Barthes, Roland, 183
S/Z, 194
Bataille, Georges, 15
Bate, Walter Jackson, 40, 46
Baudrillard, Jean, 67
"Precession of the Simulacra, The", 45
Simulations, 193
Beat movement, 28, 32–3, 160, 189
Bechdel, Alison, 173
Fun Home, 164, 175–7, 180
Beckett, Samuel, 30, 38, 160
Watt, 151
Beck, Ulrich
Individualization, 26
Beck-Gernsheim, Elisabeth
Individualization, 26
Beetle Leg, The (Hawkes), 33
Being and Event (Badiou), 79
Bel Canto (Patchett), 39
Bell, Alice, 193, 195
Bellow, Saul, 15, 36, 150
Beloved (Morrison), 58, 62, 78–80, 82–3,
89–90, 96, 99, 111, 117, 119–20, 123,
129
Bend in the River, A (Naipaul), 53
Berkhofer, Robert
Beyond the Great Story, 96
Bernhard, Thomas
Loser, The, 60
Berry, Wendell, 16
Beyond Ethnicity (Sollors), 128
Beyond the Great Story (Berkhofer), 96
Bhabha, Homi
Location of Culture, The, 113, 114, 128
pluralism, 113, 114, 116, 119
science fiction, 143
Big Money, The (Dos Passos), 154
bildungsroman, 144, 157, 158
black history, 89, 117, 119
black nationalism, 54, 115
Black Panthers, 115, 170
Black Thunder (Bontemps), 24

fragmentation
  digital fiction, 182, 184
  of discourse, 159
  formal, 29
  modernist, 47
  of subject, 99, 102, 133, 157
  see also multiplicity
Frankenstein (Inkle), 188, 196
Franzen, Jonathan
  Corrections, The, 59, 60, 62
  Freedom, 59, 62
  Kraus Project, The, 59, 62
  periodization, 29, 41, 42
Freedom (Franzen), 59, 62
Friday Book, The (Barth), 161
Freud, Sigmund, 17, 24
Frost, Robert, 29
Fuentes, Carlos, 160
Fun Home (Bechdel), 164, 175–7, 180
Fussell, Paul, 42
Futurism, 165

Gaborieau, Marc, 24
Gaddis, William
  JR, 18, 156
  as postmodern precursor, 28, 33, 34, 38, 60
  Recognitions, The, 33, 48, 154
Galatea (Short), 184, 194
Galatea 2.2 (Powers), 38–9, 46
game, as concept, 76
gaming, 58, 181, 183, 189, 191
García, Cristina
  Dreaming in Cuban, 36
Gardner, Colin, 195
Gardner, John
  Gardner–Gass debates, 148–50
  Grendel, 31, 149
  modern–postmodern split, 33, 39
  On Moral Fiction, 149
  postmodern styles, 148–50, 151, 159
  Sunlight Dialogues, 149
Garvey, Marcus, 24
Gass, William H.
  Fiction and the Figures of Life, 149
  Gardner–Gass debates, 148–50
  In the Heart of the Heart of the Country, 149
  image and text, 167
  Omensetter's Luck, 148, 149
  postmodern styles, 28, 148–9, 150, 151, 159
  Tunnel, The, 48, 149

Willie Masters' Lonesome Wife, 149, 163–4, 167–8, 179
Gates Jr., Henry Louis
  ethnic writing, 36, 37
  Signifying Monkey, The, 46
Gay, Peter, 81
gaze, 108–9
Gazelle (Ducornet), 59
Geek Love (Dunn), 108–9, 111
gender
  constructedness of, 6, 98, 99–100
  depth models, 32
  essentialism of, 101, 109
  feminine, 6, 97, 98, 101, 103–9
  gay, 105–7, 175
  and language, 98, 99, 103–4
  lesbian, 99, 101
  masculine, 6, 97, 98, 101–7, 118
  performativity, 97
  pluralism, 122
  queer, 115, 121, 161
  science fiction, 144
  and sexuality, 97–111
  theory, 63, 67, 69, 71
Gender Trouble (Butler), 110
genealogies (and influences), 14, 18, 22, 50–1, 53–7, 61, 67, 128
Generation P (Pelevin), 53
Genet, Jean, 15, 160
Genette, Gerard, 189, 196
genres
  narrative, 8
  postmodern, 7, 32, 131–3, 155–8, 166–7, 169, 181, 184, 186
geography
  and history, 125–7
  and identity, 114–16
  and pluralism, 119, 121–7
Gibbon, Edward
  Decline and Fall of the Roman Empire, 34
Gibbons, Alison, 197
Gibson, William
  cyberspace, 3
  multiplicity, 71
  Neuromancer, 4, 8, 133–4, 135, 146
  postmodern succession, 38
  science fiction, 133–4, 135
Gide, André, 13
Ginsberg, Allen, 33
Girl Who Was Plugged in, The (Tiptree), 191
Giroux, Henry, 147
Gladstone, Jason, 26, 61

INDEX

Cambridge Companions To ...

AUTHORS

Edward Albee edited by Stephen J. Bottoms

Margaret Atwood edited by Coral Ann Howells

W. H. Auden edited by Stan Smith

Jane Austen edited by Edward Copeland and Juliet McMaster (second edition)

Beckett edited by John Pilling

Bede edited by Scott DeGregorio

Aphra Behn edited by Derek Hughes and Janet Todd

Walter Benjamin edited by David S. Ferris

William Blake edited by Morris Eaves

Boccaccio edited by Guyda Armstrong, Rhiannon Daniels, and Stephen J. Milner

Jorge Luis Borges edited by Edwin Williamson

Brecht edited by Peter Thomson and Glendyr Sacks (second edition)

The Brontës edited by Heather Glen

Bunyan edited by Anne Dunan-Page

Frances Burney edited by Peter Sabor

Byron edited by Drummond Bone

Albert Camus edited by Edward J. Hughes

Willa Cather edited by Marilee Lindemann

Cervantes edited by Anthony J. Cascardi

Chaucer edited by Piero Boitani and Jill Mann (second edition)

Chekhov edited by Vera Gottlieb and Paul Allain

Kate Chopin edited by Janet Beer

Caryl Churchill edited by Elaine Aston and Elin Diamond

Cicero edited by Catherine Steel

Coleridge edited by Lucy Newlyn

Wilkie Collins edited by Jenny Bourne Taylor

Joseph Conrad edited by J. H. Stape

H. D. edited by Nephie J. Christodoulides and Polina Mackay

Dante edited by Rachel Jacoff (second edition)

Daniel Defoe edited by John Richetti

Don DeLillo edited by John N. Duvall

Charles Dickens edited by John O. Jordan

Emily Dickinson edited by Wendy Martin

John Donne edited by Achsah Guibbory

Dostoevskii edited by W. J. Leatherbarrow

Theodore Dreiser edited by Leonard Cassuto and Claire Virginia Eby

John Dryden edited by Steven N. Zwicker

W. E. B. Du Bois edited by Shamoon Zamir

George Eliot edited by George Levine

T. S. Eliot edited by A. David Moody

Ralph Ellison edited by Ross Posnock

Ralph Waldo Emerson edited by Joel Porte and Saundra Morris

William Faulkner edited by Philip M. Weinstein

Henry Fielding edited by Claude Rawson

F. Scott Fitzgerald edited by Ruth Prigozy

Flaubert edited by Timothy Unwin

E. M. Forster edited by David Bradshaw

Benjamin Franklin edited by Carla Mulford

Brian Friel edited by Anthony Roche

Robert Frost edited by Robert Faggen

Gabriel García Márquez edited by Philip Swanson

Elizabeth Gaskell edited by Jill L. Matus

Goethe edited by Lesley Sharpe

Günter Grass edited by Stuart Taberner

Thomas Hardy edited by Dale Kramer

David Hare edited by Richard Boon

Nathaniel Hawthorne edited by Richard Millington

Seamus Heaney edited by Bernard O'Donoghue

Ernest Hemingway edited by Scott Donaldson

Homer edited by Robert Fowler

Horace edited by Stephen Harrison

Ted Hughes edited by Terry Gifford

Ibsen edited by James McFarlane

Henry James edited by Jonathan Freedman

Samuel Johnson edited by Greg Clingham

Ben Jonson edited by Richard Harp and Stanley Stewart

James Joyce edited by Derek Attridge (second edition)

Kafka edited by Julian Preece

Keats edited by Susan J. Wolfson

Rudyard Kipling edited by Howard J. Booth

Lacan edited by Jean-Michel Rabaté

TOPICS